INDUSTRIAL POLICY IN ITALY, 1945–90

CENTRAL ISSUES IN CONTEMPORARY ECONOMIC THEORY AND POLICY

General Editor: **Mario Baldassarri**, *Professor of Economics, University of Rome 'La Sapienza', Italy*

This new series is a joint initiative between Macmillan and SIPI, the publishing company of Confindustria (the Confederation of Italian Industry), based on the book collection MONOGRAFIE RPE published by SIPI and originated from the new editorial programme of one of the oldest Italian journals of economics, the *Rivista di Politica Economica*, founded in 1911. This series is intended to become an arena in which the most topical economic problems are freely debated and confronted with different scientific orientations and/or political theories.

The 1990s clearly represent a transition period in which the world economy will establish new international relationships and in this context, new challenges and new risks will have to be faced within each economic system. Fundamental issues on which economic theory and policy have long based their reasoning over the last two or three decades have to be critically reviewed in order to pursue new frontiers for theoretical development and economic policy implementation. In this sense, this new series aims at being a "place of debate" between professional economists, an updated learning tool for students and a specific reference for a wider readership aiming at understanding economic theory and policy evolution even from a non-specialist point of view.

Published

Industrial Policy in Italy, 1945–90

Edited by

Mario Baldassarri
Professor of Economics
University of Rome 'La Sapienza'

St. Martin's Press

in association with
Rivista di Politica Economica,
SIPI, Rome

First published in Great Britain 1993 by
THE MACMILLAN PRESS LTD
Houndmills, Basingstoke, Hampshire RG21 2XS
and London
Companies and representatives
throughout the world

A catalogue record for this book is available
from the British Library.

ISBN 0-333-58705-7

Printed in Great Britain by
Antony Rowe Ltd
Chippenham, Wiltshire

First published in the United States of America 1993 by
Scholarly and Reference Division,
ST. MARTIN'S PRESS, INC.,
175 Fifth Avenue,
New York, N.Y. 10010

ISBN 0-312-08975-9

Library of Congress Cataloging-in-Publication Data
Politica industriale in Italia dal '45 ad oggi.   English
Industrial policy in Italy, 1945-90 / edited by Mario Baldassarri.
p.   cm.
Includes index.
ISBN 0-312-08975-9
1. Industry and state—Italy—History—20th century.
2. Industrial promotion—Italy—History—20th century.   3. Italy-
-Economic policy.   I. Baldassarri, Mario, 1946-   .   II. Title.
HD3616.I83P6513   1993   92-28595
                                                       CIP

Contents

North-South:

PART III: INNOVATION AND COMPETITIVENESS

Preface

During the last few decades, Italy's economic development has been tumultuous and, in many ways, contradictory. Its main features have been the growth and the coming of age of an industrial system which is firmly ranked among the first five or six most industrialized countries in the world, and which, despite the risk and the difficulties involved, has always been the cornerstone of the nation's economy. In short, it was during these years that Italy became a strong and modern industrial economy.

It will therefore be interesting to reexamine some of the key aspects of this development, not only to gain insight into the 'great race' and the successes of this period, but also to note the errors, limitations, problems, and defeats. This will enable us to better define the 'strategic position' of Italian industry and industrial policy, or the possibilities and the risks in store at the beginning of the 1990s, a time of radical change. Within an international context of economic and financial integration, increased competitivity abroad and industrial specialization present both opportunity and risk, in the form of new prospects arising from changes in East–West relations, and in the form of growing contrast between the northern and southern hemispheres.

The creation of the single market in western Europe and the integration with East European countries both provide positive examples. However, an example of the dangers involved is the 1991 crisis in the Middle East which, though certainly fuelled by the hegemonic aspirations of one regime, may nonetheless (or at least, in part) be a signal of a widening discrepancy between North and South.

In any modern industrial economy, it is always difficult to evaluate the role and the impact of economic policy, or more specifically, industrial policy, as a guide and a stimulus to industrial development. Indeed, its primary role must be to influence the decisionmaking and strategy of firms, and to make full use of the capacity which exists within every industrial system. Although economic and industrial policies can promote or stymie decisionmaking processes, they are incapable of 'inventing' the firm or industrial development on their own. As a consequence, the interaction between industrial policy, economic policies and development is difficult to define.

Theoretical debate in favour of macroeconomics or microeconomics, economic policy or industrial policy, interventionism or laissez-faire, controlling aggregate demand or supply-side policies, by-sector or by-factor objectives, and guaranteeing or differentiating the rules of the game has ebbed and flowed, but has certainly not subsided.

Empirical evidence from the leading industrialized countries reveals a vast array of experiences evolving over time within each nation: among these are the 'compactness' of German and Japanese industry; the more sweeping changes of the English system, French 'dirigisme', the American neo-free-enterprise, and the 'atypical' Italian situation, which is the subject of this monograph and of the papers which follow.

This book is divided into three parts.

The first section outlines the theoretical frame of reference and the empirical experiences of the Italian economy during the last few decades. The volume begins with a paper by Pippo Ranci, *Macroeconomic Policies and Industrial Policies,* which introduces the industrial policy 'issue', its role, its sphere of activity, and the various combinations created in macroeconomic and microeconomic scenarios. It is followed by a critical view of the framework, the turning points, the major issues, the philosophy and the approaches in connection in the study by Romano Prodi and Daniele De Giovanni, *Forty-Five Years of Industrial Policy in Italy: Protagonists, Objectives, and Instruments.*

The second section examines three fundamental 'links' between Italian economy, industry and industrial policy. Firstly, the public and private sectors are analyzed in depth in the paper written by Fulvio Coltorti, *Phases of Italian Industrial Development and the*

Relationship between the Public and Private Sectors and in a special study by Paolo Leon, *Public Enterprises and Industrial Policies*.

Secondly, large- and small-sized firms are dealt with in papers written by Gian Maria Gros-Pietro, *The Restructuring of Large-Sized Industrial Groups*, and by Patrizio Bianchi, *Industrial Policies for Small and Medium Firms and the New Direction of European Community Policies*.

Thirdly, the regional development gap becomes the subject of study in *The Tortuous Road of Industry through the Mezzogiorno*, by Mariano D'Antonio, and in *Industrial Policies and Territorial Development in Northern and Central Regions of Italy*, by Maurizio Tenenbaum.

A common denominator can be found among all of the contributions in the first two sections: each work stresses the need for industrial policy to focus primarily on two synergic and interrelated objectives, innovation and competitivity. Major developments in this process were achieved during the 1980s, with the tumultuous beginnings of technological and organizational innovation in a context of growing integration and of international challenge. Moreover, innovation and the competitive struggle moved out of the realm of individual firms to encompass the entire economic and industrial system. The innovation and competitivity of companies became a part of the innovation and competitive survival of the system and of the country as a whole.

The third section analyzes this message in the paper by Bruno Lamborghini and Cesare Sacchi, *Industrial Policy and Technological Innovation*. As in the other studies, the experiences of recent decades are re-evaluated not only to 'understand' what actually occurred but also to evaluate the Italian industrial system so as to meet the challenges presented within the international economic system and the Italian economy leading up to the year 2000.

Of course, an introduction is no substitute for the detailed study of each individual paper, and can hardly include all of their nuances and results in a few lines. Nonetheless, an attempt to identify and to link the basic messages of each work may have its merits.

After having examined the role, the flexibility and the essence of industrial policy, Pippo Ranci summarizes the various schools of thought adhered to by economists and provides a useful classification for the theoretical aspects of this issue. However, in the light of empirical experiences, these theoretical approaches began to meld with one another, thereby losing their individual characters and the ideological rigidity that had fuelled debate over the decades. Although mixtures and combinations were created, they were all characterized by a healthy basic tendency to distinguish the autonomous role of the firm and of industry from the role of public intervention, which should involve more general macroeconomic policies and more specific industrial policies. 'Everyone should do his own job' is the basic message here. The confused roles and unclear objectives within the private and public sectors should be abandoned in favour of the synergies between clear, forward-looking industrial strategies which Italian economic and industrial policies must provide in order to win the competitive race against other systems.

The major phases of Italy's industrial development and of industrial policy are closely examined in the paper by Romano Prodi and Daniele De Giovanni. The introduction presents several basic conclusions:

1) the Italian industrial system has gradually moved toward European integration and during the last decade has made major progress toward the single market. However, industrial policy has not kept up with this progress, and stubbornly retains its unrealistic local and national perspective;

2) despite several changes, Italian industrial policy has always been characterized by the objective of maintaining the status quo. This can scarcely be considered a far-reaching plan for industrial policy, nor can it provide firms with a strategic direction;

3) private- and public-sector dualism was actually institutionalized by the creation of two separate ministries, Industry and State Participations. State-owned firms are particularly resistant to change, and impede mergers, restructuring and

concentrations. These operations are the minimum requirement for strategic international competition;

4) the problems of unemployment and the Mezzogiorno have formed a giant knot which is becoming increasingly tangled, despite the imminence of European integration; as a consequence, regional disparities are accentuated, and solutions become more difficult and complex.

Even during the postwar reconstruction, the initial phase of Italian industrial development, Prodi and De Giovanni perceive a lack of strategy and confused objectives. Since then, 'general objectives of stabilizing investments and promoting development in poorer areas of the country took precedence over the traditional objectives of industrial policy and increased competition'.

Indeed, the main objective of the first pieces of relevant legislation was to control the everyday lives of firms. Debate falsely juxtaposed a 'guided and sheltered' reconstruction strategy with a policy of increased international competition. The first significant step occurred during the 1950s and 1960s, when the initial postwar phase of sustained development was interrupted by the first signs of economic crisis. During this period, the creation of a plan, which was announced but never put in place, caused economic and industrial policy to develop a 'schizophrenic' character. The dichotomy between 'intellectual vision', which at times wished to chart the course to be followed by Italy's economy and industry, and actual economic and industrial development, was readily apparent.

Changes in the real economy, domestically and internationally, began to outpace the prognostications of intellectuals and planners alike. Industrial policy was considered a part of planning policy, aimed at demand and designed to allocate production; however, it was continually unable to match the speed of the system. The highly criticized shower of incentives leading to the creation and the growth of small- and medium-sized enterprises (by virtue of the defective Law 623, for example) was re-evaluated. As Prodi and De Giovanni correctly point out, the adverse effect of this policy is the fact that the public sector had delegated its role of administrator to the banking system, thereby accentuating its lack of efficiency and effectiveness compared with other governments.

Another important step is the fact that certain large-sized public-sector firms, such as ENI, became responsible for vertical planning within their sector, leaving only 'horizontal' planning to be accomplished by the public sector. Further, economic planning began in Italy without the consensus of the interest groups involved. Here, the authors seem to be mildly chastising not only the government, but also the unions and Confindustria. In their opposition to planning strategy, albeit for different reasons, the latter two were in effect excluded from it. It is as though a script were written, but the actors, at times explicitly refused to play their parts. Hardly surprising, then, that the five-year plan for 1965–69 evolved into the 1966–70 and 1967–71 plans: the lengthy debate produced no concrete results.

Just as the curtain fell on this period of planning, the crisis of the 1970s began. This period was characterized by a restructuring policy unable to keep pace with fresh developments. While other countries formed the mergers and strategic alliances which would give rise to the new European oligopoly, bailouts and increasing the sphere of action of the public sector were the Italian priorities. A timid attempt to apply the American Chapter 11 principles to Italian industrial policy came in the form of the Prodi law; however, this law has once again been disowned by its creator. The law was twisted out of shape, and became a mere source of subsidization. During the late 1970s, a serious industrial policy was attempted by means of external European Community intervention. Given the lack of courageous decisionmaking at the national level, this external support was certainly helpful, but the strengthening of Italian industry could scarcely be considered an appropriate objective for EEC regulations. At the same time, attempts to untie the legislative tangle were being made by regrouping the measures in Law 183, in the Presidential Decree of 9 November 1976 and in Law 675.

Omnibus legislation was resorted to once again, making it impossible to devise or to execute long-term strategy.

Whereas the 1980s signalled the beginning of a new era worldwide, this was the decade of missed opportunities for Italian industrial policy. To be sure, Law 46 on technological innovation and Law 696 were significant improvements. Nonetheless, Italy still has far to go. Prodi and De Giovanni end with several conclusions and a question. The conclusions are as follows: a) no new leading companies have been created; b) industrial policy has in effect been developed within firms themselves; c) state-owned firms are impervious to change; d) in spite of efforts at restructuring large-sized companies, not enough of these firms exist, and no new ones have been created; e) small- and medium-sized firms seem to have no place in the picture, since they are protected by absurd public-sector intervention 'shelters'. Hence the question: can Italy survive with only small- and medium-sized firms?

The three major relationships between industry and the economy in Italy are examined in the second section of this volume, beginning with a paper by Fulvio Coltorti which focuses on the complex theme of public- and private-sector interaction during each phase of Italian industrial development.

Four periods are examined. During the first phase, from reconstruction to the economic miracle (1950–64), the public and private sectors, despite some confusion, adhered to roles which led to positive results: public-sector firms were responsible for the steel and energy industries, while textiles and metals were the province of the private sector.

During the second phase, from 1964 to 1975, state intervention was granted in unprecedented amounts, but had never before been as confused and inefficient. The public-sector sphere of action continued to grow, while industrial and economic policies tied private sector development and management to negative real interest rates. This in turn caused a debt crisis, and led to an excessive growth of capital-intensive processes encouraged by the constraints of industrial relations and the use of labour. Moreover, industrial development in the Mezzogiorno became an objective of public-sector firms. This objective was pursued using capital-intensive equipment to further primary industry, which had virtually no local or regional induced effects. At the time of the energy crisis, the Italian public and private sectors were rife with structural weaknesses, and leaning dangerously toward primary industry.

The third phase, 1975–83, involved an ostrich-style policy, since restructuring decisions were delayed, and heads were hidden in inflation and devaluation.

During the final phase, 1982–83, private- and public-sector industry were clearly delineated. Bound by rigid monetary and foreign-exchange constraints, the private sector was compelled to restructure and seemed to take flight. Industrial and organizational innovations recreated profit margins, and financial management began to flourish. Private-sector firms were now able to operate independently on the open market, free of public-sector interference and subsidized financing. Internationalization led to the creation of strategies based solely on cost-efficiency and realized with one's own financial means and/or with funds raised on the market and managed without benefit of a public-sector scheme. Despite major restructuring, Italy's state-owned firms fell far behind the European and international oligopolies. Although individual areas of public sector industry were set to proceed, no overall industrial policy was developed. Instead, the institutional dichotomy, the Ministries of Industry and State Participations, quickly reduced such strategy to ineffectual debate, thereby paralyzing vital merger and integration processes. At the same time, companies on the international market were merging so as to occupy leadership positions.

The role of public-sector firms, and more specifically, the system of state-owned firms widely used in Italy as an industrial policy instrument, is examined in depth in a study by Paolo Leon. The paper analyzes the objectives related to the promotion of industrial development and the cases in which decentralized market decisions frustrated strategic objectives, leading instead to market failure.

The shortsightedness of the microeconomic decisions of

individual firms has long been recognized in economic literature. Because of long-term deadlines, high financial requirements, and the high cost of research and development, individual firms are compelled to decide against certain investments which are actually a determinant factor of overall industrial progress. Empirically, the Italian case reveals that shortsighted private-sector decisionmaking is often accompanied by farsighted public policy, leading to an over-abundance of objectives and the misdirection of resources away from increased profitability and efficiency. One example is the lengthy debate concerning the applicability of the social discount rate to decisionmaking within the public sector.

As regards theory, private-sector nearsightedness and public-sector farsightedness revealed the need to direct investments and the development of public-sector firms, as well as the need to subject public-sector firms to the same selection criteria for investment imposed on their private-sector counterparts.

The second relationship involves industrial policy concerning the development and restructuring of large-sized firms and the dynamic and complex system of small- and medium-sized enterprises, dealt with respectively by Gian Maria Gros-Pietro and Patrizio Bianchi.

One of the most detrimental characteristics of the Italian economy is the small number of large-sized firms, the majority of which are state-owned. Gros-Pietro also points out the lack of industrial policy strategy, and, in particular, the absence of an industrial strategy for the public sector. State involvement in large-sized firms could have been used as a means of coordinating strategy during the late 1960s, when the need to shift resources to sectors with higher value-added became increasingly evident. Instead, in the absence of clear objectives and roles, safeguarding employment began to take precedence. This inefficient allocation of resources adversely affected the ability of the system to create new jobs.

In the late 1960s and early 1970s, large-sized firms were also faced with the problem of changing market strategy. For much of the 1970s, the burdensome constraints on industrial relations and on the labour market and the macroeconomic policy framework (negative real interest rates, inflation and a weak lira) caused companies to gradually increase the ratio of capital to labour, thereby creating further technological rigidity. In an effort to increase economies of scale, workers were laid off; this decline in employment was formally hidden by government regulations and subsidies. Moreover, negative real interest rates caused a debt crisis which only served to fuel this process, since firms could scarcely raise large amounts of risk capital on Italy's small stock exchange. The context of uncertainty ruled out the possibility of raising funds on foreign markets.

At this stage, Gros-Pietro identifies five industrial policy objectives for large-sized firms, and dedicates the latter part of his study to the changes and plans for improvement made during the 1980s.

The author's findings are extremely interesting: until 1980-81, more than half of public-sector transfer payments were used to offset financial operating losses, principally those of state-owned firms; in 1987, the percentage of transfer payments used for this purpose fell to 6%. During that period, Gros-Pietro asserts, industrial policy was made not so much for large-sized firms in general as for the 'great losers'. The major developments which took place from 1983 onward include a more coherent strategy aimed at fostering technological innovation and exports. Although this more recent industrial policy direction seems justifiable, it is found to be sorely lacking when compared with the qualitative and quantitative reality of other industrialized countries.

As regards the industrial policy situation, the author outlines the autonomous action of large-sized firms during the last few years. One important step is the shift from old-style industrial decentralization of the 1970s to the 'network company' concept, which decentralizes production even as it recentralizes and coordinates strategic functions, decisionmaking and resource management (the difficulties involves in carrying out a similar process aimed at small- and medium-sized firms are examined in the paper by Patrizio Bianchi). The ever-changing international scene, clearer (albeit insufficient) industrial policy direction and the great effort of firms have carried Italian industry through the difficult period of the 1970s and 1980s. The five industrial policy requirements, Gros-Pietro concludes, have remained more or less the same: 1) to restore financial health to state-controlled companies; 2) to restore financial health to specific troubled public and private industrial sectors; 3) to encourage large-sized private-sector firms to move toward more sophisticated products and technology; 4) to free the major banks from loans accumulated by certain large-sized firms; 5) to develop a capital market capable of meeting the needs of Italian industry.

The other side of the relationship, small- and medium-sized firms, is analyzed by Patrizio Bianchi, with particular emphasis on the creation of the single market and on the need to bring Italian policy into line with Community regulations. According to Bianchi, the essence of the industrial policy question lies in the fact that the individual firm is generally targeted. Small- and medium-sized enterprises in Italy are unable to develop coherent strategies, and do not have sufficient resources to execute them. In addition, the incentives provided by industrial policy are often 'out of reach'.

The problem of industrial policy is twofold: on the one hand, it consists of the reality of integrated industrial districts while on the other it concerns the need for individual entrepreneurs to adopt an industry-wide or district-wide perspective when making decisions. However, the many risks and difficulties faced by small- and medium-sized firms lead the author to ask, as Prodi and De Giovanni did at the end of their paper: can small- and medium-sized firms survive, and what are their chances of development?

During this postwar period, the regional relationship very gradually became more complex. Nowadays, in the Mezzogiorno, giant steps in industrial progress exist alongside deepening poverty and underdevelopment. To be sure, the effects of industrial development have largely been positive; nonetheless, they stand out in stark contrast to the underdevelopment ever present in certain areas of southern Italy. In the central and northern regions, the old industrial triangle is complemented by major development to the east, primarily along the Adriatic coast. Here, too, the industrial progress of certain areas highlights the lack of development in others. For this reason, it was considered appropriate to deal with this relationship in two separate studies. The paper by Mariano D'Antonio examines the problems of the South, while the paper by Maurizio Tenenbaum analyzes the problems of regional development in the Centre-North.

The study by D'Antonio begins with the most recent experiences of the 1980s, which he defines as a period of missed opportunities to industrialize the Mezzogiorno once and for all. Despite the significant changes which had occurred, weaknesses in the two traditional pillars of industrial policy for the South, the investment of state-owned firms and the granting of incentives (particularly financial relief) began to show, and they very gradually broke down. New specific and national legislation did little to improve the situation.

The author's well-documented conclusions are analytical, detailed, and of great interest. The work ends with a hard-hitting point: 'the big question concerning the southern Italian industrial apparatus is how to create, over the next few years, a steady flow of exports, and how to include small enterprises in this flow. Incentive policies must either find a suitable answer to this question, or risk being accused and suspected of acting as a curtain to southern Italian entrepreneurs, shutting out not only foreign competition, but also international markets.

The analysis by Maurizio Tenenbaum provides new insight into industrial policy and regional development in central and northern areas. This work is largely based on cross-comparison analysis by sector and by region, used for the first time in a study of this kind. The case studies included in the appendix will undoubtedly be of interest. Detailed analysis of the documentation and a keen critical sense led Tenenbaum to develop a working plan focusing specifically on the development of small- and medium-sized firms. Decisions on the type of instruments to be used vary with each different scenario. The objectives included in this proposal are indeed justifiable, and are the subject of study elsewhere in this collection.

In our view, the exhaustive nature of this volume and the diverse subjects, opinions and viewpoints of the authors provide an interesting mix of analyses, conclusions and proposals. However, each work is subtly yet clearly linked to the others. This link is the need for Italian industrial policy to develop an accurate, rigorous strategy of intervention, and to leave behind the differing and often incoherent objectives which in past decades created a bureaucratic structure resistant to change. The strategic focus needed for industrial policy and technological innovation is of prime importance.

This is the subject examined by Bruno Lamborghini and Cesare Sacchi in the final paper of this collection. The two authors begin with an analysis of what they call the 'driving forces' of innovation during the past few decades: the external action of government, and the internal action of firms. A dangerous situation is created, then, if the internal force drives companies toward innovation while the external force of government action is on the wane. The conclusions made by Sacchi and Lamborghini at the end of their paper are representative of the entire collection:

1) during the 1980s, a sharp upturn in Italian industry brought companies out of the crisis of the 1970s;

2) this transformation was largely due to the 'driving forces' of firms;

3) though insufficient, the innovative effects of industry on small- and medium-sized firms as a result of the transformation of large-sized firms have been positive;

4) developments in industrial policy, especially innovation policy, though insufficient, have been positive. Incentives for applied research, technological innovation and new plant and equipment in the case of small- and medium-sized enterprises, recent legislation for the Mezzogiorno, measures to promote research and innovative services, and the signing of planned contracts between the state and enterprises are all positive steps. Most of these measures, aimed at providing direct assistance, were fraught with difficulties, delay and uncertainty as far as the

access to funds and actual payment were concerned. This ran counter to the turn of events in other leading industrialized countries, such as France and Germany;

5) the transformation and redress of the industrial apparatus enjoyed a favourable international economic climate of sustained growth of industrialized economies, and low-cost raw materials. The persistent inequality of domestic costs in Italy in a context of increasingly fixed exchange rates may be a major obstacle to development over the next few years;

6) it is now obvious that competitivity involves entire economic systems. The lack of clear industrial policy direction is therefore a major handicap for Italian industry, especially as regards innovation policy. However, policymaking in support of innovation, Lamborghini and Sacchi conclude, implies 'policymaking to promote the development and modernization of infrastructures, networks and services in industry' and 'creating the necessary conditions for a truly competitive market, fitted into the Community-wide framework and open to international comparison. Markets, industry, network and services must be closely interconnected to meet the competitive challenge of the 1990s.'

Industrial policy and innovation policy lack 'true synergy between the driving forces of innovation internal and external to firms. A context of real competitive market conditions must be created in which the presence of the state is quantitatively lower, and yet qualitatively higher.'

Mario Baldassarri

I - SURVEYS

Macroeconomic Policies and Industrial Policies

Pippo Ranci
Irs, Milano and Università di Bergamo

In a market economy, industrial policy is not automatically assumed to be a part of economic policy. According to traditional political economy, the burden of proof lies with those who defend the usefulness of industrial policy, and in most cases, the evidence provided is hardly conclusive. Industrial policy is suspected, not entirely incorrectly, of being primarily a product of corporate interests, a relic of the protectionist past, an expression of the interventionist pretensions of politicians or bureaucrats, or some mixture of the above. Yet governments routinely take specific action to promote industrial development and to sustain a given industrial sector or even a single firm.

Without a doubt, a contradiction exists between the intellectual hegemony of the free-enterprise view, which denies the legitimacy of industrial policy (and, in some cases, goes as far as to oppose interference with aggregate demand) and the widespread and perhaps permanent acceptance of interventionist practices.

One way of dealing with a contradiction is to ignore it. This is easier to do when decisions of vital importance to industrial development are made in a setting which, though legally considered to be part of the private sector, is closely connected to government. The result is that supply-side policy is implemented, but not called public policy. In some respects, the German and Japanese systems call such a solution to mind.

At other times, industrial policy is explicitly pursued. Not only does this bring the contradiction into sharper focus, but it also requires great effort by analysts to reconcile the two opposing factors in a logical way.

Generally speaking, industrial policies are explicitly requested when things go awry, and when an expedient means of improving the terms of a particular trade-off (between inflation and unemployment, or between domestic and external equilibria) becomes necessary. Aggregate demand policies can shift the economy along the trade-off curve, but if the entire curve is to be shifted, then some other factor is needed, something which has been found in incomes policy and in industrial policy.

For a brief period during the late 1960s, industrial policy elicited the interest of the United States, when the combination of recession, inflation and a weak dollar made it necessary to find an alternative solution to the traditional policy based on agregate demand (Norton [12] (*)).

During the same period, industrial restructuring became a central theme of economic policy debate throughout the West, and the OECD developed a strategy "for positive adjustment". European Community action included: reactivating the interventionist procedures of the ECSC treaty to restructure the steel industry; doing everything possible, given the lack of power of enforcement, to extend the interventionist approach to chemicals and fibres; and developing a system of financial incentives for industrial restructuring to be granted in addition to aid provided nationally.

In Italy, interest in industrial and incomes policy reached its peak during those years, sparked by the same negative factors present in the United States economy, and encouraged by tradition and general opinion.

During the 1980s, the climate was much less conducive to industrial policy. In the United States, the conditions which prevailed during much of the decade were diametrically opposed to those of the previous ten years. From an economic perspective, gains in produc-

---

(*) *Advise:* the numbers in square brackets refer to the Bibliography in the appendix.

tion and employment, lower inflation, and a strong exchange rate masked the persistent weaknesses in technological and structural competition with Japan and other dynamic economies. As for current thinking, the wave of faith in the market was in harmony with the direction of economic policy (at least official policy) toward deregulation and laissez-faire, and with the adoption of neoclassical schemes by economists. The conflict between theory and practice moved to the macroeconomic realm, where Keynesian policies existed in a context of decidedly anti-Keynesian ideas and strategies (the most recent RPE monograph; see Baldassarri [2]). Industrial policy had gone out of style.

In Europe, even though the employment situation was much less encouraging, and the fear of structural decay and technological ostracization more acute, the outlook was generally optimistic. Two oil shocks had been weathered without seriously jeopardizing the system, and with relatively low costs. Faith in the market economy was renewed, not only owing to the ideologies which prevailed, but also because of the cost of failed intervention experiments and because of the fall of radically alternative systems. The long-awaited revitalization of the European economy was a function of increased competition, brought about by the creation of the single market and by specific national initiatives.

The industrial policy of the 1980s could be described as being primarily directed at strengthening competition. At first glance, this appears to be the antithesis of traditional industrial policy, which favoured government action to develop specific sectors, to guide investment, to bail out troubled firms and to reorganize groups. Thus from one decade to the next, an abrupt change in policy direction occurred.

Nonetheless, the old objectives of increased competitivity and improved trade-off terms still exist, and not all of the policy measures have changed completely. Privatizations have created private-sector oligopolies to be watched and regulated; deregulation frequently poses problems of re-regulation; the rising cost of research, and more specifically the rising minimum efficient scale in research projects, requires either increased state involvement or industrial concentrations, which must be supervised by the public sector. In other words, just as the macroeconomic dispute between the neoclassical and Keynesian modes of thought has not yet been settled, the industrial policy issue is nowhere near a solution.

1. - A Classification

Do these two disputes reflect the same basic opposition between laissez-faire and interventionism? Can economic policies be divided into two main currents, to some extent because of analytical differences, but principally on ideological grounds?

Oversimplifications such as this one should be avoided: though based on truth, they seek to impose an interpretation on political theory and action, thereby distorting the actual meaning. As De Cecco (in Baldassarri [2] pp. 96-7) notes polemically: «we must remember that Keynes was the greatest defender of free enterprise, . . . the one who tried to minimize state intervention so as to leave things under the control of the private sector . . . It is especially important to stress this point, because in many countries, the US in particular, Keynes is associated with public-sector intervention at any cost . . .».

Ideologies should therefore be kept at arm's length, despite their major role as support for the work of scientists and as a guide for the decisions of policymakers. It is wiser to avoid shortcuts between the general and the specific.

Nonetheless, classifications are necessary because they provide a sense of order. When not expressed outright, they manifest themselves through the unwarranted interpretation of certain aspects (this is probably the explanation for the American interventionist view of Keynes referred to above).

Simply put, policies should be grouped under four, rather than two, main headings focusing on the macroeconomic and structural areas of economic policy. The major options could be divided into two groups in each area: Keynesian policies involving the management of aggregate demand and neoclassical-monetarist policies are macroeconomic in scope, while interventionist industrial policies and measures aimed at boosting competition are structural.

Each decision is based on at least one analytical premise. Keynesian and neoclassical policies differ on the usefulness and feasibility of stabilization, the main objective of macroeconomic policies. Industrial and structural policies (whether interventionist or aimed at boosting competition), reveal a dispute on how to pursue the structural competitivity objective, measured by the level of productivity, by the strength of firms, by the frequency of innovations, and by the share of production targeting the most dynamic and profitable segments of demand.

Moreover, there are two cross effects. Macroeconomic conditions do influence structural competitivity. Similarly, the conditions of structural competitivity affect the possibility of achieving an equilibrium of high employment and low inflation.

These four issues for analysis will be examined below.

1.1 *Macroeconomic Policy and Stabilization*

This question regards the capacity of the system to automatically stabilize itself at sufficiently low levels of unemployment and inflation. A line can be drawn between the yea-sayers (whom we will call neoclassical) and the nay-sayers (whom we will call Keynesians). The choice of school of thought should be neutral with respect to the empirical criteria (expansion or contraction of aggregate demand) used to evaluate macroeconomic policy. Keynesian interventionism and neoclassical abstentionism should therefore be equally conducive to expansion or contraction. In fact, however, Keynesian policies are usually associated with increasing demand while the neoclassical view tends to be linked to recessive policies.

The reason for this is probably that prices have never decreased over the last 50 years; only their rate of increase has changed. Within this context, the definition of neutral monetary policy is crucial: if we define it according to Friedman, as the rule of thumb of the creation of money expressed as a ratio to real growth plus a "desired" rate of inflation, the resulting monetary policy will invariably be too restrictive to lower unemployment, at least in the short term. Here, neutral and restrictive policies are one and the same.

The area of conflict between the two macroeconomic policy directions is the capacity of the economy to transform, within a reasonably short time, the underutilization of factors of production into lower prices (or a slowdown of inflation). More specifically, the speed and the magnitude of this change are at issue. In a situation of excess demand, the divergence normally disappears. Thus, when the conflict is apparent, we can say that if it is believed that the system is capable of quickly transforming underused factors of production into disinflation, then policies will generally be restrictive; conversely, if it is believed that Keynesian conditions have been created, then policies directed at expansion will be recommended. The conventional division of macroeconomic policies into expansive-Keynesian and restrictive-neoclassical (monetatist) is thus sufficiently consistent with theory to be acceptable. This concept was referred to recently in Tobin's impassioned plea for a European policy primarily directed at expanding demand to reabsorb unemployment (Tobin [15]).

In a small, open economy, reducing demand may be more tempting. Restrictive polices are doubly effective against inflation (as a higher exchange rate contributes to disinflation) and less harmful to increases in production (export-led expansion counterbalances the restriction of domestic demand). By including the above effects in the Prometeia model, Andreatta and D'Adda [1], who are not anti-Keynesian in principle, were able to assert that more restrictive monetary policies would lead to more rapid disinflation without lowering employment in Italia during 1974-1980.

It has been widely known for a long time that the widespread use of restrictive policies, though justifiable for each single country, would increase the risk of an overall recession. The solution should be international cooperation in planning and executing macroeconomic policy, a stategy routinely advocated by Keynesians, and, just as routinely, called futile by those who consider a recession to be a short-term phenomenon which will disappear on its own.

1.2 *Industrial Policies and Structural Competitivity*

The multitude of theories on the most effective policies to direct industrial development toward increased competitivity cannot be forced into a dichotomy.

At one end of the spectrum, we can place the faith in competition, the ideal context for the stimulus to optimize and for the selection of operators. Since this is precisely what the mainstream doctrine holds, no clarification is necessary. Instead, it is interesting to note the evidence from empirical studies: for instance, comparison of the innovative capacity of industrial systems (Ergas [8]) underscores the strategic value of competition among firms. M. Porter's enquiry into the different national performances yields similar indications (Porter [14]). On the contrary, active policies fostering innovation and restructuring have as their basis the existence of strong externalities and dynamic relationships which make today's structure dependent on the decisions of previous periods rather than on present comparative advantage (Dosi *et al.* [7]).

If the first category prevails, then industrial policies will be directed toward privatization, deregulation, and stimulating competition; if the second category prevails, then governments will promote programmes focusing on development, industrial restructuring, fostering research and innovation, and perhaps even a little well-aimed protectionism. For the sake of convenience, we will label the first category "competition" policies, and the second "intervention" policies.

1.3 *Macroeconomic Policies and Structural Competitivity*

Let us consider the cross effects.

In the interest of simplification, two opposite positions can be identified here as well: expansion can be considered to have a positive effect on structural development; alternatively recession can be seen as a more favourable context.

The former premise can be proven by referring to the debate on the positive relationship between increased production and increased productivity, known as the Verdoorn law and used by Kaldor to investigate the causes of slow economic growth in the U.K. during the 1960s (for details on the Verdoorn law and its possible interpretations, see Vaglio [16]). The analytical basis of the relationship can be found in increased economies of scale, in accumulation of capital, in the improved quality of capital stock (embodying innovations) if it is renewed more rapidly, and the learning-by-doing processes linked to industrial growth.

A resemblance can be seen with some hypotheses recently proposed to explain the persistently high levels of unemployment in Europe during the 1980s. If the purely Keynesian argument (Tobin [14]) is set aside, then we must accept the more widespread belief that the level of structural unemployment (or Nairu, non-accelerating inflation rate of unemployment) has risen in Europe. Although the reason why this rate should have risen from 2% in the 1970s to 10% in the 1980s is not easily identifiable, the idea of a hysteresis of unemployment is nonetheless appealing: Nairu would then be tied to the actual unemployment rate (Krugman [11], Gordon [10]).

What the Verdoorn law and the hysteresis of unemployment concept have in common is a causal relation going from short-term macroeconomic behaviour, influenced by aggregate demand policies, to structural change. Keeping demand on a course of high expansion, closely following productive capacity, would cause not only a rise in productive capacity itself, but also qualitative improvement, meaning higher productivity and more efficient use of the labour force. Expansive macroeconomic policies would have a positive effect on structural competitivity.

The opposite theory, asserting that recession is beneficial to the economy, has only been supported in reference to specific cases and short-term recessions. In a context of expansion which makes life easier for firms, the effect of shrinking demand could be to force a selection process among operators, to make speculation less attractive and to stimulate improvements, which had been neglected during the easy times.

Pre-Keynesian theories on business cycles may be recalled here. The same idea has emerged in a recent debate on the Italian economy's small "miracle": the jump from the vicious inflation devaluation cycle and the industrial crisis during the seventies to the stabilized prices, profits and productivity of the 1980s. A respected explanation stresses the positive effect of the European Monetary System and the subsequent refusal of monetary authorities to adjust exchange rates to reflect the inflation differential between Italy and its competitors. The stern warning of monetary authorities induced firms to resist wage demand and to focus more on industrial restructuring (this debate was covered by the author in Ranci [13]).

1.4 *Industrial Policies and Stabilization*

If the neoclassical view of macroeconomics is accepted, then the only way to effect stable increases in economic growth without inflationary pressures is to improve supply, since efforts to stimulate demand may be harmful or ineffectual. Macroeconomic objectives should be carried out by means of structural (or industrial) policies.

The neoclassical scenario requires a structural policy capable of increasing competition as much as possible while keeping public-sector regulation to a minimum. However, the application of neoclassical principles to macroeconomic issues and their application to microeconomic issues are two separate topics. Mistrust of demand management and belief that supply conditions are vitally important to macroeconomic equilibrium can coexist with recognition of externalities and dynamic relationships. One may reject macroeconomic activism and yet conclude that a rise in productivity and structural competitivity requires an active policy aimed not so much at promoting competition as at removing constraints and promoting research and development. This would allow use of public procurement, subsidies to firms and action by nationalized enterprises, aimed at breaking into new industrial sectors, despite the initial risk involved.

De Cecco's observation that Keynes was an advocate of free enterprise (for our purposes, a Keynesian macroeconomic policy is naturally accompanied by a free-market structural policy) can be reversed: it is possible to be macroeconomically anti-Keynesian and microeconomically interventionist. Is this combination only a possibility, or does the evidence exist to support it? Examples, rather than statistical analyses, can be found in the German economy, and perhaps in the Japanese system as well. To paraphrase De Cecco, the peculiarity of this combination, so unlike the dichotomous division, may have caused German economic policy to be considered more of a free market than it actually is.

2. - Combinations

If both instruments, macroeconomic and industrial policy, each have only two possible results, contraction-expansion and competition-interventionism, then four situations may be created. In principle, they can be easily described; however, the search for concrete examples must be based on approximation.

The contraction-competition scenario is true to neoclassical economic principles, and is clearly based on faith in competitive markets. One concrete example is Great Britain over the past ten years.

Conversely, an expansion policy with government intervention can be found in France during 1980-1982. The extraordinary development of Japan's economy over several decades also belongs in this category, but with two caveats: Japanese industrial policy is widely interpreted as focusing on planning and interventionism but there are different interpretations; and Japanese macroeconomic policy can be considered expansionary of one looks at the exceptionally high rates of industrial expansion, but less so if one observes that it always allowed for a sizeable current account surplus.

Expansion accompanied by a policy to promote competition seems to be an acceptable description of the Reagan policy, whether expansionism was deliberate or not.

Two distinct examples of the recessive macroeconomic policy and interventionist industrial policy combination can be found.

Some governments are inclined toward active policies, but are hampered by the external constraint. This was Italy's situation after the first oil shock, and to a lesser extent after the second shock; the situation in France was similar, interrupted only by the attempt at expansion during the early 1980s. Other governments, such as Germany, adopt policies which officinally stimulate free enterprise, but are actually performed within the context of a corporatist culture; where consultation is usual, externalities and dynamic relationships are naturally taken into account. One extremely interesting combination is European policy during the late 1970s and 1980s involving the creation of the European Monetary System and the Internal Market.

Macroeconomically, the anti-inflationary strategy of the Bundesbank dominated monetary policy.

The creation of the European single market can be considered a large-scale deregulation and liberalization, or an industrial policy designed to stimulate competition. However, the famous 300 directives included in the Internal Market programme not only supersede more stringent national regluations, but they also create new legislation, especially in areas previously overlooked in many countries, such as environmental protection and financial markets. On balance, liberalization can still be considered to be the dominant factor (as is the case in studies of the global impact of this strategy). New legislation meets the social and technological requirements of economic development and would have been introduced in any event, albeit at different times.

The overall result of "Europe 1992" will be improved structural competitivity and increased growth of the European economy; because of increased emphasis on dynamic effects, this economic growth should surpass the estimates of the Cecchini report (Cecchini [4], CER-IRS [5], Baldwin [3]).

3. - Variations

Although the division into four subgroups is more realistic than simply distinguishing between free-market and interventionist policies, it is still too rigid to accommodate a wide variety of experiences. In reality, some economic policy measures, such as specific taxes or social benefits, are not easily dealt with using the traditional instruments of macroeconomic or industrial policy, even though they effectively further the same objectives. Moreover, a policy may appear to be a combination of instruments belonging to different areas of economic policy, and may produce results because of the extent and time sequence of action. This was the context of Italian economic policy from 1975 to 1989, according to Giavazzi and Spaventa [9].

Because of the oil shock, the high level of inflexibility of real income in the Italian economy signalled, in the conventional view, the need for recessive policies (including the defence of the exchange rate to break the vicious inflation-devaluation circle), and structural policies aimed at increasing competition on the labour market. This was precisely the strategy put in place, but only from 1980 onward. During the late 1970s, accommodating macroeconomic policies prevailed, and repeated devaluations in nominal terms led to the real depreciation of the lira. Profits were supported through the reduction of social security contributions. In the end, real profit margins were maintained with the help of inflation-induced redistribution in favour of debtors, or companies.

Giavazzi and Spaventa assert that this policy was more effective than both the strategy based on conventional wisdom proposed by the OECD, and the stabilization policy effected in Great Britain. Given the inflexibility of real revenues, the Italian solution seems to have been second best. Indeed, maintaining high levels of demand and safeguarding profit margins throughout the initial phase caused a rise in productivity and an investment flow which eased the external constraint. In the early 1980s, when worldwide disinflation caused by the second oil shock and by Italy's joining the European Monetary System led to the long-awaited recession, the Italian economy was in the best position to deal with it, partly because of the climate of cooperation with the trade unions (1).

In reference to the classification used earlier, the reasoning is as follows: to achieve stabilization, it was essential that macroeconomic policy keep domestic demand in check after the oil shock had already reduced demand. The subsequent recession could have assumed exceptional proportions, and its structural consequences would have been all the more grave. As we have seen, a recession can either create a healthy shake-out, or act as a damaging disincentive to investments. The positive aspects prevail if the economy is already in a position of strength, that is, if profits are high, if the capital stock is new, and if the economy has the momentum of a recent period of increased production behind it, as in Italy's case. The negative effects

---

(1) In their analysis Giavazzi and Spaventa stress the fact that the reduction in social security charges was financed through the increase in tax revenue from household income, especially labour-related income, by means of fiscal drag. However, this aspect does not play a major role in the relationship between macroeconomic and industrial policy.

take precedence if the reverse is true. Examples of this are the UK economy and possibly what would have happened to the Italian economy if a policy of excessive disinflation had been implemented from the 1970s onward without corrective measures.

The very simple sheme used above to classify policies must be stretched somewhat to accommodate the views of Giavazzi and Spaventa. Whether or not a single act may satisfy a given objective cannot be decided on the basis of scholarly beliefs. The outcome depends on verifiable conditions within a specific context and the equally verifiable means of implementation of the economic policy concerned.

BIBLIOGRAPHY

[1] ANDREATTA N. - D'ADDA C.: «Effetti reali o nominali della svalutazione? Una riflessione sull'esperienza italiana dopo il primo shock petrolifero», *Politica economica*, n. 1, 1985.

[2] BALDASSARRI M. (ed.): «Keynes e le politiche economiche negli anni '80», Collana di monografie, Roma, Sipi, *Rivista di politica economica*, n. 1, 1989.

[3] BALDWIN R.: «The Growth Effects of 1992», *Economic Policy*, n. 9, 1989.

[4] CECCHINI P.: *La sfida del 1992*, Milano, Sperling & Kupfer, 1988.

[5] CER-IRS: *Un'industria in Europa*, Bologna, il Mulino, 1987.

[6] DORNBUSCH R.: «Europe 1992: Macroeconomic Implications», *Brookings Papers on Economic Activity*, n. 2, 1989.

[7] DOSI G. *et al.* (eds.): *Technical Change and Economic Theory*, London, Pinter, 1988.

[8] ERGAS H.: «Why Do Some Countries Innovate More Than Others?», *Ceps Paper*, n. 5, 1984.

[9] GIAVAZZI F. - SPAVENTA L.: «Italy: the Real Effects of Inflation and Disinflation», *Economic Policy*, n. 8, 1989, e Collana di monografie diretta da Mario Baldassarri, Roma, Sipi, *Rivista di politica economica*, n. 7-8, 1989.

[10] GORDON R.: *Back to the Future: European Unemployment Today Viewed from America in 1939*, «Brookings Papers on Economic Activity», n. 2, 1988.

[11] KRUGMAN P.: «Slow growth in Europe: conceptual issues», in LAWRENCE R.Z. - SCHULTZE C.D. (eds.): *Barriers to European Growth: a Transatlantic View*, Brookings Institution, Washington, 1987.

[12] NORTON R.D.: «Industrial Policy and American Renewal», *Journal of Economic Literature*, vol. XXIV, 1986.

[13] RANCI P.: «La strategia della Banca d'Italia vista dal sistema delle imprese», in NARDOZZI G. (eds.): *Il ruolo della banca centrale nella recente evoluzione dell'economia italiana*, Progetto finalizzato Cnr, Struttura ed evoluzione dell'economia italiana, F. Angeli, Milano.

[14] PORTER M.E.: The Competitive Advantage of Nations, London, McMillan, 1990.

[15] TOBIN J.: «La teoria keynesiana: è uno strumento ancora utile nella realtà economica odierna?», *Rivista di politica economica*, n. 4, apr. 1989.

[16] VAGLIO A.: «Fatti stilizzati» ed interpretazione teorica: il caso della legge di Verdoorn», *L'industria*, n. 1, 1990.

Forty-Five Years of Industrial Policy in Italy: Protagonists, Objectives and Instruments

Romano Prodi - Daniele De Giovanni
Università di Bologna

1. - Introduction

Limiting the detailed analysis of almost half a century of industrial policy to a few pages is an impossible task, and it is not our purpose to attempt the impossible. It is considered more useful and feasible to highlight a few of the specific points of interest in postwar industrial policy in Italy. Our objective, therefore, will be as follows: though less than systematic, the observations herein will seek to identify the themes underlying the Government and the regulatory action of industry in Italy.

Foremost is the observation that although the Italian industrial system gradually succeeded in matching those of other European countries, the same does not hold true for Italian industrial policy. Strategic shortsightedness has not only set Italian policy apart from that of almost every other EEC country, but has also caused it to run counter to the strategic guidelines created by the Commission of European Communities.

Regulatory action of industry in Italy has always been characterized by its improvisation, by the absence of a clear long-term strategy (the paucity of structural objectives), and especially by the deep-rooted prejudice, dualism (North-South, public-private) and dichotomies (small-sized firms against large-sized firms) which have always been a part of our economic and institutional systems.

One by one, each intellectual innovation, such as the granting of priority status to staple-sector investment, the indiscriminate support of small- and medium-sized enterprises to the point of placing troubled firms under state control, was tried and rejected. The excessive availability of formal aid stymied regulatory action, now fragmented within an unfocused system devoid of recognizeable points of reference. As a consequence, the measures put in place became virtually inaccessible to those who wished to make use of them.

The lack of strategic vision of industrial policy was often accompanied by inefficient measures and increasingly distorted effects. Unlike the balance of payments disequilibria and unemployment during the 1950s, the problem of southern Italy, rather than improving with the passage of time, became an increasingly dominant factor in industrial policy, further distancing the latter from those of France, Germany and Great Britain (Prodi [15]) (*).

The dualism and the dichotomies are, in our view, the main reason why Italy will always be compelled to implement policies aimed at maintaining the status quo and not at creating an institutional framework attuned to European economic integration.

There is, however, one aspect of postwar Italian industrial policy that makes it an appealing and, in many ways, frustrating object of study. We are referring to the divergence (unparalleled in any other country) between debate and the resultant legal measures (on one side) and actual administrative decisions (on the other).

True industrial policy, which resulted in administrative decisions, more often than not maintained its traditional course, only vaguely acknowledging the new legislation which arose. Rarely did this result in major changes, stemming from the new legislation, in public-sector administration and in the strategy of individual firms.

This also implied the absence of the often unwritten strategic understanding between enterprises and public-sector administration, which forms the basis of industrial policy in France, Spain and, with some differences, Germany.

This is not to question the importance and the role of public-sec-

---

(*) *Advise:* the numbers in square brackets refer to the Bibiography in the appendix.

tor administration. We simply wish to point out that it was limited to the administration of laws, and at times trifling laws, geared toward the support (or even the propping up) of firms rather than contributing to the development of long-term strategy. At no time has the Ministry of Industry suggested (through the appropriate channels used in other European countries) a strategy of mergers or the development of joint ventures and projects, among firms on their own.

Although the decisional aspect of industrial policy was emphasized, it is impossible to ignore the adverse effects of dividing the decisionmaking process between the ministries governing private- and public-sector enterprises. The need to unify the decisionmaking of Italian industrial policy by abolishing the Ministry of State Holdings was readily apparent almost twenty years ago (Prodi [17]). Since then, experience has shown all too clearly that in a historical context in which the barriers of national industry are surrendering to the onslaught of the European oligopoly, the dualism inherent in the Italian system can only cause irreparable damage.

The failed attempts at the reorganization (through the creation of so-called pools) of the aerospace industry, railway equipment, energy, food and banking sectors are all examples of foregone opportunities to strengthen the present and future competitiveness of Italian industry. These concentrations, which other countries succeeded in forming in the 1960s, were rendered impossible because the Ministry of Industry was never able to exert authority over Italian industry as a whole, since its sphere of action was limited to the private sector. Further evidence is provided by the fact that in coalition governments, the two portfolios have always been assigned to ministers of different parties, and in single-party governments, to ministers of differing schools of thought.

The Ministry of State Holdings, therefore, became increasingly adept at placing obstacles in the path of the much needed rationalization of industry; this despite its natural consequence, a decline in the minister's power. By the 1970s and 1980s, each minister did little more than check the success of his ministry in undermining the rationalization of the industrial system. During the past few years, the damage has spread even further. Attempts to justify this anomalous situation have caused the old dualisms of public- and private-sector firms, left for years in the shade, to be resorted to once again.

Dualism in the distribution of power, coupled with the need to justify its existence in hindsight, impeded all attempts to clear away, in Italy in the 1980s, the relics long since discarded in other countries.

By no means is the implicit or explicit adoption of Reagan-inspired industrial policy being advocated. This type of dualism in industrial policy serves little purpose other than to jeopardize what used to be known as «national industry», and is nowhere to be found, not in Great Britain under Thatcher, nor in traditional Germany, nor in French or Spanish neo-Socialist policies. Also deserving of mention is the change which occurred over a very short period in Spain, where Italian dualism was viewed at first as an interesting experiment, and then as a stumbling-block to the Europeanization and to the rationalization of the system. Dualism was then summarily dispensed with wherever possible.

2. - The Reconstruction Phase

The overall characteristics of Italian industrial policy (summarized above) were already manifest during the reconstruction phase. An analysis of Italian government intervention of the period clearly reveals the absence of a long-term plan for industrial policy and the "administrative parcelling" involved in the management of intervention measures. In addition, this was the period which saw the expansion of public-sector firms. These firms were given the overall objectives of stabilizing investment and fostering the development of impoverished areas of the country, rather than the more traditional industrial policy and increased competition.

This decison signalled the existence of different rules governing Italy's economic system, even as it conferred on public-sector firms a character distinct from that of private-sector firms. This distinct character was to play a decisive role in shaping the regulatory action of industry in Italy.

The Italian institutional framework of that period contained several fundamental contradictions caused by the coexistence of decisively free-market measures (such as the removal of several forms of public-sector control created under Fascist rule) and initiatives clearly aimed at underscoring the role of government in the economic development process. Such initiatives made Italy similar to a country with a centrally planned economy.

On the one hand, Italy was working toward "controlled reconstruction" based on the traditional Keynesian use of public expenditure; on the other hand, Italians in favour of free enterprise, and thus economic development centred exclusively on the modernization of industry to grow increasingly sceptical. The opposition of these two approaches provided Italy with ideas, rather than methods of government (Amato [1]) this burden would continue to weigh the country down to this day.

The reconstruction phase is by definition based on short-term objectives, in this case the reconstruction of an industrial system devastated by war. Nevertheless, this phase came to be known as one of the most intriguing periods of the postwar economic debate, because of the wide variety of perspectives on Italy's future destiny which emerged. The conflict pitted believers in autarchic (weak) Italian industry against those who foresaw the scenario of the 1950s, in which Italian firms engaged in international competition.

According to the latter view, enterprises would ease the pressure of the trade deficit by increasing the competitiveness of national products on foreign markets. To this end, a restructuring policy was needed which had as its base the modernization of industrial structures and the achievement of economies of scale.

By creating the Interministerial Committee for Reconstruction (CIR), the government was to coordinate "the reconstruction plans developed by each administration" and to set up the general plans for reconstruction. These included the 1946 plan to impose a ceiling on industrial imports and the 1946-1947 plan for imports and exports, expected to invigorate national industry (1).

---

(1) This experiment, which brought about the first signs of government planning of Italian industry (Saraceno 1945), revealed the role and the power of the state in the reorganization of the productive activity of firms. As several authors have pointed out, regulatory action of industry at that time expressed, though not explicitly, the concept of planning that lies between forecasting and decisionmaking mentioned by Saraceno in reference to the 1960s (AMATO [1]).

Even during this first phase, it is possible to detect the absence of coordinated regulatory action. In their original versions, the plans tended toward unifying public- and private-sector projects; however, this was only a rare occurrence, and plans for public-sector intervention in infrastructures gradually began to reflect internal interests, to the exclusion of the growing need for structural change in the economy.

Its plans aside, industrial reconversion policy provided for the management of foreign aid (the IMI-ERP Fund of 1947), the granting of assistance to small- and medium-sized enterprises (Decree Law 1419 of 15 December 1947) and the financing of machinery and equipment purchases (Law 922 of 4 November 1950).

The industrial policy experiment involving plans clearly revealed which powers the state wished to reserve for itself and how it intended to exert them. Government intervention began to be based not on overall industrial policy, but on bureaucratic control over the everyday lives of enterprises. This trend (already present in the management of the IMI-ERP and FIM Funds (the latter financing the metals industry) was accepted with little protest by enterprises, each one believing that it could derive special benefit from its privileged relationship with public-sector administration. The role of the latter changed from principal regulatory measure to mediator of individual interests.

3. - The 1950s and 1960s: From Central Planning to a Schizophrenic System

With the worldwide economic recovery and the intensifying of international trade of the early 1950s, the Italian economy entered a new phase during which it achieved unprecedented results. Italy began to change, transformed by the thousands of key players who created new enterprises, at first in the traditional development areas and then chiefly in the Centre-North and, to a limited extent, in certain areas of the Mezzogiorno. Although the term "miracle" would be slightly out of place, there can be no question but that the vitality of the economy during the first half of the 1950s led (for better or for worse) to the most profound changes in Italian history.

Confronted with a situation which surpassed by far all previous predictions, policymakers focused largely on devising a rational plan to regulate the actual behaviour of thousands of key players (especially new ones) in the Italian economy. Industrial policy thus became part of a planning policy based on expected demand aimed at allocating production to firms. The intellectual debate attributed iron-clad coherence and predictability to phenomena which, operating within an increasingly open economy, could only frustrate attempts to categorize constantly changing reality.

This distancing of policy proposals from Italy's actual problems was exemplified in the so-called Vanoni Plan, considered to be a fundamental policy measure during that period replete with major changes.

Closer scrutiny of the industrial policy debate of the period reveals the chasm between the school of thought in favour of planning and the reality of an international market that cannot be compared with the conditions which prevailed during the prewar period. Expressed in another way, the divergence between "intellectual vision" and real economic developments has been referred to as schizophrenia.

Nonetheless, examination of the measures adopted in some cases shows a surprising ability to provide concrete answers for the problems plaguing Italian industry. Though not particularly refined, these solutions were principally directed at the plight of small- and medium-sized enterprises. Industrial policy of the 1950s and 1960s, though highly criticized for having introduced a veritable shower of incentives, is in fact composed of legislation designed to foster the creation and the growth of small- and medium-sized enterprises. It cannot be doubted that the piece of legislation which has most often come under fire for its lack of strategic vision (Law 623 of 30 July 1959) produced the most beneficial effects for postwar Italian industry.

That the initial development of thousands of enterprises was attributable to Law 623 is worthy of note. However, the industrial policy which prevailed in Italy during the 1950s and 1960s can hardly be considered totally free of blame, since the fundamental weakness

Table 1

OUTLINE OF THE MAJOR INDUSTRIAL POLICY MEASURES IN EFFECT IN POSTWAR ITALY

Reconstruction phase: 1945-1950

Measure		Objective
Plan of	1946	Aid for raw materials imports
Plan of	1947-1948	Aid for imports and for exports
D.L.C.P.S. 891 of 11 September 1947		Setting up of IMI-ERP Fund
D.L.C.P.S. 1598 of 14 December 1947		Industrialization of southern Italy
D.L. 1419 of 15 December 1947		Credit to small- and medium-sized enterprises (SMEs)

The 1950s and 1960s

Measure		Objective
Law 157 of	22 June 1950	Financing of SMEs
Law 922 of	4 November 1950	Assistance in the purchase of machinery and equipment
Law 949 of	25 July 1952	Creation of Mediocredito Centrale
Law 298 of	11 April 1953	Increased credit to industry in southern Italy
Law 135 of	16 April 1954	Increased credit to SMEs
Law 634 of	29 July 1957	Mezzogiorno development incentives
Law 623 of	30 July 1959	Incentives to SMEs
Law 1470 of	18 December 1961	Financing of reconversion plans
Law 1329 of	28 November 1965	Subsidies for tool machinery purchases
Law 614 of	22 July 1966	Subsidies for depressed areas in central and northern Italy

TABLE. 1 *continued*

The 1970s

Measure		Main features
Law 184 of	22 March 1971	Creation of GEPI
Law 853 of	6 October 1971	Mezzogiorno subsidies
Law 183 of	2 May 1976	Regulation of subsidized loans
Law 902 of	9 November 1976	Regulation of subsidized loans to industry
Law 675 of	12 August 1977	Fund for the Reconversion and Restructuring of Firms
Law 787 of	5 December 1978	Restoring financial stability to firms
Law 91 of	29 March 1978	Subsidized credit
Law 95 of	3 April 1979	Management of troubled firms
Law 784 of	28 November 1980	Rise in GEPI capital stock

The 1980s

Measure		Objective
Law 46 of	17 February 1982	Setting up of the Fund for Technological Innovation
Law 696 of	19 December 1983	Subsidies for the purchase of tool machine
Law 64 of	1 March 1986	Special intervention for the Mezzogiorno
Law 399 of	3 October 1987	Subsidies for the purchase of tool machine

mentioned earlier, the dearth of administrative structures geared toward the management of intervention measures, continued to persist.

Indeed, during this twenty-year period, state bureaucratic structures very gradually unravelled, and much of the responsibility for enforcing laws was conferred on external structures, such as the banking sector. In the 1970s, when policy in favour of bailouts and sector-by-sector restructuring caused decisionmaking authority to shift back to the supervisory body, the bureaucracy designed to regulate industry, it was discovered, had been virtually destroyed. During this period, each of the Ministers of Industry sought to circumvent this problem through the use of non-bureaucratic structures, for the most part external commissions largely made up of university professors.

Despite our favourable opinion of the above-mentioned shower of incentives, there can be no question that the industrial policy of the 1950s and 1960s lacked strategic vision, even as regards a point of reference for enterprises and for policymakers. This role could certainly not be played by the bureaucratic structure in its chronically weakened state.

One of the factors which inhibited the creation of a strategic industrial policy was undoubtedly the role of public-sector firms first undertaken in the early 1950s. Although the objectives of state-owned firms during the reconstruction phase (the reconversion of wartime industry and the reconstruction of devastated productive structures) were extremely simple and useful to all, the 1950s and especially the ENI "scandal", opened debate concerning the function of public-sector enterprise, a debate which divided not only policymakers, but also the broad public view.

The underlying themes of the debate are in themselves contradictory, as public-sector firms are correctly viewed as a key element in the destruction of firmly established monopolies (as in the case of fertilizers) while also being used to provide political support.

Even though, on the one hand, some of the objectives of public-sector firms showed foresight and were perfectly in tune with the economic needs of the time, on the other hand the decision to formally sanction the differentiation between firms in the public and private sectors through the creation of the Ministry for State Participations cannot be regarded as positive, either in principle or on the basis of facts.

Diametrically opposed to the emphasis placed on public-sector firms were the attempts to introduce antitrust legislation. In the 1950s, debate on the safeguarding of competition was just beginning in Italy. In spite of their differing perspectives, the draft bills proposed as a result unanimously supported the view that antitrust laws should not impede the development of Italian industry (2).

Thus, a blatant contradiction existed. Although competition was acknowledged as being central to economic change, increased state involvement was nonetheless encouraged to ensure balanced development. The paradox extended even to the draft bills proposed. By blatantly favouring the public sector, which was virtually exempt from legislation, antitrust regulation took Italy one step closer to that perilous division between laws governing public-sector firms and laws governing private-sector firms.

With the restructuring of Italian industry, the government was faced with the task of lowering the unemployment rate, pushed upward to inprecedented levels during the reconstruction phase while industrial policy focused on the reconstruction of industry rather than on the expansion of Italy's industrial base. In the meantime, policymakers and many economists began to express the conviction that Italian economic development, if left to continue unchecked, would be ill-equipped to eliminate either the dualism between North and South or the other structural weaknesses of the economy. This conviction became the cornerstone of a theory of economic planning (on a large scale) with a view to creating industrial policy solely for the purpose of redressing the disequilibria created during reconstruction.

The growing importance attached to unemployment in socio-political debate (3) in Italy during the early 1950s, and the increasingly

---

(2) The draft laws included those of Malagodi-Bozzi of 1955, Lombardi-La Malfa of 1966, Tremelloni of 1958 and Carcaterra of 1959.

(3) A particularly significant role was played by the second national congress of the Cgil trade union where the so-called Working Plan was developed. In some respects, the features of this Plan preceded the Vanoni Plan.

widespread approval in principle of the theory of economic planning led to the sanction of the *Ten-Year Plan for the Development of Employment and Income in Italy from 1955 to 1964*, otherwise known as the *Vanoni Plan*. Even though it cannot be considered as the true starting-point of economic planning, since it was never implemented, the Plan revealed the need for the decoupling of Italian industrial policy from the old liberal-protectionist intervention schemes put in place during the reconstruction phase.

In spite of its attempts to introduce substantial changes in the regulation of industry, the *Vanoni Plan* served no other purpose than to express the need for the "liberal interventionism" which had initially provided the impetus for industrial change. Within this new context, since it was not believed that industry was capable of reabsorbing the unemployment it had created, regulatory action should have consisted of a new phase of development to eliminate the disequilibria caused by reconstruction. This did in fact occur, albeit through the use of measures not set out in the Plan, and with the exception of southern Italy. The parameters for industrial policy-related assistance were constructed in part on the bases of the findings of the Committee for the Development of Employment and Income, set up to remedy the lack of appropriate measures mentioned in the *Plan*. Of the sector-by-sector analyses conducted by the Committee, the most important was the cornerstone of the Steel Plan, the first plan prepared for an Italian industrial sector.

The notion that the *Vanoni Plan* could redirect the regulation of industry toward well-coordinated forms of intervention was immediately refuted by the measures introduced by government in the late 1950s and the early 1960s. Small- and medium-sized enterprises blossomed in a shower of incentives, and a steady stream of public funds was directed toward state-owned firms.

The subsequent disappearance of the *Vanoni Plan* met with the full approval of the Italian economy. This phase of self-propelled development succeeded in achieving and at times surpassing even the most far-reaching objectives set out in the *Plan* without making use of the regulatory action which the *Plan* recommended. Development stemmed in part from entrepreneurial activity, which in the meantime had come into its own (4), and in part from the future prospect of a European single market.

The rise in market growth and an industrial system which had almost succeeded in matching the other leading West European countries were not viewed by the state as an opportunity to define its role or the resultant regulatory action. With global economic strategy in the shade, the government could do little more than indiscriminately provide financial support to enterprises, leading to a proliferation of incentives. Aside from the positive results mentioned earlier, this increased assistance led in turn to the development of an ambiguous relationship between government and firms. The emergence of a cadre of new professionals known as "incentives" experts, each with appropriate political contacts in the capital, was a direct consequence of public-sector weakness.

Initially, the incentives system should have conformed to the view of industrial policy taken by the *Vanoni Plan*. The proposed objective was in fact the selective granting of aid based on a "strategic" view of industrial policy. Signs of this intention are also present in the legislation of the period, which seemed to promote, at least in theory, a distancing from the liberal protectionism which had formed an integral part of the incentives system during the reconstruction phase (5).

The new developments in the action of industry during the early 1950s all concern the creation of new institutions. On the one hand, the legislation had been created for the organization of financing measures aimed at small- and medium-sized enterprises which culminated in the creation of the Mediocredito, the institute for medium-term credit, under Law 949 (6) of 2 July 1952 and in the

---

(4) Entrepreneurial development was one of the effects of incentives policy; this aspect is frequently overlooked in criticisms of the regulatory action of industry during the latter half of the 1950s.

(5) Two of the discriminatory factors introduced in legislation are worthy of note: the focus on the Mezzogiorno, and the emphasis on small- and medium-sized firms, both of which benefited from special forms of financing.

(6) The need for an efficient, decentralized system for extending credit to small — and medium — sized enterprises had already been signalled in Law 445 of 22 June 1950, which invested the Treasury Ministry with the power to set up regional institutes to provide small- and mid-sized firms with medium-term credit.

granting of medium-term credit to foster industrial development in southern Italy by special sections of Banco di Napoli, Banco di Sardegna and Banco di Sicilia through the Institute for Economic Development in Southern Italy (ISVEIMER), Credito Industriale Sardo (CIS) and the Regional Institute for the Financing of Industry in Sicily (IRFIS) under Law 298 of 11 April 1953.

On the other hand, seemingly in contrast with Amato's interpretation [1] (7), a policy to create infrastructures in the Mezzogiorno was being developed. This objective, which led to the creation of the southern Italian savings bank, Cassa per il Mezzogiorno, was not only set forth in the above-mentioned law but was also confirmed by the absence of plans to increase income and employment.

From the mid-1950s on, industrial progress was accompanied by a system whose deterioration was fueled by an overextended incentives policy, frustrating all attempts to impose more coordinated regulatory action. A wide margin of discretion, coupled with an ineffectual supervisory framework, created a rift between the measures put in place and the objectives for which they had originally been created; as a consequence, these measures gradually came to be used as tools for the self-preservation of government.

Institutions began to play the role of "notary" to firms, the true centres of industrial planning. Indeed, sector-by-sector policies were pursued by the major Italian public- and private-sector industrial groups, which left only horizontal industrial policies, such as incentives and transfer payments to enterprises, to be dealt with by means of regulatory action (Scognamiglio [19]).

The shortcomings and inefficiencies of regulatory action in the 1950s were first officially revealed during the discussion of a report by the Minister of Special Intervention in March of 1961. From that debate arose the first formal approach to economic planning aimed at transforming the market into an "institution" manageable by regulatory action on the economy.

Viewed from this angle, economic planning was an institutional

---

(7) Amato asserts that during the early 1950s, policy concerning aid to southern Italy experinced a noticeable shift away from the building of infrastructures and toward increased incentives. In our opinion, the facts do not seem to support this view.

model capable not only of departing from the liberal protectionism of the reconstruction years, but also of surpassing the concepts of global economic strategy of the early 1950s. Regulatory action on industry was part of a predetermined plan no longer geared toward spontaneous industrial development (8).

Supported by leftists, this position rekindled debate. On one hand, it was thought that the market was not the appropriate setting in which to execute policy related to industry as a whole, while on the other hand the granting of incentives was the only planning activity that could be conceived of to achieve gains in efficiency in health, education and transportation services.

From the outset, the planning experiment was therefore widely criticized, for the most part, by the general public and was regarded with disapproval by industry and trade union leaders. The Saraceno Commission report proposed a five-year plan for 1965-1969 which was subsequently approved by Parliament as the *National Economic Plan for the Five-Year Period 1966-1970.*

The planning debate continued for years at every decisionmaking level, with public involvement bordering on obsession. In many respects, this was a period of widespread involvement and a high level of democracy. This is why it is so surprising to note that no tangible results ensued. With the approval of the *Plan,* a collective sigh of relief could be heard across the country, as though a great problem had been solved. As for the stage of industrial development currently under review, this *Plan* simply produced no results, positive or negative.

Developments in industrial policy were destined to be rejected during the 1960s, not only because no means had yet been found to organize the incentives provided by state-owned firms or by the Ministry of Industry, but also because the only sector-by-sector plan in place, concerning the chemicals sector, exemplified the errors of industrial policy. It contained rigid quantitative forecasts of production levels, and developed plans of action and roles for firms which

---

(8) Thus defined, an economic planning strategy limits economic development caused by spontaneous private-sector initiatives, but is not opposed to a market economy: "It renders private decisionmaking subordinate to the broader interest of balanced economic development" (Confindustria, 1963).

were in no way inspired by trends in market growth or by current domestic and international competition.

The creation of the Ministry for State Holdings heralded the advent of dualism in regulatory action on industry, a major factor causing the industrial policy gap between Italy and the other European market economies. Not only did the Ministry fail to strengthen planning activity, but it also represented the further fragmenting of power, hardly a positive influence on regulatory action on industry (9).

As regards reconversion, while France, Germany and Great Britain took advantage of high rates of growth to restructure troubled sectors (10), Italy's broad economic incentives for reconversion, which should have been considered an economic planning priority, consisted of very few pieces of legislation (11), which underscored the practice of providing fragmented and ill-timed assistance, based almost entirely on one measure, financial incentives.

The failure of institutions to produce new regulatory action on industry caused negative effects on the industrial system. The rapid pace of Italian industry, which had almost matched the standards of productivity and efficiency of the other EEC countries, was slowed considerably by factors such as the lack of technological continuity, the inability to diversify products, and especially the failure of restructuring and reconversion projects which a few years later would play a key role in easing the tensions of the market for factors of production.

4. - Industrial Policy of the 1970s: Ill-Timed Efforts at Restructuring

The 1970s were a period of turmoil for Italian industry. International competition had become an everyday event in the lives of firms,

---

(9) The simplification process that should have begun with the creation of the Ministry for State Participations was stymied by the fact that decisionmaking in connection with public-sector firms was far beyond the Ministry's jurisdiction (PRODI [17]).

(10) For a complete list of industrial bailout incentives in Europe, see PONTAROLLO [11].

(11) During the 1960s, only one restructuring measure was approved: Law 1470 of 18 December 1961, on the financing of industrial programmes for the completion of reconversion programmes, which did little more than increase the "power to grant financial subsidies" of the Ministry of Industry.

sending traditional products and production methods into a crisis state. The growing danger of the collapse of all large-sized enterprises caused industrial policy to aim at halting the spread of this crisis to Italian industry as a whole.

The choice of instruments used to avert danger represented one of the most dangerous differentiations from the policies of other European countries. The crisis of firms was not viewed as an opportunity to carry out the necessary regrouping and rationalization dictated by the new competitive framework; rather, bailouts became the order of the day. Large-sized enterprises received this assistance from state-owned firms (IRI in particular), while enterprises less likely to benefit from such aid became the responsibility of GEPI, set up at the beginning of the 1970s for the specific purpose of preventing the failure of troubled firms.

Created by virtue of Law 184 of 22 March 1971 to «aid in the maintenance and in the increasing of employment levels jeopardized by the short-term difficulties of industrial enterprises», GEPI ought to have provided incentives on the basis of restructuring and reconversion plans.

Initially, Law 184 had set out selection criteria for the granting of assistance through GEPI; however, these criteria were quickly abandoned following deliberations at the interministerial committee (CIPE) level, and incentives were provided even when no real plan existed for restoring financial health to firms. The degeneration of GEPI activity was sanctioned by Decree Law 9 of 30 January 1976 (12) and by Law 784 of 28 November 1980.

The Decree Law led to the creation, by GEPI, of the Institute for the Promotion of Employment (IPO) which was to hire and immediately grant redundancy fund assistance to the employees of enterprises selected by CIPE (13); for its part, Law 784 bundled 24 firms with a total of 9000 employees into GEPI, compelling the agency to create new businesses to hire them. Once geared toward assisting troubled firms, GEPI, had become a job-creation agency, and consequently an instrument for the easing of social tensions.

---

(12) The selection criteria had simply been approved by the CIPE.
(13) For the most part, this involved agencies whose crises were caused by the misuse of foreign capital.

Whereas it is true that the 1970s were critical years for other European countries as well, examination of the industrial policies adopted abroad reveals that this was the decade in which mergers and strategic alliances were formed among national firms in order to play a leading role in the new European oligopoly.

In Italy, increased bailouts brought about a one-way expansion of the public sector, but in a completely random fashion. This lack of logic (or better yet, this randomness) prevailed in the reorganization of the food sector, the expansion of the public-sector steel industry and, in the worst case, the creation of an aerospace-sector nucleus.

In every instance, changes in ownership obeyed no industrial logic whatsoever; this objective was achieved owing to pure chance. Of course, pro-public-sector opinion took advantage of this good fortune, labelling this or that industrial sector as "strategic" as though the term were a stamp of approval for the bailing out of firms by making them a part of the public sector.

Italian industrial policy is so far removed from strategic objectives that no attempt is made even to place complementary firms in the same agency. The compulsory objectives of synergy are thus ignored, not only between public and private sectors, but also within the public entity itself.

As the number of troubled firms continued to rise, the ability of the system to absorb them was increasingly called into question. this led to the approval by government of intervention instruments which, though designed to bring Italy's industrial system in line with normal market conditions, inevitably formed a part of the bailout package received by large-sized firms, yet another sign of the inadequacy of regulatory action on industry (14). This can hardly be considered surprising. That the system should degenerate into an approach merely based on aid was more or less to be expected, since restructuring was widely understood to mean the bailout of firms at any cost.

Also deserving of mention is the fact that more sophisticated observes pointed at the lack of legislation providing for special

---

(14) This refers to Laws 184 of 22 March 1971, of 1 December 1971, and 464 of 8 August 1974. For further information, see PONTAROLLO [12].

measures to ease the plight of large-sized firms as partial justification for this behaviour. Law 95 of 3 April 1979 (more widely known as the Prodi law), clearly inspired by legislation in existence abroad in particular by *Chapter 11* in force in the United States, attempted to remedy this situation. Nonetheless, the conditions for the application of the law where very gradually extended until they frustrated the objectives of the law itself, reproposing the indirect use of bailout policies.

This fledgling attempt was followed by more effective measures, and a policy for the control of direct subsidization to firms was adopted by the European Economic Community. Thus, external intervention acted as a partial substitute for Italy's lack of legislative and administrative action, but not without adverse effects. Community-wide policy can hardly be expected to strengthen the position of Italian industry within the common market, as other European countries had surmised.

During the late 1970s the industrial policy debate began anew as the policy of subsidies and bailouts in place from 1965 to 1975 met with widespread opposition. The many interesting discussions which ensued led to the introduction of important legislation, including Law 183 of 2 May 1976, the Presidential decree of 9 November 1976 and, in particular, Law 675 of 12 August 1977.

These three pieces of legislation were designed to foster the reorganization of all financial subsidy measures existing under current law, largely in an effort to establish procedures which clearly distinguished adminstrative areas of responsibility — those of government — from the technical role of banks. However, even this attempt to set a new course for industrial policy fell victim to the old vices. The presence of the Interministerial Commitee for the Coordination of Industrial Policy (CIPI) and the action which followed made for an even more complicated decisionmaking framework.

Law 675 of 12 August 1977 ought to have represented the final breakthrough, with the application for the first time of principles discussed in the 1970s. Nonetheless, as Momigliano point out, the complex Byzantine legislative innovations simply reconfirmed the old errors. Italian restructuring and reconversion was considered to be "a new myth replacing the failed myth of economic planning of the

1960s, or the failed myth of a new development model of the 1970s" (Momigliano [8]).

Article 17 of Law 675 abolished the industrial restructuring measures previously in place (15) while inheriting the administrative procdures associated with them. Also worthy of note is the fact that the law contained noticeable contradictions. Although legislation was geared toward redesigning regulatory action of industry, this should have been complemented by the reorganization of the administrative responsibilities involved. The law did not result in concrete changes; indeed, new measures became entangled in old administrative procedures.

According to the law, sector-by-sector plans were the intervention instruments which would be made available to the CIPI to further this new approach. These plans were of little use in rendering regulatory action on industry more selective. During two CIPI meetings held on 24 February 1978 and 8 July 1980, trade-union preassures ensured that reconversion programmes were extended to 12 industry sectors; however, the programmes were so broad in scope as to include most of the country's industrial system (16).

Few tangible results were produced by this law, which had given rise to so many expectations. Its failure can only be attributed to the factors mentioned many times earlier. What seems to be the worst offence of a strategic measure, as the law on industrial restructuring strove to be, is without a doubt the lack of overall long-term strategy concerning individual incentives. Perhaps because of its arduous passage through Parliament, Law 675 contained several ambiguities regarding the directions to be taken and the methods to be applied. What should have been a reorganization measure looked more like a law for reform, introducing but not defining the framework for the planning of regulatory action on industry (17).

In addition, Law 675 once again underscored the lack of decisions concerning regulatory action, as well as their conservative

(15) Laws 1470 of 128 December 1961, 1101 of 1 December 1971, Article 9 of Law 464 of 8 August 1972 and Titolo I, Articles 1, 2, 3 and 4 of Law 184 of 23 March 1971.

(16) At the same time, certain, sectors were being more broadly defined. Among these were tool machinery, steel and electronics; the latter was extended so far as to include household appliances with electronic parts.

(17) For a review of the debate on industrial planning, see RANCI [18].

nature (18). Examples of the latter are the distribution of the funds made available under the law (19) and the large amount of assistance provided purely for the purpose of industrial bailout (20).

5. - The 1980s: Foregone Opportunities

The early 1980s brought sweeping radical change to the economic environment under review and to international debate on economic policy, especially industrial policy.

The disapproval of widespread public intervention and of bailout policies was accepted by all, while measures geared toward economic liberalization and the privatization of firms (21) were being created and applied virtually everywhere, albeit in varying degrees. The context, therefore, was one of radical change, both in form and in substance.

In Italy these innovations were put in place after some delay and with several reservations, if compared with those of the United States, Great Britain and France, to name a few. The drawbacks of incentives policies were brought into sharper focus, especially because of their adverse effects on the daily lives of many firms.

Thus, at the beginning of the 1980s, incentives policy was shunned in favour of new developments in industrial policy, such as public demand, payment for real services to firms and the moderniz-ation of the entire public sector.

Confindustria proposed that industrial policy be directed toward accepting the challenge of new international trade by means of a policy which focused on the factors of production. The adoption of the by-factor policy and the shelving of the by-sector policy, though not an all-encompassing programme, was nonetheless regarded as an acceptable expression of changing times (Confindustria [6]).

---

(18) Also of note is the delay in making the payments provided for under the law and the lengthy disputes with regard to its interpretation, especially with the Commis-sion of European Communities.

(19) Traditional sectors (automobilies, chemicals and steel) received 80% of fun-ding.

(20) An example is given by the basic Chemistry plan.

(21) For a review of privatization processes in Europe, see VICKERS - WRIGHT [20].

Even legislation seemed to take a new turn. As Law 675 had been shattered by administrative chaos and EEC action (22), new industrial policy directions were the order of the day. These included Law 46 of 14 February 1982 on technological innovation and Law 696 of 19 December 1983 on incentives for the purchase of high-level production equipment by small and medium-sized enterprises.

In theory, Law 46 should have caused a turnaround in Italian industrial policy. However, owing to the recurrent ills of regulatory action on industry in Italy, not all of the answers provided met the needs of the Italian industrial system. Aside from the problems and delays associated with its readings in Parliament, the law was hampered by the lack of institutional innovations to coordinate intervention, and by the myriad compromises built into the law itself (Momigliano-Antonelli [10]).

What played a major role in tying Law 46 to traditional Italian industrial policy was the creation of the «Innovation Fund» overlapping Ministry of Industry responsibilities with those of the Ministry for Scientific Research.

Although the intellectual climate had changed, regulatory action continued to lack the measures and the administrative structure needed to keep pace with new developments. Since nothing really new had happened to regulatory action despite the radical change in Italian public opinion, government industrial policy met with growing scepticism and indifference.

Privatizations are certainly the best example. No legislation on this subject was created either to deal with general policy or to determine the procedures to be followed if privatizations occurred. When the situation of state-owned firms grew so alarming to jeopardize their survival, policymakers somehow managed to tolerate the new privatization and rationalization policies involving firms and industry sectors for some little time; however, once the crisis abated, the old policy re-emerged as though nothing in the world had happened during the 1980s.

As in the previous case, no new legislation was adopted, and no

---

(22) For a review of the relationship beteween Italian industrial policy and Community-wide legislation, see CAGLI [3].

new strategy was developed. Nonetheless, the references made at the time to the "strategic" or "singular" nature of the public sector served to illustrate the continued prevalence of government, and the control of policymakers over the lives of firms.

A few years ago, this would have sparked controversy, and given rise to heated debate and opposition. Nowadays, it is calmly treated as inevitable, a phenomenon common to the entire poltical scene. Something will be done about it in the future, probably as a consequence of judgements pronounced by Brussels, but it will undoubtedly be too late to efficiently reorganize Italian industry. In many cases (especially in public procurement industries, such as railway equipment and capital goods for energy production), it is already late in the day to become leaders in international markets. At this stage, nothing more can be done.

In other cases, it will become clear that it is too late in five or six years.

Italy's role in international competition (23) is increasingly dominated by sectors primarily composed of small- and medium-sized enterprises, sheltered by their very nature from public intervention, which no longer acts in the interest of industrial policy, but, rather, as an unwelcome interference in the daily lives of firms, impeding their every decision. One may well ask whether a country like Italy can subsist on small- and medium-sized enterprises. The answer, nonetheless, seems perfectly clear.

6. - Conclusions

Within a context where European integration, despite several delays, is moving ever closer to its objective, the single market, Italian industrial policy does not seem to have emerged from the quagmire which over time has rendered it obsolete and ineffectual in fostering the transformations needed by Italian industry to play a more significant role on international markets. Not only must more favourable conditions for market activity be created, as debate in the 1980s had

---

(23) On this subject, see PORTER [13].

rightly concluded. Antitrust legislation and a more limited sphere of public activity for public-sector firms are fundamental aspects of any plan for industrial freedom of choice, but cannot replace regulatory action on industry, which by now seems to be completely paralyzed.

The reasons which explain why Italy has experienced the longest postwar period devoid of new industrial policies derive not so much from failed attempts at imposing French-style regulatory action as from government inability to introduce new industrial policy in keeping with the spirit of the European Community, which is no longer willing to accept industrial policy measures based on the granting of subsidies.

BIBLIOGRAPHY

[1] AMATO G. (ed.): *Il governo dell'industria in Italia*, Bologna, il Mulino, 1972.

[2] BIANCHI P. - PRODI R.: «Il dibattito di politica industriale», *L'industria*, vol. V, n. 2, 1984.

[3] CAGLI A.: «La politica industriale italiana tra sovranità nazionale e vincoli comunitari», in BIANCHI P. - GIORDANI M.G. (eds.): *L'amministrazione dell'industria e del commercio estero*, Bologna, il Mulino, 1990.

[4] CER-IRS: *Terzo rapporto sull'industria e la politica industriale italiana*, Bologna, il Mulino, 1989.

[5] CONFINDUSTRIA: *L'impresa industriale nella società italiana: proposta Confindustria per uno statuto dell'impresa*, Roma, Sipi 1977.

[6] — · — : «Per una politica industriale: le proposte degli imprenditori», Atti del convegno, Genova, 9-10 October 1981, *Rivista di politica economica*, August-September 1982.

[7] GOBBO F. - PRODI R.: «La politica industriale italiana», *Note economiche*, n. 5-6, 1982.

[8] MOMIGLIANO F.: «Ristrutturazione e riconversione industriale, politica industriale e programmazione economica», *Rivista di economia e politica industriale*, vol. V, n. 1, 1979.

[9] — · — (ed.): *Le leggi della politica industriale in Italia*, Bologna, il Mulino, 1986.

[10] MOMIGLIANO F. - ANTONELLI C.: «Politiche per la ricerca applicata, l'innovazione, l'ammodernamento e il trasferimento teconlogico» in MOMIGLIANO F. (ed.): *Le leggi della politica industriale in Italia*, Bologna, il Mulino, 1986.

[11] PONTAROLLO E.: *Il salvataggio industriale nell'Europa della crisi*, Bologna, il Mulino, 1976.

[12] — · — : «Le politiche di ristrutturazione industriale in Italia dal 1961, al 1977», *L'industria*, vol. 1, n. 3, 1980.

[13] PORTER M.: *The Competitive Advantage of Nations*, New York, Free Press, 1990.

[14] PRODI R.: «I problemi dell'economia italiana», *Atti del convegno nazionale di studi della Democrazia cristiana*, Perugia, Cinque Lune, 1972.

[15] — · — : «L'Italia», in VERNON (ed.): *L'intervento pubblico nell'industria: un'analisi comparata*, Bologna, il Mulino, 1974.

[16] — · — : «Per una riconversione e ristrutturazione dell'industria italiana», in PRODI R. - GOBBO F. (eds.): *Per una ristrutturazione e riconversione dell'industria italiana*, Bologna, il Mulino, 1980.

[17] PRODI R.: «La crisi delle partecipazioni statali: Conseguenze economiche di faticosi processi di decisione», *L'industria*, vol. I, n. 1, 1981.

[18] RANCI P.: «La legge sulla Riconversione come strumento di politica industriale», *Economia e politica industriale*, n. 20, 1978.

[19] SCOGNAMIGLIO C.: «Strategia industriale e programmazione», in GRASSINI F.A. - SCOGNAMIGLIO C. (eds.): *Stato e industria in Europa: Italia*, Bologna il Mulino, 1979.

[20] VICKERS J. - WRIGHT V.: *The Politics of Privatization in Western Europe*, London, Frank Cass, 1989.

II - THREE LINKS

Phases of Italian Industrial Development and the Relationship between the Public and Private Sectors

Fulvio Coltorti (*)
Ricerche e Studi (R & S), Milano

1. - Introduction

The purpose of this essay is to describe the phases of recent postwar Italian industrial development, with particular focus on the interaction between public- and private-sector firms. More specifically, public-sector enterprises are defined as state-owned industry, while the term industry is used in its broadest sense to describe the activity involved in the production of goods and services.

First of all, we think it helpful to set out the phases of development and their marks. Even though we are aware of the historical continuity, we think it convenient to hold a frame of reference which could serve to arrange some sort of "travel notes". The underpinnings of such a scheme can be found in Graph 1, which outlines trends in Italian production from 1950-1989 according to ISTAT indices. Though essentially steady, the expansion revealed seems nonetheless to have been characterized by three major setbacks in 1964, 1975 and 1983. These interruptions create a natural division of events into four sufficiently homogeneous phases: 1) 1950-1964: postwar reconstruction followed by the economic miracle; this phase ended with the first tightening of monetary base by the Central Bank; 2) 1964-1975:

(*) The Author assumes sole responsibility for the opinions expressed.

heightened public-sector intervention in the economy took the form of economic planning and policy to stimulate development in the South: the recession caused by the first oil shock marked the end of this period; 3) 1975-1983: this phase began with rising inflation, the financial crisis of industry and its subsequent structural adjustment, and ended with the second major recession of the Italian economy; 4) 1983 to the present: the highlights of this phase are renewed entrepreneurial vigour, innovation and recourse to the financial market.

For easier reference, the following specific information on each phase is provided in several tables attached: the quantity supplied of selected major goods (Table 1A); transactions made by the principal state-owned industrial agencies (Table 2A) and by the leading private-sector industrial groups (Table 3A); essential economic and financial data concerning the major state-controlled and private-sector firms (Table 4A and 5A); selected time-series data from the profit-and-loss statements of Italian enterprises (Table 6A).

2. - Postwar Reconstruction amd the Economic Miracle: 1950-1964

The second world war left Italian industry with plant and equipment which, although not seriously damaged, could be considered obsolete and underutilized. Most of Italy's population (over 40% of the labour force) was employed in the agricultural sector. Solid primary industries (steel, energy, chemicals) were lacking and unemployment was rampant throughout the country. Moreover, very low real wages made for an extremely impoverished domestic market. A sizeable portion of industry remained under government control, as a result of failed attempts at privatization during the banking-sector restructuring of the 1930s: state holdings were primarily concentrated in steel, shipbuilding, sea transport, a part of the electric power industry, the mechanical and the electromechanical industry (1). Autarchic

---

(1) The principal areas of operation were those of cast iron Finsider and Cogne representing (80% of national output), steel (45%), shipbuilding (80% in terms of national output capacity), railway rolling stock (25% of national output capacity), oil refining (AGIP and ANIC presenting 52% of national output), telephone services (57% of

policies placed constraints on market structures; by limiting foreign competition, these measures stunted the growth of the domestic market and inevitably led to the creation of monopolies (2). Thus, firms relied heavily on the state, both explicitly (being government-owned), or implicitly through the sale of supplies to the public sector.

Private industry consisted mainly of textile firms (especially cotton and wool mills), metalworking enterprises and producers of the energy necessary to operate these factories (3). the scarcity of raw materials and the abundance of skilled and unskilled labour aided those industries in which "the labour factor [was] of great importance" (4). Small-sized enterprises accounted for a significant share of production; on 5 November 1951 (when the first postwar census was taken), just under 595,000 firms employed fewer than 100 workers, or 53% of the labour force (Table 1). These firms were directly linked to large-sized enterprises, and more often than not were their suppliers (5). It should be noted that the economy made use of nationally supplied energy, primarily in the form of hydroelectric power (this type of energy accounted for just under 90% of 1950 production; see Table 1).

These conditions engendered the steady development and sustained rates of growth which continued until the 1960s. Known as the economic miracle, this phase of growth was to shape future develop-

---

customer access lines in service), merchant vessels (18% of tonnage) and electric power (30% of production). The labour force were over 218,000. The labour force was over 218,000. See MINISTERO DELL'INDUSTRIA E DEL COMMERCIO [23], vol. I, pp. 19-21.

Numbers in square brackets refer to the Bibliography.

(2) See the *Country Study* on Italy commissioned by the United States Congress in 1949, a few months after the institution of the European Recovery Programme (ERP), see VILLARI L. [32], pp. 624-625.

(3) «In its fundamental structure Italian industry appears to include a strong textile industry and a large scale electric industry, a continually developing mechanical industry, a limited but sound chemical industry, a mining industry, proportionate to the shortage of resources, an active building industry and an important food industry susceptible of further developments», an excerpt from the report submitted by the Italian government delegation to the 5th UNRRA Council, August 1946, in COMITATO INTERMINISTERIALE PER LA RICOSTRUZIONE [11], p. 43.

(4) Giovanni Falk, managing director of the Falk steel mills, expressed this opinion before the *Commissione Economica della Costituente* at the March 1946 hearing.

(5) According to a study conducted in 1959 by the Mediobanca research department and T. Bianchi, A. Mauri and M. Arcelli, the supplies of small- and mid-sized enterprises already equalled about half of the total supplies of the automobile industry, accounting for a 1/4 share of turnover.

TABLE 1

CENSUS DATA ON MINING AND MANUFACTURING INDUSTRIES

Employment size of units	1951	1961	1971	1981
Number of local units				
up to 5	543,055	463,872	403,277	469,130
6 - 50	47,402	80,945	95,957	141,882
51 - 100	4,023	6,624	7,784	8,307
101 - 500	3,467	4,899	5,943	6,300
501 - 1000	452	503	563	575
over 1000	278	274	326	309
total.....................	598,677	557,117	513,850	626,503
Number of employees				
up to 5	877,247	845,398	747,134	904,077
6 - 50	682,889	1.173,471	1.425,519	1.978,225
51 - 100	283,628	462,810	546,308	580,457
101 - 500	720,089	986,396	1.183,212	1.219,000
501 - 1000	315,286	351,486	390,186	389,987
over 1000	578,843	620,083	826,243	747,391
Total	3.457,982	4.439,644	5.118,602	5.819,137
Average number of employees per local unit				
up to 5	1.6	1.8	1.9	1.9
6 - 50	14.4	14.5	14.9	13.9
51 - 100	70.5	69.9	70.2	69.9
101 - 500	207.7	201.3	199.1	193.5
501 - 1000	697.5	698.8	693.0	678.2
over 1000	2082.2	2263.1	2534.5	2418.7
Total	5.8	8.0	10.0	9.3

Source: ISTAT

ments. Regarding the population, two major changes occurred: workers abandoned the countryside, benefiting industry and a somewhat rapid, sprawling urbanization process; there was a strong tendency toward dual growth involving migratory flows from South to North. This phenomenon would play a significant role in future decisionmaking with regard to public-sector intervention and mounting social tensions. Also worthy of note: *a)* firstly, the reconstruction was chiefly of interest to northern industry, which could purchase modern machinery from the United States, undisputably the leading industrialized nation at that time (6); *b)* secondly, this phase required relatively simple investment decisions: by definition, the reconstruction was not a time for strategic policymaking, one reason for its rapid progress (7).

One obvious measure of industrial growth during the initial phase was the rise in certain areas of production from 1950 to 1959: electric power supplies doubled; automobiles and merchant vessels more than quadrupled, while the quantity of steel and cement produced nearly tripled. Low wages and high exports were the key factors contributing to this development.

Even in 1959, according to Eurostat figures, the hourly cost of labour in Italian industry was 20% lower than that of West Germany and 14% lower than that of France. These differences were probably much more dramatic in smaller enterprises. Italy succeeded in concentrating certain labour-intensive areas of production whose marketing was controlled from abroad. Examples are the household appliance industry (developed through *terzismo*, that is, the supplying of a product by the firm to another, which in turn sells that product under its own brand name, and to some extent, the clothing sector. As

---

(6) From 1948-1952, Italy received approximately $1.5 billion, or 11% of the Marshall Plan funds (known officially as the European Recovery Programme). See CASTRONOVO ([8], pp. 269) and VILLARI ([32], from p. 583). Equipment was purchased from the US primarily by the metallurgic industry, by the electric power industry (committed to a plan to build thermoelectric plants) and by the metal and mechanical industry. Finsider, Edison and Fiat were the companies most involved (CASTRONOVO [8], p. 270). One important element of the Marshall Plan was the sending of teams of personnel from European industrial enterprises to visit their countarports in the United States in order to learn about American production and organizational techniques. These visits were undoubtedly useful, despite discordant views as to their actual effectiveness (UNITED NATIONS ECONOMIC COMMISSION FOR EUROPE [30] p. 11).

(7) As regards speed: «I believe that reconstruction will only take one or two years, rather than 8 or 5 years» (A. Costa, president of Confindustria). As regards the lack of difficulty: «Our main concern is to ensure as quickly as possible that the facilities are able to generate product as it was generated before, and that processes are carried out in the best way possible as far as quality and cost are concerned [...] Other responsibilities must be dealt with as well, such as moving toward old-style mass production (see Valletta, general manager of Fiat) (both statements were made in 1946 at the Ministero per la costituente hearing on the Italian economy. The war caused more damage to public-sector industry than to the private sector. Among the hardest hit were steel mills (99% of cast iron and 87% of steel production facilities were respectively destroyed), shipyards (60%) and factories of railway stock (65%). See MINISTERO DELL'INDUSTRIA E COMMERCIO [23], vol. III, pp. 377-9.

for exports, Italy's share relative to 14 other Western countries remained at 1-2% during the early 1950s, rose steadily in subsequent years reaching pre-war levels in 1958 and continued rapidly thereafter to 4.5% in 1959, to 5.3% in 1961 and to 7.3% in 1964 (8). In 1957, membership in the European Common Market led to the elimination of the bottleneck effect, the otherwise ineluctable consequence of an impoverished domestic market (9).

During this period the presence of the state was considered inevitable in sectors with high financial requirements. The capital market was too restricted, and no private-sector entrepreneurs could afford to provide the financial backing for the capital-intensive sectors in which growth was highest. Thus, the traditional goals of public-sectors intervention satisfied two main requirements (10): while providing assistance to industrial firms necessary to the country during their initial stages of development, it supported the service sector, which included public utilities and energy sources. In this phase of Italian industrial progress: *a)* entrepreneurial strategies tied to these objectives were generally decided on by management, which enjoyed sufficient autonomy (11); *b)* during its initial stages, at least, the private-sector accepted and tacitly justified the presence of state-owned industry (12).

Public industry thus became involved in far-reaching strategic developments, two of the most important affecting the steel industry and energy production. The advent of modern integrated-cycle steel

----

(8) These data may be found in the study of exports by V. Balloni, in Fua [15], pp. 401.

(9) «Autarchic policies should be avoided. There is a strong tendency in some Italian circles to consider economical and desirable any investment which leads to reduced imports. For a country with such a small domestic market and limited natural resources, this sounds like a desperate view. The direction of Italian development must be toward expansion [...] hence the nation's dependence on foreign trade» (see the *Country Study* quoted in Villari [32], p. 620).

(10) See Ministero dell'Industria e Commercio [23], vol. II, from p. 42.

(11) «In the newly formed IRI, the guidelines, checks and balances imposed on firms were formulated within the agency» (see the interview given by P. Barucci to P. Saraceno in Banca Toscana [5]. See also Bottiglieri [6], p. 102.

(12) «From an economic perspective, if we thought that industry could absorb IRI, then we could say: 'let's get rid of IRI by selling it off to the private sector'. But nowadays, we can't imagine a private-sector company able to take on an Ansaldo, for example» (statement made by the president of Confindustria, Angelo Costa, at the *Commissione economica della Costituente* hearing in March 1946).

production had been hindered in the past by the lack of raw materials (iron and coal) and by the amount of capital necessary for the undertaking; these resources were more readly available in central European countries. The Italian postwar plan was implemented also in order to rebuild seriously damaged plants and was aided by changes in the supply of raw materials: the discovery of new mines in countries outside Europe (especially Canada, Brazil and Australia) with very low costs of excavation made Italian mineral imports profitable. As a result, the Iri-Finsider plan created by Oscar Sinigallia focused on the construction of large-scale integrated-cycle plants located along the coast and heavily oriented toward flat rolled sections. In 1954, the Genoa-Cornigliano centre was started in addition to the existing plants at Naples-Bagnoli and Piombino (13). The programme greatly increased the competitivity of the public-sector steel industry, and profits grew steadily in later years. Annual net profits rose at a constant pace, from some L2 bn in 1954-1955 to L16 bn in 1962-1963. During the latter two-year period, Fiat and Edison were the only publicly quoted companies to realize higher profits. The Sinigallia plan did not carry over to the private sector, because private businesses lacked the means to finance such a large-scale project, and because this programme was carried out according to the division of the market agreed on during the autarchic 1930s, a time when national production should have been based on no more than 50% scrap metal (the raw material predominantly used by the private sector). The Sinigallia plan gave way to a further expansion of public-sector industry, resulting in the opening in 1961 of the fourth integrated-cycle facility, located at Taranto.

Public-sector industrial expansion occurred in tandem with that of private-sector industry, composed of several large-sized groups primarily involved in the more intricate areas of production (Falck, Fiat, Redaelli), and a number of small- and medium-sized firms located in or near Brescia. Despite their concentration in the poorer areas of the steel industry (reinforced concrete rods and other long products), firms in the latter category succeeded in surviving the

---

(13) The financial requirement for the Cornigliano facility was about L100 billion at the prices of that period. ERP funds financed one-quarter of overall expenditure.

competitive struggle through the effective management of plant innovations (electric furnaces, and later casting techniques) which,
coupled with intensive specialization, led to exceptionally high levels
of productivity.

Government involvement in the energy sector, largely due to the
stimulus provided by Enrico Mattei, produced entirely different
results. Intervention centred on AGIP, which had been set up to reach
some level of autonomy in procuring oil supplies (14), so as to release
Italy from the monopoly power of foreign producers. The company
undertook a successful exploration programme in the Po valley,
where large natural gas reserves were discovered (15). This led to the
creation of ENI, to which AGIP was transferred along with other
state-owned firms in the petroleum sector (including Romsa, ANIC,
SNAM and the assets of Ente Nazionale Metano, which then wound
up). ENI also obtained the exclusive drilling rights in the Po valley.
Natural gas production grew rapidly, reaching over 6 billion cubic
metres by the end of the 1950s. Another area of impressive development was the system pipelines necessary to distribute the gas; this
network covered some 6,000 kilometres in the early 1960s. Unlike
steel, the energy plan represented an innovation for Italian industry.
This novelty lay not so much in actually finding and exploiting the gas
(which, again, called for an investment that private industry could not
have afforded), but in the policies pursued by the government agency
regarding the use of gas. Indeed, in 1953 the groundwork was started
to develop a programme for the production of synthetic rubber and
nitrous fertilizer based on natural gas. The programme bore fruit in
1958, with the opening of plants in Ravenna; these led to the

---

(14) The *Azienda Generale Italiana Petroli* (AGIP) was set up in 1926 because the
government considered it «necessary to create a paragovernmental organization which,
without obstructing private-sector initiatives, undertook to: search for petroleum in
Italy; search for petroleum abroad; [...], extract petroleum from existing fields; operate
refineries [...]».

(15) AGIP was the first in Europe to use the reflection shooting method of oil and
gas exploration. The first major natural gas deposits were found in 1944 and 1945 at
Caviaga, near Lodi. In 1948, smaller deposits of petroleum were discovered in
Cortemaggiore, where the first oilwell was built. Of note is the fact that the means
available at that time were scarce: «Mattei obtained major results with limited means.
Even in 1953 the total natural gas reserves confirmed in the Po valley were and would
remain for several years lower than the deposits located in 1974 with a single well in
Malossa» (CUZZI [12], p. 7).

Montecatini loss of leadership in fertilizers (with state-controlled plants fixing their prices at 15-20% less than the market average), and to the first profitable synthetic rubber production, reducing the sale price to levels lower than that of the products imported thus far from North America. The dynamism of the group was exhibited in the rise in equipment and machinery, from L174 bn in 1954 to L549 bn in 1960. In the early 1960s, growth was even more rapid, doubling the book value of fixed assets. The factors contributing to such a change were new investments in the chemical and energy sectors, and acquisitions of firms, frequently as a results of political pressure. In 1962, the controlling stock of Lanerossi was the third major acquisition which overstepped the original objectives; the other two were the purchase of Pignone in 1953 and of the daily newspaper *Il giorno* in 1959.

Also deserving of mention is the concentration in Stet of telephone-service stakes held by private investors near the end of the 1950s (the Ericsson-controlled Set, and Teti, a subsidiary of La Centrale); the telephone service companies were merged into SIP in 1964, beginning a programme of remodernization and expansion in the telecommunications industry.

Early in the postwar period — as mentioned above — the principal areas of private-sector production were textile and mechanical manufactures which accounted for about half of exports:

EXPORTS IN 1951

	billion lira	%
Yarns and fabrics	302	29.3
Mechanical products	186	18.1
Food and farm products	159	15.5
Chemical and rubber products.................	108	10.5
Other	274	26.6
Total	1,029	100.0

The level of concentration reached in each sector was a credit to producers of electric power and the chemical industry as well. Textile producers were primarily small- and medium-sized firms using extremely labour-intensive technologies. The low cost of labour caused profits to be particularly high; however, these profits were chiefly invested in real estate (16) rather than in plant modernization. So it was that this favourable cost situation did little to expand production, which — at least according to the official cotton-industry statistics — ranged from 300,000 to 400,000 tonnes annually. The industry structure was composed primarily of production-oriented companies (such spinners or weavers which sold products to be manufactured by domestic and foreign apparel industries), which paid little attention to the market trends. The mechanical industry was made up of a large assortment of companies generating intricate products. The main area of production was the automobile industry, whose leading private-sector firm, Fiat, had struck a deal with public-sector Alfa Romeo, which targeted a different market segment. Fiat grew very quickly by focusing on an informed product policy (based on low-power, low-priced models) and on the achievement of economies of scale. With regard to the latter, 1956 saw the beginning of the progressive expansion of the Turin Mirafiori factory which was become the largest concentration of workers in the country. The total labour force employed by Fiat rose from a prewar figure of 40,000 to 71,000 in 1952 and climbing 100,000 between 1960 and 1961. Also worthy of note was the position of Olivetti, which during the 1950s developed its production of electromagnetic calculators, and became the leading supplier worldwide (17). In the early 1950s, the chemical industry was dominated by Montecatini which concentrated mainly on base industries (18); the plant owned by this firm was not always competitive (in

---

(16) The Cotonificio Cantoni, the leading cotton producer, was also a major real-estate owner. According to a study conducted by Ricerche e Studi in 1973, more than 7,300 rooms were owned. Similarly, the manufacturing firm Rossari & Varzi owned a total of 2,300 hectares in farmland distributed over 7 properties in addition to several rooms and parcels of land during the late 1960s. In 1969, this company made large-scale investments in real estate, while allocating less than L50 million to its production facilities. Shortly thereafter, the firm became insolvent.

(17) In 1959, Olivetti also gained control of Underwood with 34% of shares purchased at $8.7 million), the American firm whose founder had invented the most famous typewriter in the world in 1896 (CAIZZI B. [7], p. 243).

(18) Shortly before the second world war, the Montecatini group market shares were estimated at 70-75% of national sales of base chemicals, fertilizers and pesticides, 20% of pharmaceuticals, 80-85% of organic dyes (whose production was actually

the past, they had benefited from the heavy tariff barriers), and a large-scale reorganization had become necessary. Montecatini acquired the Natta patents for polypropylene and, during 1949-52, built the first European petrochemical plant at Ferrara. The chemical sector made important strides after the war. To diversify its interest, Edison invested heavily in southern Italy, creating SINCAT (1954), Celene and ACSA (1957). Moreover, in 1955 Edison acquired control of Chatillon, a chemical fibre producer. The industry leader was SNIA Viscosa, which expanded its activities and entered the textile sector (its main transaction was the purchase of controlling interst in Cotonificio Olcese cotton mill in 1948 (19). However, electric power utilities could be considered the most important of firms. While forming a tightly knit oligopoly which controlled the main source of predominantly hydroelectric energy:

	1950	1960
	(percentage of total production)	
Hydroelectric energy	87.5	82.0
Thermoelectric energy	7.3	14.3
Geothermoelectric energy	5.2	3.7

these groups were well represented on the stock exchange, and accounted for a sizeable proportion of listings (Table 2). The largest group, Edison, headed some 100 companies; the other electric power groups were SADE (with 65 firms under its control at the end of the 1940s), La Centrale (a holding company whose investments were centred predominantly in the electric power industry), SME (in which IRI held a minority stake) and Finelettrica, set up in 1952 to regroup

controlled by the German group I.G.-Farbenindustrie, a partner in the Italian firm operating in this sector), some 35-45% of the paint, pigment and allied product market and 50% of aluminium (RICERCHE E STUDI [27], p. 34).

(19) Expansion in the chemical fibres sector occurred mainly through licensing agreements with foreign firms. Rhodiatoce began producing synthetic fibres in 1947 under licence of Du Pont de Nemours, and in 1953 produced polyester fibres under licence of ICI; ACSA produced acrylic fibres under licence of Monsanto (RICERCHE E STUDI [28], p. 19).

TABLE 2

MARKET CAPITALIZATION OF THE MAJOR ITALIAN COMPANIES QUOTED ON THE STOCK EXCHANGE

Company	Industry	Market capitalization at year-end		
		1948	1960	1960-1948
		(billion lira)		(no. of times)
Montecatini	chemical	56	682	12
Edison	electric power	58	655	11
Fiat	motor vehicles	22	610	28
Stet (IRI)	telecommu-nications	6	298	50
Finsider (IRI) ..	steel	8	291	36
Pirelli Spa	rubber	25	280	11
Snia Viscosa	chemical fibres	37	224	6
Sme Meridionale Elettricità	electric power	18	216	12
Italcementi	cement	14	203	15
Sip (IRI)........	electric power	19	196	10
La Centrale	holding company (1)	7	172	25
Finelettrica (IRI)	electric power	— (2)	169	—
Bastogi	finance	21	164	8
Anic (ENI)......	chemicals	10	150	15

(1) With significant holdings in electric power utilities.
(2) Finelettrica was set up in 1952 and listed on the Stock Exchange as of 1953.
Source: MEDIOBANCA: *Indici e dati (1948-1965)*

the IRI operations in the sector. As mentioned earlier, these groups benefited from development induced by growth in the national industry: from 1950 to 1960, energy production and consumption doubled. However, from the mid-1950s on the share of power produced by hydroelectric sources began to decline, largely in favour of thermoelectric energy obtained from petroleum-based fuel oil (20). Profits

(20) It should be borne in mind that during this period, the first European projects for the construction of nuclear power plants were launched. The first experimental reactor was built by Fiat and Montecatini in 1960 at Saluggia, Vercelli. The nuclear power programme was never continued because of low oil prices, and was abandoned altogether in the 1980s because of strong social opposition to the building of new power plants.

remained consistently high, even though the cost of petroleum-based products was initially competitive.

The early 1960s witnessed the "miracle", buoyed by the significant expansion of the industrial sector resulting from improved productivity and the steady rise in foreign demand (21). The tendency to bring Italian wages in line with those of other Common Market countries led to a worsening of Italian industry even as labour disputes became increasingly bitter. Thus, during 1963-1964, there was a noticeable slowdown of activity, the first during the postwar years. This slowdown marked the end of a period in which the social unrest of the latter stages urged government to take more incisive action regarding the development process and, more specifically, to redress the territorial imbalances which in the meanwhile had grown even more pronounced.

3. - State Intervention: 1964-1975

During this second phase, the tendency of Italian industry toward expansion continued. From 1961 to 1971, the average number of employees per firm grew largely as a results of the changes arising in units with staff of 1,000 or more: these firms increased both in number and in average size (Table 1). The above-mentioned tendency also appears in Table 3, which outlines the characteristics of major production facilities in 1975: during that year, 29 factories employed over 290,000 workers, with the attendant overcrowding in the workplace and environs.

The main characteristic of this period was the stepping up of state intervention. The major undertaking was the nationalization of the electric power industry, involving the creation of ENEL (*Ente nazionale energia elettrica*) under a law issued in December 1962. Given the climate of political change in which it occurred, this nationalization was to be of great importance. However, although the development of a source of energy essential for economic growth could have

---

(21) According to Bank of Italy estimates, production increases from 1950 to 1964 accounted for 50% of increases in productivity (BANCA D'ITALIA [2], p. 484).

Fulvio Coltorti

TABLE 3

MAJOR ITALIAN MANUFACTURING FACILITIES AS AT END-1975

Location	Owner company	No. of employees at end 1975	Industry
Turin Mirafiori	Fiat	50,389	motor vehicles
Taranto	Italsider	19,518	steel
Arese (MI)............	Alfa Romeo	18,200(1)	motor vehicles
Turin Rivalta.........	Fiat	15,676	motor vehicles
Pomigliano d'Arco (NA)	Alfasud	15,573(1)	motor vehicles
Genoa	Italsider	13,955	steel
Milan	Sit Siemens	12,460	telecommunications equipment
Porto Marghera (VE) ..	Montedison	9,853	petrochemicals
Turin Lingotto	Fiat	9,739	motor vehicles
Milan Bicocca	Industrie Pirelli	9,099	rubber
Turin Ferriere	Fiat	8,394	steel
Porcia (PN)	Zanussi	8,250	appliances
Bagnoli (NA)..........	Italsider	7,765	steel
Pontedera (FI)	Piaggio & C.	7,200(1)	motorcycles
Piombino (LI)	Acciaierie di Piombino	6,916	steel
Terni	Terni	6,709	steel
Dalmine (BG)	Dalmine	6,702	steel tubes
Castelletto (MI)	Sit Siemens	6,456	research
Priolo (SR)...........	Montedison	6,268	petrochemicals
Biandronno (VA)	Ire Philips	6,034(2)	appliances
Sesto S. Giovanni (MI)	Ercole Marelli	5,700	electromechanical
Monfalcone (GO)	Italcantieri	5,433(1)	shipbuilding
Sesto S. Giovanni (MI)	Falck	5,220	steel
Turin	Michelin	5,000(1)	tires
Arezzo	Lebole Euroconf	4,540(2)	apparel
Crescenzago (MI)......	Magneti Marelli	4,484	electromechanical
Ivrea (TO)	Olivetti	4,433(1)	office equipment
Scarmagno (TO)	Olivetti	4,322(1)	office equipment
Gela (Cl)	Anic	4,249	petrochemicals
Total		288,537	

(1) As 31-12-1976.
(2) As 31-12-1977.
Source: R&S

been organized in a unified and efficient manner (22), the financial
effect of the processes involved in nationalization weighed heavily on

---

(22) In 1970 the production of electric power war divided as follows: private-sector
firms, 46%; IRI-controlled companies, 24%; self-sufficient firms, 18%; municipalized
agencies, 6%; Ferrovie dello stato (including Larderello), 6%. Private-sector firms did

the Agency performance, in real terms, of subsequent years. These repercussions were felt by the public-sector Agency and by the private sector as well. ENEL was compelled to pay compensation worth L1.65 trillion over ten years at 5.5% interest annually. contrary to what was forecast (based on the pre-nationalization profits of private sector firms, which enjoyed more favourable financial conditions), the current cash flow was insufficient to finance the compensation. As the Agency had no endowment fund, it had to resort to indebtedness. Moreover, the decision to maintain tariffs at virtually the same level until 1974 (23) placed yet another burden on Agency management. This was not without consequences on subsequent Agency investment policy. For the private sector, the receipt of compensation resulted in large amounts of capital to be reinvested.

The nationalization of the electric power industry occurred at a time when the state was principally entrusted with planning-oriented responsibilities. Aid to the southern regions was a prime example. Even in 1950, with the creation of the Cassa per il Mezzogiorno a singular programme was instituted to remedy the lack of development in the South. For the first ten years, a total of L1 trillion was set aside for the modernization of agriculture and for the construction of an initial infrastructure. The financial commitment to southern develop-ment policy was later increased, and in 1957, Law 634 launched a more direct intervention programme for the region, which would receive 40% of capital expenditure made by state-owned firms. All of the institutes for medium-term credit (and not only Isveimer, IRFIS and CIS, the three southern "special" institutions set up for support-ing Mezzogiorno development) granted subsidized credit to industry using the funds of the Cassa. During the early 1960s, however, the realization that public-sector expenditure for infrastructure stimulated

---

not have the problem of technical inefficiencies, but suffered instead from a tendency to take advantage of the natural monopoly held by this industry. Territorial inequalities also existed. For example, until 1961 tariffs had not been standardized nationwide and the cost of electricity in the southern regions was much higher than in the North.

(23) See ZANETTI - FRAQUELLI [33], pp. 14-5. Similarly, telephone service rates were not brought in line with costs, compelling the company providing the service to use indebtedness to fund the expansion of the network. These pricing policies were changed during the 1980s.

northern industry spawned through state-owned firms. The five-year plan for economic development for 1966-1970 defined public-sector firms as means of "policy designed to partially of wholly fulfill the goals and objectives established within the plan"; however, it also safeguarded their "entrepreneurial function", requiring them to operate "in keeping with strict criteria as regards cost-effectiveness". Implicit in this concept was the assumption that the failed industrialization of the Mezzogiorno was no so much a result of unfavourable business conditions (hidden by expressly created tax and financial incentives) as it was a consequence of large-sized firms reclutance to change the location of their production facilities. The investment plans of state-owned firms and ENEL were subject to the approval of CIPE (24). This intervention in the management of the firms embodied the growing involvement of the "hidden political shareolder"; examples of this input were almost invariably anti-entrepreneurial in scope (25). The "political control" of public-sector firms involved the setting of objectives concerning the cost-effectiveness constraint that were almost unfailingly contradictory. This situation reached a climax in the 1970s, resulting in the following developments for state-owned firms: *a)* the abandonment of the cost-effectiveness constraint and of the benchmark accounting data used to evaluate financial performance; *b)* the acquisition of a host of troubled private-sector industrial firms; *c)* repeated requests for endowment fund increases to cover growing financial requirements.

That management cost-effectiveness had fallen out of favour is clearly revealed in Table 4*A* in the appendix. In 1975 (conventionally regarded as the upper mark of this phase), not only did every public-sector agency post financial losses, but each one was on the verge of an uninterrupted deficit trend whose effects would become manifest a few years later. With the heavy financial toll came requests

---

(24) This expanded the Ministry's sphere of action. One reason was «for the purpose of strengthening its powers of control and vigilance, the Ministry for State Holdings must authorize the purchase or sale of state-owned firms effected by Agencies either directly or thorugh subsidiaries». Rather than limiting acquisitions, the provision actually established a sort of political supremacy as regards operational decisionmaking.

(25) For more on this subject, see MINISTERO DELLE PARTECIPAZIONI STATALI [24], p. 11.

for enormous amounts of refinancing. This is when the first noteworthy endowment fund increases occurred:

1968-1975 CHANGE

	billion lira
IRI	1,293
ENI.....................................	697
EFIM	287
ENEL	200
Total	2,477

Investments also rose significantly: for the three major agencies (IRI, ENI and ENEL), this figure went from L1.272 trillion in 1968 to L4.135 trillion in 1975. Also deserving of mention is the gradual expansion of the *Ente partecipazioni e finanziamenti industria manifatturiera* (EFIM), set up in 1962 to oversee public-sector holdings in mechanical concerns (the Breda group in particular) and subsequently extended to include many other sectors. Public-sector firms were responsible for projects of great importance: expanding the highway network (which grew from 1,656 km in 1964 to 5,329 km in 1975), increasing investments in the telephone system (the number of customers grew from 4.2 million in 1964 to 9.7 million in 1975), enlarging the Italsider facility in Taranto to double its previous output capacity, building the Alfasud plant in Pomigliano d'Arco (26) and completing the network of oil pipelines linking Italy to central Europe. However, not all of these expenditures were fruitful to the same

---

(26) «Indeed, the type of organization, the style of executive management and the corporate behaviour within an industrial group such as IRI are suitable for creating and managing largesized firms which form the main support of entire industrial sectors [...] The achievement of maximum entrepreneurial efficiency within each firm in the group is one of the central goals of our plan» (IRI [18], pp. 29-30).

extent. If we examine the public-sector firms surveyed by the Mediobanca research department, the data for 1968-1975 are as follows:

	1968	1975
	(billion lira)	
Profit + depreciation	38	142
% of turnover	7.9	0.8
Net worth	2,121	2,670(*)
Financial debts	4,813	16,304
Debt/net worth (no. of times)	2.3	6.1

(*) Not including increase resulting from monetary revaluation

The decline in cost-effectiveness was accompanied by a lack of
accounting transparency. Only ENI released a consolidated balance
sheet voluntarily; EFIM was required by law to issue one from 1972
on, while IRI did not make these figures available until 1974. The
absence of standard accounting principles rendered these data
virtually meaningless, and analysis was frequently laden with difficulties (27).

Acquisitions were made in totally disparate sectors, and touched
not only the areas of activity of large-sized groups specializing in
primary industry but also small- and medium-sized manufacturing
sectors. Generally, these buyouts served to remedy the labour-related
concerns of the workers involved, and not to execute a coherent and
explicit strategic plan (28). The first major transactions involved:
1) the purchase by ENI of a large number of clothing and texile firms
from the mid-1960s onward (a process which culminated in the
creation of Tescon holding in 1974); 2) the absorption of the Motta,
Alemagna, Cirio and Star food concerns from 1968 to 1972 by SME,
of which IRI had acquired full control during the same period; 3) the

-----

(27) For example, in 1975 Italsider recorded provisions for depreciation that were
57% lower than ordinary rates used for tax purposes, while Dalmine rates (another
member of the IRI-Finsider group) were 47% higher according to the same parameters.

(28) See the study on acquisitions by R. GALLO in VARIOUS AUTHORS [31], from p.
270.

purchase of the Montedison aluminium business by EFIM in 1972-1973.

Of more importance was the subsequent setting up of the «*Ente Autonomo di gestione per le aziende minerarie metallurgiche*» (EGAM). Created in 1958, EGAM's operations began in 1971 with the concentration of public-sector holdings in Cogne, a national firm (which produced integrated-cycle steel with moneylosing blast furnaces located in Val d'Aosta), in AMMI and in SICEA. The Agency began to acquire failing companies so rapidly that its aggregate turnover for 1974 reached a high of L670 bn, and the number of employees hovered near 25,000 (29). Nonetheless, the Agency's accounts were far from balanced: during 1974-1975, losses amounted to L144 bn.

The 1960s were problematic years for private industry. Indeed, many firms had weak ownership structures, made up in many cases of cross participations. The nationalization of the electric power industry also required a rethinking of the strategic objectives of certain large-sized groups. However, new directions were taken without due consideration of new strategy; further, the management of these groups did not always seem equal to the task of satisfying new requirements (30). During this period, growing industrial relations constrains led to inflexibility in the use of labour and to an increase in labour costs, which reached a high in 1969 as a results of the "hot autumn" disputes. Profits also declined in the private sector in the midst of an expansion phase, as outlined in the data on production contained in Table 1*A*; indeed, steel production (of both public- and private-sector firms) nearly doubled, the production of cars reached record levels in 1973 and the supply of electric power (which gives some information about the performance of user sectors) doubled. This situation could not have been resolved with capital increases. Apart from the weakness of controlling syndicates mentioned above,

---

(29) This was yet another example of organizational deterioration within public-sector firms. Acquisitions were made without regard for pre-determined procedures, and according to criteria which were clearly not in favour of the public-sector agency (see the comments of G. La Malfa in G. LA MALFA in CEEP [9], p. 12).

(30) Firms whose businesses were nationalized used compensations and to finance acquisitions in the food sector (such as SME or La Centrale). These adjustments led to Montecatini-SADE merger and later, in 1966, to Montecatini-Edison merger.

the economic climate created fears of further nationalizations, thereby discouraging investments. The search for capital contributions
necessary for investment funding was taken outside the firm, to the
banking sector. Financial indebtedness rose significantly; Mediobanca
data reveal the following changes for private-sector firms from 1968 to
1975:

	1968	1975	Change
	billion lira		
Turnover	10,330	30,548	20,218
Net worth	3,812	4,507(*)	695
Financial debt	3,556	10,640	7,084
Financial expenses	250	1,414	1,164
Net profit or loss.............	150	− 718	− 868

(*) Not including increase resulting from monetary revaluation.

As we can see, for each lira of net worth increase, there were 10
lire of new financial debt; the burdens on these debts were such that,
with worsened business conditions, financial outcomes changed from
positive to negative. Also, this period was characterized by a sizeable
increase in debt propensity; in fact, the incentives system in place
made it possible to reduce nominal rates to a large degree so that
when inflation was taken into account, real rates were negative.
Moreover, issuing shares was not a convenient means of raising
capital, given market rates of interest. This was the period which saw
the emergence of new industrial enterprises whose growth was based
on indebtedness. The principal groups were those whose controlling
interest centred on Liquigas and SIR. The former, originally limited to
the trade of petroleum-based products, expanded through direct
investments in petrochemicals during the late 1960s; in the 1970s, it
continued to grow, diversifying into other sectors. SIR, on the other
hand, operated almost exclusively in the chemical sector and had
increased in size largely as a result of direct investments (the most
significant of which was the petrochemical plant at Porto Torres,
Sardinia during the 1960s); investments were also effected through
Rumianca, a medium-sized publicly quoted chemical firm acquired

during the late 1960s. In order to gain some idea of its size, it is enough to remember that the net equipment and machinery of SIR, Rumianca and Liquigas combined surpassed that of Montedison (31).

The combination of fiscal and financial subsidization available permitted capital-intensive enterprises investing in the Mezzogiorno to achieve the highest gains. The major private-sector transactions in this region generally involved capital-intensive plant in the petroleum refining and petrochemical industries; these facilities were unable to provide sufficient stimuli for the development of surrounding areas (as such, they came to be known as "cathedrals in the desert"). One important point is that refined raw materials quadrupled during 1960-1970.

The early 1970s were also marked by important internationalization initiatives within the private sector. Given the scarcity of available resources, a policy of forming alliances prevailed. One of the most important examples, in the rubber industry, was the union of Pirelli and Britain's Dunlop (1970). After unsuccessfully attempting a merger with Citroën (1970), Fiat participated in a joint venture first with the American firm Allis Chalmers (1973, earthmoving machinery) and later with the German KHD (1974, resulting in the creation of Industrial Vehicle Corporation IVECO).

Interplay between the public and private sectors was either competitive or collusive. On the one hand, there was competition for available financial assistance. As mentioned earlier, subsidized financing was the main financial resource, and whether or not a firm obtained it affected both future rates of growth and the type of production processes put in place. The "chemical warfare" which pitted private-, public- and parapublic-sector firms against one another was perhaps the prime example of this mutant strain of competition. On the other hand, there was collusion which originated in political circles, and aimed at shifting the most financially ailing companies onto state-owned firms. This process reached its peak in 1971, with

(31) It should be noted that investment costs were divided among several firms in the same group so as to maximize the tax and financial benefits reserved for small- and medium-sized firms. The SIR group made the most use of this outlet: during the late 1970s the Porto Torres complex was owned by nearly 50 firms simultaneously (ALZONA [1]). These companies formed subgroups in which the existence of bearer shares made it possible to hide ownerships.

the setting up of GEPI. Although originally conceived as a temporary intervention measure for troubled firms which would be resold, GEPI became in fact a political tool used to bail out overextended small- and medium-sized firms. At year-end in 1975, some 100 firms employing 40,000 workers had received assistance totalling L330 bn. Accumulated losses (L86 bn) had risen higher than the initial capital allocation, resulting also in this case in repeated requests for refinancing (32).

To be sure, the increased state intervention which occurred during this second phase brought improvements in the country's infrastructure. Nonetheless, there is some question whether the investments promoted, all told, were indeed effective. The reason for this can be traced not only to declining profits; government assistance was also granted without an overall view and without adequate consideration of the opportunity cost involved. The objectives presented to public-sector firms were generic and lacking in operational detail; when planning activity became more specific (as in the case of the plans for the renascence of Sardinia or for the development of individual sectors), the necessary links with the rest of the economic system were nonexistent (33). From a more operational viewpoint, the growing emphasis on general objectives gradually undermined the traditional vigilance of the credit system as regards the creditworthiness of the ventures financed (34). A clear example of this approach is

---

(32) GEPI was set up by IMI (with 50% of capital) and three public-sector agencies, IRI, ENI, and EFIM (with 16.67% each), to which the Treasury then allocated the amounts necessary to fund the projects.

(33) For more on this subject, see FRATIANNI M. - LA MALFA G. - TREZZA B. [14], pp. 98-9. As these authors point out, the expansion of the public sector stimulated the demand side only, leading to price and external-sector disequilibria.

(34) The remarks of Governor Paolo Baffi are of extreme importance: «The difficulties facing a part of the financial system are the mirror image of the crisis in important sectors of the economy brought about by international and domestic factors, not the least of which is the subsidized credit mechanism designed to promote development and regional balance within Italy [...]. Two contrasting trends began to emerge in the activity of the financial intermediaries — on the one hand, increasing risk as investment was stepped up and concentrated in areas with little or no industrial tradition and, on the other, declining autonomy in decision-making as the range of projects judged to be consistent with the country's development aims was widened. Moreover, in several instances the agencies providing finance had a special legal status, so that their governing bodies were direct or indirect appendages of the very government departments responsible for granting credit concessions». (BANCA D'ITALIA [3], p. 379).

the CIPE decision in 1971 to invest over L1.1 trillion (according to initial forecasts) in the construction of a new integrated-cycle steel mill at Gioia Tauro, Calabria, the absurdity of which became evident as the steel market subsequently collapsed.

The first oil shock (in 1973) hit a chronically weakened Italian industry, both public and private. Moreover, financial fragility combined with industrial rigidity, since a large portion of investment expenditure had been allocated to primary industry (especially chemicals and steel) rather than to more advanced stages of production. The competitive position of Italian industry on the international market was slowly eroded by NICs (newly industrialized countries), which targeted similar market segments (consumer goods and products based on low, proven technology). Monetary authorities succeeded for a short time in pursuing a policy of sustaining exports by following a strategy of "differentiated devaluation"; thus, during the early 1970s when the dollar began to lose ground to the deutsche mark, the Bank of Italy guided the lira along the middle of the road so as to foster a revaluation of the dollar (the currency in which the prices of many fundamental imported raw materials were set) and, at the same time, a devaluation of the deutsche mark (the currency in which the sale prices of a large number of exported goods were set) (35). Nonetheless, the effects on certain Italian industry sectors were significant. One of the most noteworthy was the textile industry, whose employment levels in cotton, wool and silk production (formerly at the forefront of Italian export trade) fell by over 131,000 workers from 1961 to 1971 (36).

4. - Crisis and Restructuring: 1975-1983

The two oil shocks (1973-1974 and 1979-1980) caused price increases which in our country were added to the inflationary trend

---

(35) For more on this subject, see GRAZIANI [17].

(36) These data are the industry census results reported in the Ministry of Industry *Programma finalizzato per il sistema della moda* (Plan for the Fashion Industry) developed in 1978.

Industry association data reveal that from 1964 to 1975, the number of cotton producers fell from 632 to 498, closing down 175 production facilities.

inherent in the system. The strong inflationary pressures called for credit restrictions which necessarily had repercussions on the financing mechanisms of firms, and especially on those of large-sized groups which were the most heavily indebted. For these groups, servicing the debt became important for at least three reasons: *a)* the higher cost of funding could not be offset by raising the prices of products sold, since these were predominantly bulk goods whose demand was on the decline; *b)* the amount of indebtedness was such that new debt had to be incurred to finance payments once old debt expired; *c)* the rise in the cost of servicing the debt caused a growing financial disequilibrium, since it was practicable in the short term (as in the case of current interest charges, payments on the principal of expiring loans, and new debt incurred to meet financial requirements).

The financial crisis accompanied the above-mentioned structural weaknesses of property and management, with disastrous results. Thus, a reorganization process began which involved the removal from the market of the most heavily indebted firms, and the reorganization of production processes within the surviving large-sized industry.

Of the groups expelled from the market, the most noteworthy examples are the Monti group (which sold off almost all its industrial assets, mainly in the petroleum refining sector), Liquigas (which went into receivership) and SIR. To aid the latter, the Ministry for State Holdings set up an Intervention Committee which underwrote 60% of the capital of the *ad hoc* SIR Banking Consortium; this Consortium was assigned the responsibility of balancing the debt position of the group with respect to its creditors (37). ENI was entrusted with the creation of a plan to reform industrial assets by deciding which concerns were salvageable and which should be liquidated. To this end, in 1981 Enichimica was set up, comprising SIR plants and some

(37) Those with real guarantees on plant used them in part to offset previous losses, and converted the remainder into non-yield-bearing certificates with a ten-year term released by the *Cassa depositi e prestiti.* This was the largest amount of postwar banking activity related to the industrial sector. Toward the end of 1978, the SIR group had accumulated financial debts amounting to some L2.75 trillion (pricipally with public-sector banks: IMI, and special credit institutions in the South), compared with net worth of L139 billion, half of which would be allocated for deferred charges as yet undepreciated. The share capital of the Società Italiana Resine — the company appearing to be the parent of the group — was barely L5 billion.

of the companies which headed Liquichimica (formerly owned by the Liquigas group). ENI — acting on political orders — began a large-scale expansion of its chemical sector, largely through the absorption of firms resulting from ineffective investment plans (38). The other private-sector groups whose financing structure was based on debts were nonetheless compelled to change, sometimes radically, their ownership structures (39). The industrial restructuring projects were aided legally by certain pieces of legislation; one of these was the right of banks, by virtue of Law 787 of 1978, to participate in the creation of consortia which refinanced troubled firms by buying shares which would be resold once the recovery plan had expired. The major consortia aimed at supporting Pirelli and Montefibre. The consortium initially created to grant assistance to SNIA did not become operational since the refinancing of firm was rendered possible through recourse to the stock market. Montedison started a recovery plan whose financing was based on a capital increase of L640 bn (made at end-1981) underwritten by a consortium of major credit banks which had also supported the acquisition of majority interests by Germina, a private-sector financial company.

The main characteristic of the restructuring plans was a new group structure achieved by dismantling specific sectors and transferring them to subsidiaries usually created for the purpose. On the one hand, this phenomenon led to a sort of "counter-reform" based on the decentralization and resultant emphasis on the capabilities (and responsibilities) of peripheral managers, as opposed to the monolithic management style which had prevailed thus far. On the other hand, this was an important opportunity for firms to revalue their assets. These revaluations were used to offset previous losses, and to record "real" depreciation levels in an effort to regain what was lost because of inflation. Fiat is the prime example: in the 1960s, it had concentrated all of the firms involved in an integrated process, from production to the sale of goods and services. Despite its divisional structure, it was difficult to identify the individual areas of activity and financial

---

(38) It should be pointed out that the government bailouts of these firms (partly in the form of credit extended by public- sector banks) made it all the more difficult to restructure and to restore financial health to the private sector.

(39) See BANCA D'ITALIA [4], pp. 641-3.

outcomes. The hiveoff of operational sectors began in the early 1970s and was completed in 1980 with the creation of a legally separate entity called Fiat Auto, concentrating the automobile operations. At the same time, all of the major private-sector firms and some of the leading public-sector firms adhered to this reorganization model, setting up groups controlled and serviced by a holding company. This process of integration in reverse was accompanied by the decentraliz-ation of production processes which led to the transferral of a significant portion of value-adding operations to small- and medium-sized firms. This decentralization was aimed firstly at restoring flexi-bility in the use of labour (40) and at locating production facilities away from the traditional concentrations of workers in the industrial triangle. Census data reported in Table 1 provide an accurate descrip-tion of this phenomenon: in 1981, for the first time during the postwar years, the number of manufacturing units with more than 500 employees declined, and the number of firms employing fewer than 500 increased. Within this context, the paring down of the labour force employed by large-sized enterprises was of particular impor-tance. Table 4 outlines the data concerning the major groups, in which employment levels declined by an average of 28%. With regard to the 1988 situation of the major facilities included in Table 3, a sharp fall, 46%, is revealed. These declines were made possible not only by creating an exodus (of golden handshakes and early retirement plans), but also through the use of the *Cassa integrazione guadagni* (the state redundancy scheme) (41) which served as a sort of parking lot

---

(40) There were already several examples showing the right path to follow. One of these was the situation of the major domestic appliance producers. In the late 1970s the most efficient producers were the Merloni group (made up of several small single-product factories located in the Marches interior) and the Candy group (composed of specialized firms which decentralized some of the production). The Zanussi and Indesit groups, which had gambled more heavily than the others on achieving economies of scale because of the high concentration of output facilites, faced mounting obstacles which led to a change of ownership in the former case, and to liquidation in the latter. The worst fate awaited the company (in this case Indesit) which had accumulated the most consistent store of liquid assets: these reached: in 1976 a level not far from the net value of plant and equipment.

(41) The launching of employment restructuring policies is usually identified with the «Fiat/Union dispute» in 1980, when a prolonged standoff between management and the unions which ended in favour of the former was supported by the workers and by the Turinese in the "March of 40,0000". As for the social issues linked to restructuring,

and as a substitute for unemployment insurance. From 1979 to 1983, the number of *Cassa Integrazione* hours devoted to special assistance tripled, reaching L413 million, or one year of work for 250,000 people.

TABLE 4

CHANGE IN THE LABOUR FORCE
OF THE MAJOR ITALIAN INDUSTRIAL GROUPS

Group	Number of employees at year-end		Change
	1979	1983	
Fiat	358	244(1)	− 114
Montedison	115	73(2)	− 42
Pirelli	73	64	− 9
Olivetti	56	48	− 8
Zanussi	33	27	− 6
Snia Bpd	31	20	−11
Bastogi	25	15	− 10
Philips italiana	18	14	− 4
Michelin italiana	15	14	− 1
Falck	16	12	− 4
Piaggio & C.	13	11	− 2
Rizzoli editore	11	9	− 2
Total	764	551	− 213

(1) Of which 15,00 Fiat Auto workers have been placed on the redundancy scheme.
(2) Of which 6,000 workers have been placed on the redundancy sheme.
Source: R&S, 1984

During the same period, policy was created to promote entre-preneurial activity in an effort to facilitate the reinsertion into the labour force of workers considered redundant as a result of industrial

a 1985 survey of workers who left Italtel (IRI-STET group) during 1981-1983 showed that 71% had not found work, while 5.5% worked occasionally. Self-employed re-spondents were shown to have entered the less advanced services sector. Thus, even sustained economic recovery did not create enough jobs to replace those lost as a consequence of technological innovations, since different skills were required (see the *Introduction* by BELLISARIO M. to the survey compiled by DALLA CHIESA n. [13]).

restructuring (42). The processes described above were accompanied by the expansion of peripheral areas in the central Northeast including Veneto, Emilia-Romagna, Tuscany and the Marches, and in the southern Adriatic strip (Abruzzi, Molise, Apulia). In these areas, a new structure of industrial firms emerged, based on small size and on the compartmentalized industrial activity (43). The progress of electronic technologies aided this growth model considerably by lowering the size threshold of entry into many sectors. There is often some question whether these developments are the result of a new structure adopted by firms as a response to technological and social change, or more simply as a consequence of the policies of firms aimed at reducing the amount of product attributable to labour. Both hypotheses may be equally correct. In any event, the network of small-sized firms has come to represent a dominant force, rather than a transitory one, within the Italian economy.

The above considerations hold true for the most part as far as the private sector is concerned; public-sector firms were principally involved in staple industries, in which decentralization of production processes could be undertaken in a more difficult way. Moreover, these firms faced longer term constraints in the form of trade union inflexibility. A further consideration is that this was the period which revealed the effects of purchases of businesses by the private-sector. One example is the April 1977 decision to dissolve EGAM following the detection of irregularities in the management of the agency (44). Thus, large-sized firms in the private sector were the first to post favourable balance-sheet results as of 1984 (Table 6A in the Appendix):

---

(42) See RICERCHE E STUDI [30], Ch. 3.

(43) See FUA G.: *L'industrializzazione nel nord est e nel centro*, in FUA - ZACCHIA [15]. From 1971-1981, according to the data compiled by MAZZONI [19], central- and north-east and the southern Adriatic regions accounted for 84% of the new jobs created in industry (as opposed to 49% in 1951-61 and 66% from 1961-1971). Despire the financial aid provided by the public sector, the Mezzogiorno did not register any noticeable change overall in relative terms: the number employed in Italian industry has remained at early postwar levels (15% in 1988 compared with 16% in 1951). Significant change has occurred in the area of total per capita resources (which rose from 61% to 71% of the corresponding values in southern Italy from 1951 to 1987); however, this is attributable to transfer payments and not to an autonomous growth process.

(44) The EGAM group companies were awarded in trust to IRI and ENI to evaluate the possibility of recovery or to carry out liquidation procedures.

	1974	1979	1984
	(percentage of value-added)		
Labour cost	71.9	71.6	63.8
Net operating margin	28.1	28.4	36.2
Net profit (*)...................	4.4	4.0	7.9

(*) Equal to the adjusted profit outlined in Table 6A.

Public-sector firms, on the other hand, continued to post heavy losses, reaching an all-time low during 1981-1983; the total, L20.51 trillion, was divided as follows:

	1981	1982	1983
	(billion lira)		
IRI (excluding banks)	3,134	2,896	3,315
ENEL	2,219	2,433	1,823
ENI	302	1,509	1,449
EFIM	315	370	745
Total	5,970	7,208	7,332

5. - Innovations, Profits and Finance: From 1983 to the Present

The developments set out in the previous paragraph determined to a large extent the progress of industry during the rest of the 1980s. From 1984 on, production enjoyed a period of renewed growth, reaching the highest levels of the 1980s in 1986 (45). This phase is characterized by a series of very important facts. There were new means of funding investment based on self-financing generated by the outcome of organizational restructuring. On this subject, Table 5

---

(45) This year marked the so-called "sorpasso", Italy's GDP surpassing that of Great Britain.

reports the cash flow of 1,710 Italian firms. The ratio of cash flow to investment in equipment and machinery reveals the following trend:

	1,710 firms	Private sector	Public sector
	(%)		
1980-1982	34.4	94.7	- (*)
1983-1985	83.9	146.1	36.5
1986-1988	105.2	148.8	67.8

(*) Cash flow was negative.

Thus, there was a change in the selection criteria for investments, no longer linked to the availability of financial assistance provided by government programmes with territorial or by-sector development objectives, based solely on decisions oriented toward cost-effectiveness. A significant role has been assigned to process innovation, with considerable investment in the automation of production processes. Italy's automation sector is estimated to have grown by over 80% during 1983-1988, both in terms of consumption and in terms of production (46). These investments made it possible to increase labour productivity significantly. Between 1983 and 1988, according to Nomisma figures based on Istat data, labour productivity in industry rose by 26.7%. The change in larger sized enterprises should be even more revealing: indeed, the value-added per employee calculated at constant prices on Mediobanca data shows a 27% increase during 1985-1988. It should also be pointed out that the new law enacted in

---

(46) Data were extracted from the annual ANIE survey. One of the most important aspects is the information on the use of robots in industry. According to the International Federation of Robotics, the number of robots used in Italy has risen from 450 in 1981 to 4,000 in 1985 and then to 8,300 in 1988.

Though Italian industry only has half the number in use in West Germany, it has more robots than the United Kingdom and France. Small- and medium-sized enterprises have become interested in process innovation. A recent survey of 220 firms conducted by the CENTRO STUDI F. CICOGNA [10] reveals that about three-quarters of the companies visited devoted resources to research and development.

TABLE 5

1,710 ITALIAN COMPANIES:
SOURCES AND APPLICATION OF FUNDS

	1980-1982	1983-1985	1986-1988	1980-1982	1983-1985	1986-1988
	(L. bn at current prices)			(%)		
Capital expenditure	33,742	48,678	71,661	51.1	58.4	68.1
Financial investments ..	10,019	11,385	23,719	15.2	13.7	22.5
Increase in liquid assets	4,047	9,709	4,356	6.1	11.6	4.1
Increase in net working capital...............	18,177	13,577	5,546	27.6	16.3	5.3
Total funds employed	65,985	83,349	105,282	100.0	100.0	100.0
Cash-flow	11,620	40,861	75,374	17.6	49.0	71.6
Funds provided by shareholders	13,795	19,263	6,781	20.9	23.1	6.4
Grants received	3,063	5,758	6,180	4.7	6.9	5.9
Increase in financial debt	31,426	12,678	11,411	47.6	15.2	10.8
Increase in other liabilities.............	6,081	4,789	5,536	9.2	5.8	5.3
Total sources	65,985	83,349	105,282	100.0	100.0	100.0

Source: MEDIOBANCA [22], p. XXIX

1986 to govern wage indexation has in fact eliminated the main mechanism which in the past had resulted in wage adjustments independent of productivity trends. The ratio of operating margin to value-added has thus remained consistently high, significantly higher than those registered in the late 1970s (see also Graphs 2 and 3):

NET OPERATING MARGIN AS A % OF VALUE-ADDED

	media 1977-1979	media 1986-1988	Change
Private sector	15.6	22.8	+ 7.2 p.
Public sector	11.6	14.6	+ 3.0 p.

Source: based on MEDIOBANCA data.

Profit margin increases were certainly aided from 1985 on by exchange-rate movements of the lira leading to a devaluation of the dollar (− 32% from 1985 to 1988) and, at the same time, to a revaluation of the deutsche mark (+ 14%). In addition, the relative weakness of raw materials markets and especially the sharp fall in oil prices rendered the performance of Italian industry all the more brilliant (47).

Another dominant characteristic of the late 1980s was the trans-

TABLE 6

RIGHTS ISSUES BY COMPANIES QUOTED
ON THE MILAN STOCK EXCHANGE (1)
(L. bn)

Year	Par value	Premium (2)	Total
1967	10	2	12
1968	59	190	249
1969	89	21	110
1970	68	28	96
1971	61	2	63
1972	84	3	87
1973	237	26	263
1974	43	2	45
1975	30	8	38
1976	39	10	49
1977	99	10	109
1978	445	8	453
1979	238	6	244
1980	538	119	657
1981	520	204	724
1982	206	95	301
1983	433	19	452
1984	2,022	231	2,253
1985	1,372	1,197	2,569
1986	4,161	4,825	8,986
1987	1,607	1,395	3,002
1988	726	729	1,455

(1) Figures relate to issues involving a market price for rights and exclude banks and insurance companies.
(2) Including reimbursement of expenses.
Source: Mediobanca [22]

(47) The price in dollars of crude oil purchased by ENI dropped by 47% during 1985-1988.

fer of funds to firms by means of the stock market. Growing expectations of company profits, and the tendency of households to diversify
their protfolios caused savings to flow to the stock exchange, particularly from 1985 onward. The amount of capital traded rose from L452
bn in 1983 to L8.986 trillion in 1986 (Table 6). In subsequent years,
the flow of funds was lower, but never fell below L1.4 trillion
annually. Funds were also raised on the primary market by initial
public offers.

In 1986, the balance of 37 companies registered on and removed
from the official list of firms traded on the Milan exhange is the
highest such figure ever recorded during the postwar period (48); the
number of listed firms, which during the late 1960s had dropped to
slightly more than 100 (similar to 1940s levels), rose decisively as of
1985, reaching 228 at end-1988. Again, private-sector enterprises
benefited the most from this financial market development. The
amount of funds raised on the stock exchange was higher than that
called by investment opportunities in industrial firms. The result has
been growing interest in financial activity, involving share purchases
and short-term allocations such as the purchase of negotiable securities whose yield were judged to be convenient for tax purposes, and
because of favourable real interest rates. The breakdown of expenditure effected by Mediobanca sample firms into industrial and financial allocations is as follows (49):

	1985	1986	1987	1988
	(%)			
Industrial allocations	74.1	47.2	61.4	75.0
Financial allocations	25.9	52.8	38.6	25.0

In 1987, two important privatizations occurred: the sale of Alfa
Romeo business to Fiat and that of Lanerossi operations to Marzotto.
Another important transaction, the sale of ENI chemical assets to

---

(48) Only in 1905 was a higher value ever registered (44 companies). See
MEDIOBANCA [22].
(49) For more on this development, see the notes on changes in the financial
structure of Italian firms over the past 20 years, in BANCA D'ITALIA [4].

Enimont, a joint venture with Montedison, took place in 1989 (50). However, the effects of these phenomena on the aggregate of public-sector assets was insignificant. In terms of capital expenditure, the ratio of public- to private- sector firms, after the sharp increase of 1983-1985, has returned to the levels of the early 1980s:

1980-1982	116.7 %
1983-1985	131.2 %
1986-1988	116.7 %

Source: based on MEDIOBANCA data.

Also worthy of note is the market position of government firms operating in the service sector, where sales have made it possible to realize profits (more often than not, monopoly profits), which are used at least in part to offset the losses of troubled sectors. Within the Mediobanca sample, the following results are revealed:

	Total 1983-1988 (billion lira) (*)
Total public-sector firms	− 7,897
Total state-controlled firms operating public services	+ 6,941

(*) Profits for the fiscal year, adjusted for reserve movements and accelerated depreciation.

Profits realized within the public service sector benefited from a significant price increase. During 1983-1988, public-sector tariffs rose by 44.8% as against a general wholesale price index of 26.2% and a consumer price index of 40.9%.

6. - Concluding Remarks

In our view, the points set out above lead to several observations. The first concerns the relationship between the public and private sectors. Although in recent years further instances of collusion have

---

(50) Of note is the sale of a stake in Mediobanca which, though of interest to IRI, only concerned the banking arm of the group.

occurred, events seem to indicate that the private sector now enjoys some decisionmaking autonomy. This development is of great interest, as it introduces an element of novelty into the potential management criteria of firms. In the past, industry had almost invariably linked its growth to the state, on the demand side (public-sector supplies), on the supply side (ownership of the most capital- intensive firms) and as regards financing (soft loans). Two of these factors have decreased in intensity. Firstly, the state no longer determines the size of the market; its role has been redesigned by freer market trade within Europe. This occurred for the first time in the 1950s, when Italian labour cost competitivity permitted firms to make headway on foreign markets while safeguarding at least some part of the domestic market. During the 1980s, fresh and potentially powerful impetus has been created by the "open" market conditions made possible by technical progress (notably in telecommunications) and by the attendant spread of information. Within this new environment, it is no longer possible to conceive of a thriving protected industry. The other factor which has diminished is the purchase of public finances at favourable rates.

According to Mediobanca figures, the share of subsidized financing granted fell sharply from about 50% in the late 1970s to 9% in 1988. At least two causes can be identified: self-financing levels permitting companies to cover all capital expenditure, and developments in the financial market. Here, too, internationalization is a determinant factor, making it possible to search for resources on markets abroad (51). What remains unchanged is that a large part of industry is government owned.

Nonetheless, the financial capabilities of the private sector could call this aspect into question as well (52). This is an entirely political

---

(51) Apart from the size of the Italian stock exchange, it is worthwhile to consider the gradual listing of Italian companies on stock exchanges abroad. The most notable example is London's Stock Exchange Automated Quotation (SEAQ) where trading on Italian shares rose during the first months of 1990 to several trillion lire, about one-third of the Milan exchange.

(52) According to Bank of Italy data, the net financial assets of Italian households at end-1989 equalled approximately one-and-a-half million billion lire; bank deposits accounted for about one-third of this figure, while another third was invested in government securities. Before any privatization projects could be effected, a readjustment of the portfolio of Treasury bills and certificates would become necessary.

issue: on the one hand, there is the risk that an unmindful sale to the marketplace could lead to the loss or to the dismembering of firms useful to the country in their entirety; on the other hand, we must remember that frequently firms under government control seem to be far from efficient, given that they are far from market competition. The government maintains control over public services, whose pricing policy is unconstrained by parameters related to quality and seems to be based solely on the abuse of dominant position. Add to that the noticeable lack of accountability: even today, no homogeneous, tried and true system of accounting procedures exists within the public sector. As a result, the accounts presented by certain agencies are often ambiguous.

The second observation concerns private-sector entre-preneurship. With the restructuring of the early 1980s came the unusual tendency to solve economic problems using a firm-oriented approach. Process innovation and the new prospects of electronics were probably at the root of the vigour leading to the creation and development of small- and medium-sized firms with highly competi-tive rates of productivity. Paradoxically, however, this development seems to be linked to the deterioration of a sizeable share of the industrial structure. The workers expelled from restructured facilities contributed to the spread of "irregular" jobs, with production methods which are sorely lacking, as it were; this is probably why the start of new Italian business proceeded at such a high rate toward the end of the 1980s; it should be noted that the mortality rate of firms was equally high. The creation of these new fringe elements of employment should probably not be underestimated, especially since they cannot help but be increased by the most recent demographic trends.

The third observation regards the ability of Italian industry to survive the competitive challenge. The comparison of current export-import balances with early postwar figures reveals less impressive levels of imported energy: the deficit of energy products in 1988 represented 9.5% of exports, while in 1951 the oil and coal deficit alone equalled 24%. This reduced dependency does not seem to have boosted competitivity in high technology sectors. According to a recent study conducted by the U.N. Economic Commission for

Europe, during 1970-1987 Italy's share of world exports of mechanical products fell by almost one point in the high-technology goods category and rose two points in that of low-technology (53). Similar indications can be found in a recent OECD report which stresses Italy's strong position in traditional sectors, and its chronic weakness in research intensive areas (54). The most consistent foreign-trade surpluses are realized in industries where product innovation is generally accompanied by the new underemployment phenomena mentioned above: in 1988, sweaters, hosiery and footwear registered a higher surplus than mechanical industry; the latter is the largest exporter overall, evidence of the vitality in a sector characterized by a large number of dynamic medium-sized firms. The important questions which arise concern the ability to sustain the development of medium-sized firms in markets which require ever higher doses of technology, and the real possibility of correcting the imbalance of sectors in which large-sized industry prevails (55).

The final observation deserving of mention concerns the recourse of firms to the stock market. This process — as it is widely known — led to an increase in the share of capital invested in financial assets: negotiable securities and shares. In some cases, this process was accompanied by increased mobility of the firms' controlling stock. It is difficult to throw a positive light upon these developments. On the one hand, there is the "real" risk that the continuous shifting of control over organization of production methods will jeopardize the capacity of the firm to grow and develop with long-term focus; on the other

(53) This pattern varies greatly from that of Japan, but is not so different from the European Community average. Unlike Italy, the other European countries do not seem to be directed toward expanding low-technology production, where certain recently industrialized Asiatic countries have exibited higher levels of growth. See UNITED NATIONS ECONOMIC COMMISSION FOR EUROPE [30].

(54) If we consider the index calculated as the share of product: in the total exports of country j divided by the share of this quotas of individual firms nationwide (numerator) and worldwide product in world exports ("revealed" comparative advantage) during 1984-1986, Italy shows the following figures: in traditional labour-intensive industries, such as clothing and textiles, 2.00 (USA 0.44, Japan 0.51, France 0.86, United Kingdom 0.89, West Germany 0.81); in research-intensive industries such as electronics or aeronautics: 0.66 (USA 2.33, United Kingdom 1.92, France 1.22, West Germany 0.95, Japan 0.70). OECD [25], p. 31-2.

(55) After the energy sector, chemicals, transport and metallurgy are the industrial sectors with the most consistent negative import-export balances. In 1951, the second and third sectors mentioned registered positive balances.

hand, there is the negative effect of the rise purely in nominal value of controlling interests every time that they are transferred (56). In this sense, it seems useful to maintain some degree of stability within the controlling syndicates of firms. It should be borne in mind that the increasing importance of non-industry-related trade surpluses will inevitably slow down the tendency toward growth of means of production. The recent past is replete with cases in which the accumulation of real-estate and financial wealth distinguished the industries which the market had undertaken to penalize.

---

(56) «Funds invested in securities, stocks and credit rise and then fall [...]; this goes to show the mania for groupings, dominance and link-ups that was the rage for so many years and even today has not yet been firmly discredited». (L. Einaudi, in an extract from the *Relazione al bilancio*, MEDIOBANCA [20].

TABLE 1A

ITALIAN INDUSTRIES: MAIN PRODUCTS BY QUANTITY

Year	Electric power (gross prod.) (bn kWh)	Natural gas (bn m³)	Steel (mn tonnes)	Yarns and fabrics ('000 tonnes)	Authorized merchant vessels ('000 gross tonnes)	Cars ('000)	Cement (mn tonnes)	Crude oil and other inputs processed by refineries (mn tonnes)	Refrigerators ('000)	Washing machines ('000)
1950	24.7	0.5	2.4	373	114	101	5.0	5.4	…	…
1951	29.2	1.0	3.1	399	124	119	6.0	7.4	…	…
1952	30.8	1.4	3.5	349	152	114	7.0	9.7	…	15
1953	32.6	2.3	3.5	340	270	144	8.0	12.8	65	…
1954	35.6	3.0	4.2	361	153	181	9.0	16.2	…	…
1955	38.1	3.6	5.4	312	198	231	11.0	17.6	…	…
1956	40.6	4.5	5.9	334	348	280	11.0	19.2	200	60
1957	42.7	5.0	6.8	372	453	319	12.0	20.8	370	79
1958	45.5	5.2	6.3	356	528	369	13.0	24.2	500	100
1959	49.4	6.1	6.8	380	496	471	14.0	26.4	750	164
1960	56.2	6.4	8.2	422	430	596	16.0	30.8	977	180
1961	60.6	6.9	9.1	421	330	694	18.0	35.0	1,528	262
1962	64.9	7.2	9.8	443	346	878	20.0	41.8	1,768	511
1963	71.3	7.3	10.2	453	495	1,105	22.0	48.5	2,187	916
1964	76.7	7.7	9.8	424	365	1,029	23.0	57.8	2,176	1,264
1965	83.0	7.8	12.7	347	459	1,104	21.0	69.4	2,608	1,490
1966	90.0	8.8	13.6	429	435	1,282	22.0	81.2	2,807	1,710
1967	96.8	9.3	15.9	426	482	1,439	26.0	86.6	3,205	2,245
1968	104.0	10.4	17.0	407	500	1,545	30.0	94.7	4,387	2,354
1969	110.4	12.0	16.4	431	495	1,477	31.0	104.9	5,002	2,704

TABLE 1A continued

Year	Electric power (gross prod.) (bn kWh)	Natural gas (bn m³)	Steel (mn tonnes)	Yarns and fabrics ('000 tonnes)	Authorized merchant vessels ('000 gross tonnes)	Cars ('000)	Cement (mn tonnes)	Crude oil and other inputs processed by refineries (mn tonnes)	Refrigerators ('000)	Washing-machines ('000)
1970	117.4	13.1	17.3	422	622	1,720	33.0	121.7	5,247	2,720
1971	124.9	13.3	17.5	388	875	1,701	32.0	124.9	5,257	2,705
1972	135.3	14.1	19.8	400	1,146	1,732	33.0	128.5	5,424	2,996
1973	145.5	15.2	21.0	408	744	1,823	36.0	136.3	5,307	3,325
1974	148.9	15.3	23.8	418	1,073	1,631	36.0	126.4	5,204	3,239
1975	147.3	14.6	21.8	360	903	1,349	34.0	105.4	4,953	3,041
1976	163.6	15.6	23.4	415	606	1,471	36.0	112.3	4,585	3,489
1977	166.5	13.7	23.3	383	699	1,440	38.0	115.5	4,865	3,650
1978	175.0	13.7	24.3	401	341	1,509	38.0	121.3	4,779	3,590
1979	181.3	13.5	24.3	440	149	1,481	39.0	123.0	4,486	3,615
1980	185.7	12.5	26.5	435	171	1,445	42.0	101.6	4,130	3,710
1981	181.7	14.0	24.8	431	301	1,254	43.0	98.3	4,095	3,610
1982	184.4	14.5	24.0	446	283	1,297	42.0	91.0	4,010	3,465
1983	182.9	13.0	21.8	423	180	1,395	40.0	85.7	4,157	3,346
1984	182.7	13.9	24.1	462	352	1,439	39.0	82.9	4,030	3,525
1985	185.7	14.2	23.9	447	41	1,384	37.0	79.7	3,950	3,590
1986	192.3	15.9	22.9	457	211	1,653	36.0	89.1	4,160	4,060
1987	201.4	16.2	22.9	485	...	1,712	37.0	85.4	4,376	4,185
1988	203.4	16.5	23.8	474	...	1,883	39.0	86.7	4,545	4,482

Source: ISTAT and industry associations.

TABLE 2*A*

HIGHLIGHTS OF THE MAJOR TRANSACTIONS PERFORMED BY THE PRINCIPAL STATE-OWNED INDUSTRIAL AGENCIES (1965-1989)

Year	Description
	IRI-ISTITUTO PER LA RICOSTRUZIONE INDUSTRIALE
1965	Alfa-Saviem agreement for the joint production of industrial vehicles at Pomigliano d'Arco
1966	Joint-venture with Fiat (called GMT) to produce large diesel engines
1967	Start of the Alfasud investment programme
1968	Sale of railway production business to EFIM in order to purchase electromechanical firms
	Acquisition through SME of 35% of Motta
	Quotation of Alitalia and Italcable shares
1969	Expansion of Italsider plant in Taranto to 10.3 million tonnes
	Joint-venture WITH Fiat in the aeronautics industry (Aeritalia)
1970	Purchase of the Società Italiana per Condotte d'Acqua
	Management of the Cantieri navali del Tirreno and Riuniti shipyards (formerly the Piaggio group)
	Acquisition through SME of 50% of Alemagna
	Sale to ENI of MCM and Il Fabbricone
	Quotation of the shares of the three banks of national interest
1971	CIPE (Interministerial Committee for Economic Planning) approval of a new steel mill location at Gioia Tauro, Calabria
	CIPE approval of the Aeritalia-Boeing agreement for the construction of a new civilian aircraft
	Management of the insolvent firm Pellizzari at Arzignano
	Purchase from Olivetti of controlling interest in SGS, through STET
	Acquisition of 50% of Star and collaboration agreements with the Fossati group
	Joint-venture with Fiat concerning the stell operations (Acciaierie di Piombino steel mills)
	Acquisition of Innocenti Meccanica
	Sale of Terni Industrie Chimiche to ENI
1972	Start-up up of Alfasud facility
	Setting up of NIRA (owned jointly by Finmeccanica and ENI) for nuclear plant production
	Contract to supply one million tonnes of tubing to the USSR
	purchase of Cirio Shares
1973	Trade of holdings with EFIM (acquisition of control of Breda Termomeccanica and Termosud)
	Sale to EFIM of 75% of Oto Melara

Year	Description
	New GMT facility in Trieste becomes operational
	New SIT Siemens facilities at Carini and Terni become operational
	New Spica facility in Livorno becomes operational
	Sale to EGAM of Monte Amiata mines
1974	Purchase from Montedison of 50% of Alimont (renamed Alivar), through SME
	Start of restructuring programme for naval services of national interest by virtue of Law 684 of 1974
	Start of the mechanized postal centres programme in cooperation with the Post and Telecommunications Ministry
	Purchase of shares in steel mills belonging to the Duina group
1975	Start of Finmare programme to phase out ships (including the "Michelangelo" and the "Raffaello")
	Condotte and Italimpianti win the contract to build a port in Bandar Abbas, Iran
1976	New Italsider facilities in Taranto become operational
	Fiat reduces its share of GMT by 25% and pulls out of Aeritalia
	Merger of Motta and Alemagna to create Unidal
1977	Liquidation of Unidal
	Sale of FNM (Brasil) to Fiat
	Start of colour television programming
1978	Fiat refusal to increase its holding in the Acciarie di Piombino steel mills and subsequent pullout of the company
	New Aeritalia-Boeing collaboration agreement
	Slowdown and subsequent halt of Condotte work in Iran
1979	Creation of a strategic plan for Alfa Romeo involving collaboration agreements with Nissan
	Purchase of Isotta Fraschini, Ducati and Cantiere Navale Breda from EFIM
	Creation of third RAI television network sale of CIR (paper industry) holdings to FCR, of the Fabocart group
	Start-up up of the new Dalmine medium-section mill
1980	Finmeccanica-Fiat collaboration agreements
	Reorganization of Alfa Romeo
	Delivery to ENEL of the Caorso nuclear plant built by Ansaldo
	Attenpted liquidation of Maccarese
1981	Start of Alfa-Nissan agreement
	Restructuring of Ansaldo group
	Aeritalia-Aérospatiale collaboration agreement for the construction of the new ATR-42 aircraft

Year	Description
	Restructuring of Italtel
	Reorganization of SGS
	Purchase through Alitalia of aircraft company formerly known as Itavia
	Fare increases for SIP telephone service go into effect (establishment of *«cassa conguaglio»*)
	Liquidation of Italsider
1982	Finsider-Nippon Steel collaboration agreements for the acquisition of know-how
	Agreement with Fiat to acquire Teksid steel company
	Agreement with Fiat for the joint-production of automobile parts
1983	Reorganization of Ansaldo
	Attempted sale to a third party of the agro-industrial Maccarese group
1984	Merger of shipbuilding firms to form Fincantieri
1985	Start of the IRI programme to form research consortia
	Finalizing of agreements with the Fossati group (resale of Star, acquisition of 42% of Alivar)
	Start of IRI-Union group talks
	Start of Bic project through SPI
	Completion of steel plant at Tubarão, Brazil by Italimpianti
	Attempted sale of SME and Sidalm to Buitoni
	Listing of SIRTI shares
1986	Attempted telecommunications joint venture (Telit) with Fiat
	Sale of Alfa Romeo operations to Fiat
	Listing of Aeritalia and Ansaldo
	Trasporti shares
1987	Microeletronics joint venture with Thomson (SGS Thomson Microelectronics)
	Start of the «Europa Plan» for telecommunications
	Start of the new Finmare Reconstruction Plan under Law 856 of 1986
	Listing of Società Autostrade highways shares
1988	Purchase of Italian subsidiary of American Standard (Westinghouse)
	Collaboration agreements with Belleli and Asea Brown-Boveri
	Sale of Mediobanca shares
	Liquidation of Finsider, Italsider (the new company), Terni A.S. and Nuova Deltasider
1989	Collaboration agreements with AT&T
	Start of steel operations restructuring (ILVA became operational in January)

Year	Description
	ENI-ENTE NAZIONALE IDROCARBURI
1965	Creation of Snamprogetti, hived off from SNAM
	ERIAG refinery in West Germany becomes operational
	Creation of Combustibili Nucleari
1966	completion of central Europe oil pipeline
	Creation of Chimica Larderello chemicals
1967	Completion of Trieste Ingolstadt Trans Alpine Pipeline
	Entry into nuclear fuels sector
	CIPE approval of the nationwide conversion to natural gas
1968	Purchase of Montedison shares and entry into the controlling syndicate
1969	Creation of SAIPEM, hived off from Snamprogetti
	Creation of ammonia and urea processing plants at Monte Sant'Angelo, Apulia
	Investment in Saras aromastic chemicals and cumene
1970	Purchase of MCM and Il Fabbricone by IRI group
	New ethylene production plants at Gela become operational
1971	Trade of holdings with EFIM (acquisition of controlling interest in Pignone Sud)
	Purchase of Terni Industrie Chimiche from IRI
	Agreement to import natural gas from Holland
1972	Vado Ligure coke transferred to Fornicoke (laster sold to EGAM)
	ANIC-BP collaboration agreements for the production of bioproteins in Sardinia
	Setting up of NIRA (owned jointly by Finmeccancia and ENI) for nuclear plant production
1973	Purchase through Italgas of Estigas from Esso Italiana
1974	Purchase of Shell Italiana (later IP)
	Creation of Tescon (textile industry holding)
	Agreement with Bassetti to market MCM products
	Purchase of Confezioni Monti D'Abruzzo apparel
1975	Purchase of Cotonificio Fossati Bellani and MacQueen Orland operations
1976	New fibre production facilities in the Tirso valley, Sardinia become operational
	Acquisition of 50% of the ICAM ethylene plant at Priolo
1977	Creation of AGIP Petroli, hived off from AGIP
	Acquisition and management in trust of EGAM mining, metals, and textile machinery operations
	Acquisition of 50% of Recordati
	Liquidation of Tescon

Year	Description
1978	Creation of Samim and Officine Savio for the purchase of assets formerly belonging to EGAM
1979	Start of construction of Algeria-Italy natural gas pipeline
1980	Creation of Sofegal (50% each owned by the Monti group and ENI) to gain majority control of Sarom Finanziaria
	Acquisition of 100% of the Fibra e Chimica factories in the Tirso Valley
	Management in trust of the assets formerly owned by SIR and Liquichimica
1981	Creation of Enichimica
	Creation of AGIP Carbone
1982	Acquisition of remaining 50% of Sofegal
	Joint venture with Occidental Petroleum and creation of Enoxy
	Purchase of chemical plants formerly owned by SIR (effective as at 11-12-1981)
	Purchase of plants formerly owned by Liquichimica
	Purchase of Napoletana Gas from SME (IRI)
	Renegotiation, with Treasury Ministry subsidization, of the purchase price for Algerian natural gas
	Agreements with USSR for additional natural gas imports
1983	Purchase of Montedison chemical operations
	Dissolution of Enoxy (made a part of Enichimica)
	Creation of AGIP Uranio
	Agreements with the Tonolli group and creation of Sameton
1984	Listing of SAIPEM shares
	Completion of the Algeria-Italy natural gas pipeline
	Creation of Ageni to re-employ redundant workers
1985	Creation of Enichem to replace Enichimica
	Concentration of unsalvageable textile concerns in Confezioni Monti d'Abruzzo
	Acquisition of the remaining 50% of Sameton by the Tonolli Group
	Devaluation of coal reserves by Enoxy coal
	Sale to EFIM of SIV shares
1986	Enichem-ICI joint venture for PVC and creation of EVC
	Listing of Nuovo Pignone shares
1987	Listing of Immobiliare Metanopoli shares
	Sale of Lanerossi operations to Marzotto
	Creation of Terfin
1988	Listing of Enichem-Augusta shares
	Agreements to dissolve Enoxy Coal

Year	Description
	Joint venture with Du Pont for Sclavo
1989	Joint venture with Montedison and creation of Enimont

EFIM-ENTE PARTECIPAZIONI E FINANZIAMENTO INDUSTRIA MANIFATTURIERA

Year	Description
1970	Creation of Cellulosa Calabria (a pulp-and-paper mill in Calabria)
1971	Trade of holdings with ENI (acquisition of majority control of Fucine Meridionali forges)
	Creation of Sopal (a food-industry holding company)
1972	EFIM involvement in the restructuring of Sava
	Completion of Alsar and Eurallumina plants for the production of primary aluminium
1973	Acquisition of 51% of the Augusta group, through Breda Ferroviaria
	Trade of holdings with IRI (Acquisition of majority control of OTO Melara, through FinBreda)
	Acquisition of 50% of Sava
1974	Acquisition of 94% of Alumetal (Montedison aluminium operations)
	Acquisition of 50% of Tubettificio Ligure
	CIPE approval of Sopal programme in the agriculture and food industries
1975	Start of a redistribution of Sopal activities
1977	Purchase of Saca operations at Brindisi, through the Augusta group
1979	Sale of the CDRM paper mill holdings to FCR (Fabocart group)
	Sale of Breda shipbuilding to Fincantieri (IRI)
1981	Reorganization of the Augusta group
	Purchase of OMI
	Purchase of Termomeccanica Italiana from Finmeccanica (IRI)
1982	Purchase of Officine Galileo, from Bastogi, through FinBreda
	Purchase of Breda Nardi and Bosco
1983	Purchase of Caproni Vizzola through Agusta
	Purchase of Terme Recoaro from Eagat
1985	Purchase of ENI holding in SIV
1986	Sale of Terme di Recoaro and food companies
1987	Remodernization of Porto Vesme Eurallumina plant
	Purchase from Fiat of 50% of Omeca and Ferrosud
1988	Acquisition of 50% of Sava from Alusuisse
1989	SIV-Fidenza Vetraria collaboration agreements

Source: R&S, annual reports, various data.

TABLE 3*A*

HIGHLIGHTS OF THE MAJOR TRANSACTIONS PERFORMED BY THE
PRINCIPAL PRIVATE-SECTOR INDUSTRIAL GROUPS (1965-1989)

Year	Description
	FIAT
1965	Creation of Internazionale Holding Fiat to concentrate holdings in foreign subsidiaries
1966	Joint venture with IRI (called GMT) to produce large diesel engines
1967	New Rivalta autombile plant in Turin becomes operational
1968	Construction of the Tofas automobile plant in Turkey begins
	Start of automobile production in Poland under Fiat licence
	Construction of new Vado Ligure and Termini Imerese facilities begins
1969	Purchase of Lancia from the Pesenti group
	Acquisition of 50% of Ferrari
	Acquisition of 35% of Telettra
	Joint venture with IRI in the aeronautics industry (Aeritalia)
1970	Agreements with Michelin and acquisition of 49% of Partedi (Citroën group parent company)
	Togliattigrad, USSR automobile factory becomes operational
	Purchase of Ferroviaria Savigliano
	Construction of the Cassino, Frosinone automobile plant begins
1971	Joint venture with IRI concerning the steel industry (Acciaierie di Piombino steel mills)
	Purchase of Abarth
	Sale of Italnavi
1972	Dissolution of agreements with Citroën
1973	Joint venture with Allis Chalmers in the earthmoving sector (Fiatallis)
	Construction of the Brazil automobile plant begins
1974	Joint venture with KHD in the industrial vehicle sector (Iveco)
1975-1979	Main operations involved in Fiat hive-off
1976	Acquisition of majority control of Telettra, Gilardini and Nebiolo
	Purchase of FNM (Brazil) from Alfa Romeo (IRI)
	Start of Fiat Automoveis (Brazil)
	Transfer of financial operations to Fidis
1977	Entry of Libyan investor in Fiat shareholding Purchase of Hesston Corp. (USA)
1978-1985	Purchase of minority shares in Fiatallis
1980	Sale of controlling interest in the Spanish automaker Seat
	Creation of Fiat-Peugeot joint venture in Argentina (Sevel Argentina)
1981	Participation in the creation of Gemina

TABLE 3*A continued*

Year	Description
1982	Purchase of minority shares in Iveco
	Sale of steel operations to Finsider
	Sale of Sevel Argentina
1983	Acquisition of controlling interest in SNIA
	Listing of Fidis shares
1985	Attempted agreement with Ford in the automobile sector
	Listing of Sorin Biomedica shares
1986	Purchase of Westland shares
	Iveco-Ford joint venture in Great Britain
	Purchase of Alfa Romeo operations
	Repurchase of Fiat shares from Libyan shareholder, through IFI; the Agnelli group holding then amounts to about 40% control of the company
	Listing of SNIA Fibre e Tecnopolimeri shares
1987	Fiat-Matra joint venture and creation of Ufima (65% Fiat-owned)
1989	Purchase of Cogefar from Bastogi
	Acquisition of 49% Maserati

MONTEDISON

Year	Description
1966	Montecatini-Edison merger
	Purchase of Shell stock in Monteshell Petrochimica
1968	ENI and other public-sector shareholders entry into the controlling syndicate
	Construction of the aluminium plant at Fusina, Venezia begins
	Participation in the Tirso valley industrialization programme
	Purchase of Union Carbide shares in Celene (later merged with Sincat)
1969	Joint venture with Hercules in polypropylenic fibre (Neofil)
	Construction of the aluminium plant of Fusina (Venezia) begins
	Participation in the industrialization programme of Tirso valley
1970	Expansion of the Sincat refinery at Priolo to more than 15 million tonnes of capacity
1971	Acquisition of absolute majority of Carlo Erba
	Agreement with Rhône-Poulenc to purchase its holdings in Farmitalia and Rhodiatoce
	Sale of Sisma to EGAM
	Agreements to transfer Monteponi & Montevecchio operations to Ammi (EGAM)
	Creation of Montefibre (merger of Châtillon, Rhodiatoce, Polymer, Sinteco) and Alimont (formerly known as Pavesi)
	Concentration of insurance holdings in Fingest
1972	Acquisition of controlling interest (34% of the vote) in SNIA

Year	Description
1973	Sale of aluminium operations to EFIM
	Sale of metallurgical operations to EGAM
	Agreements with Hercules to market Farmitalia antitumoral agents in the US
1974	Sale of food operations (Alimont) to SME (IRI)
	Purchase of the daily newspaper *Il messaggero*
	Fibre production facilities in the Tirso valley become operational
	Joint venture with Pirelli in the textile sector (Sicrem)
1975	Creation of a new Montedison controlling syndicate composed of public- and private-sector participants
1977	Sale of majority control of Banco Lariano to the Istituto Bancario San Paolo di Torino
1979	Sale of majority control of Fingest to the Bonomi group
	Sale of Novamont (USA) and Paular (Spain)
	Montefibre goes into receivership
1979-1980	Main operations involved in Montedison hive-off
1981	Acquisition of majority control by Gemina
	Sale of gas utility to the Milan City Council
1983	Sale of a group of chemical assets to ENI
	Agreements with Hercules and creation of Himont and Erbamont (later quoted on the New York exchange)
	Sale of majority control of SNIA to Fiat
	Listing of Selm shares
1985	Purchase of majority control of Bi-Invest
	Acquisition of control from the Varasi group
	Acquisition of control of Compo in exchange for the sale of Ausimont
1986	Purchase of Fondiaria assicurazioni insurance shares
1986-1987	Acquisition of the company by the Ferruzzi group
1987	Purchase of additional Fondiaria Assicurazioni shares
	Acquisition of majority control of Antibioticos (Spain)
	Purchase of Himont shares
	Purchase of the Total Italiana distribution network (a joint venture with Shell)
	Public offer of Farmitalia C.E. shares in exchange for Erbamont shares and cash settlement
1988	Acquisition of remaining SIR operations from the SIR Intervention Committee
	Merger of Iniziativa Meta and Ferruzzi Finanziaria
1989	Joint venture with ENI in the chemical sector (Enimont)

Year	Description
	Public offer launched on the US exchange to repurchase shares owned by third parties in Himont, Erbamont and Ausimont
	Agreements with James River and Nokia in the pulp-and-paper industry

OLIVETTI

Year	Description
1965	Dismantling and sale of large computer division to General Electric
1968	Acquisition of majority control of SGS
	Closing down of former Underwood plant at Hartford (USA)
1969	Opening of new plant at Harrisburg (USA)
	Completion of new facilities at Scarmagno
1970	New plant at Marcianise, Caserta becomes operational
1971	Sale of SGS to STET (IRI)
1978	Acquisition of control by CIR (De Benedetti group)
1980	Saint-Gobain becomes a shareholder
1983	Agreements with AT&T, which underwrites an Olivetti restricted rights issue under a standstill agreement in effect until 1990
1980-1984	Venture capital investments
1981	Acquisition of the Hermes Precisa group in exchange for the sale of other assets
1985	Acquisition of the Acorn group
1986	Volkswagen becomes a shareholder
	Acquisition of Ta-Triumph Adler group
	Listing of Teknecomp shares
1987	Listing of Tecnost shares
1988	Purchase of Scanvest Ring (Scandinavia)
1989	New AT&T-CIR agreements and transfer of the US company holdings to CIR
	New organizational structure

PIRELLI SPA

Year	Description
1970	Pirelli-Dunlop agreement and conversion of Pirelli SPA into a holding company
1971	Sale of La Centrale shares
1973	New telephone cable production facility at Battipaglia becomes operational
1974	Joint venture with Montedison in the textile industry (SICREM)
1979-1980	Main operations involved in Industrie Pirelli hive off and start of the recovery plan concerning the same firm
1980	Acquisition of majority control of Treficable (France)

TABLE 3A *continued*

Year	Description
1981	Dissolution, of Pirelli-Dunlop Union
1986	Purchase of Metzeler (W. Germany)
	Acquisition of holding in Burgo in exchange for the sale of pulp-and-paper assets
1988	Attempted takeover of Firestone (USA)
	Acquisition of control of Armstrong Tire (USA)
	Purchase of Fiergie (France) from Ceat International
	Reorganization of the controlling group
1989	Creation of Pirelli Tyre Holding

GRUPPO PESENTI

Year	Description
1967	Merger of 8 banks controlled by the group to form IBI
1969	Sale of Lancia to the Fiat group
1973	Merger of Opii with Italcementi
1976	Acquisition of majority control of bastogi from Montedison
1979	Sale of Credito Commerciale to Monte Dei Paschi
	Distribution of Italmobiliare stock to Italcementi shareholders and conversion of the former into the parent company of Pesenti group
1980	Start of the reconversion program of the supply of combustible carbon-based oil to cement factories
1982	Sale of IBI to Cariplo
1984	Sale of Banca Provinciale Lombarda to San Paolo di Torino
	Sale of Efibanca shares
1985	Purchase of E. Marelli operations through Franco Tosi
1984-1986	Sale of control of Ras to Allianz
1986-1987	Sale of Bastogi shares to Acqua Marcia
	Listing of Cementerie Siciliane and Cementerie di Sardegna shares
	Purchase of firms in the concrete sector
1987	Purchase of Cementifera Fibronit
1987-1988	Agreements with the Monti group concerning publishing operations
1988	Sale of controlling stock in the Cimsa finance company (Spain)
1989	Sale of Franco Tosi industrial operations to Asea Brown-Boveri

Source: R&S, annual reports, various data.

Fulvio Coltorti

TABLE 4*A*

SELECTED DATA ON THE LEADING
PUBLIC-SECTOR INDUSTRIAL ACIENCIES
IRI

Year	No. of employees (2)	Turnover	Capital expenditure in year	Profit or loss (1)			Endowment fund
				Banks	Industrial companies	Total	
	(thousands)			(billion lira)			
1968	273	2,593(3)	586	(4)	(4)	(4)	517
1969	292	3,012(3)	655	(4)	(4)	(4)	595
1970	340	3,659(3)	872	(4)	(4)	(4)	675
1971	384	4,116(3)	1,261	(4)	(4)	(4)	900
1972	413	4,686(3)	1,536	(4)	(4)	(4)	1,140
1973	447	6,022(3)	1,819	(4)	(4)	(4)	1,358
1974	468	7,354	1,851	27	(131)	(104)	1,586
1975	474	8,895	2,183	30	(365)	(335)	1,810
1976	476	11,145	2,584(3)	42	(392)	(350)	1,833
1977	477	13,114	3,035	51	(619)	(568)	2,180
1978	471	15,952	3,234	75	(1,039)	(964)	3,356
1979	478	18,147	3,135	86	(1,199)	(1,113)	3,269
1980	478	22,558	3,980	112	(2,221)	(2,109)	6,229
1981	465	29,004	4,659	200	(3,134)	(2,934)	8,098
1982	467	32,940	5,476	208	(2,896)	(2,688)	10,956
1983	457	36,887	6,309	266	(3,315)	(3,049)	14,920
1984	443	41,133	7,372	556	(2,929)	(2,373)	19,231
1985	420	44,960	8,426	524	(1,943)	(1,419)	22,782
1986	408	47,058	8,795	587	(880)	(293)	26,017
1987	361	43,315	9,102	404	(1,047)(5)	(643)	27,510
1988	358	49,217	10,506	508	(242)(5)	266	28,601

(1) Consolidated balance-sheet data, net of profit or loss attributable to minorities.
(2) Banks employing 60,000 at end-1988 were not included.
(3) Restated data.
(4) No consolidated balance sheet was issued.
(5) Losses resulting from the restructuring of steel operations, which equalled L. 2.24 trillion in 1987 and L. 2.681 trillion in 1988, were not included.

Source: annual reports.

TABLE 4A *continued*

ENI

Year	No. of employees	Turnover	Capital expenditure in year	Profit or loss (1)	Endowment fund
	(thousands)		(billion lira)		
1968	60	1.244	257	4	347
1969	63	1,407	308	10	418
1970	72	1,601	453	4	474
1971	76	1,865	472	(19)	684
1972	79	2,192	576	8	914
1973	81	3,058	765	38	989
1974	92	5,837	888	(44)	990
1975	100	6,745	940	(98)	1,044
1976	101	10,123	1,190	(105)(2)	1,107
1977	103	11,672	1,082	(257)	1,241
1978	120	13,404	1,188	(326)	1,871
1979	121	16,098	1,545	46	1,957
1980	123	23,495	2,607	69	2,307
1981	123	33,263	4,322	(302)	2,522
1982	144	38,999(2)	4,785	(1,509)	3,491
1983	136	44,386	4,009	(1,449)	5,234
1984	131	44,701(2)	4,949	(65)	6,291
1985	129	46,462	5,694(2)	822	7,820
1986	130	33,520	6,132	547	8,619
1987	119	31,730	6,307	687	8,805
1988	116	32,837	5,859	1,194	8,901

(1) Consolidated balance-sheet data, net of profit or loss attributable to minorities.
(2) Banks employing 60,000 at end-1988 were not included.

Source: annual reports.

TABLE 4*A continued*

EFIM

Year	No. of employees	Turnover	Capital exmpenditure in year	Profit or loss (1)	Endowment fund
	(thousands)		(billion lira)		
1968	17	(2)	(2)	(2)	42
1969	19	(2)	(2)	(2)	47
1970	21	(2)	(2)	(2)	51
1971	22	(2)	(2)	(2)	135
1972	24	204	128	(11)	169
1973	28	304	95	(7)	289
1974	41	663	124	(9)	290
1975	43	814	108	(93)	329
1976	46	1,263	149	(74)	420
1977	46	1,820	150	(102)	548
1978	46	1,918	162	(95)	742
1979	41	1,968	166	(196)	829
1980	41	2,456	188	(95)	929
1981	43	3,094	243	(315)	1,073
1982	42	3,307	255	(370)	1,391
1983	42	3,957	252	(745)	1,969
1984	40	4,401	192	(571)	2,233
1985	39	4,839	200	(485)	2,981
1986	36	4,182	261	(217)	3,667
1987	36	4,544	554	(104)	3,712
1988	37	4,623	471	(48)	3,834

(1) Consolidated balance-sheet data, net of profit or loss attributable to minorities.
(2) Banks employing 60,000 at end-1988 were not included.
Source: annual reports.

ENEL

Year	No. of employees	Turnover	Capital exmpenditure in year	Profit or loss (1)	Endowment fund
	(thousands)		(billion lira)		
1968	102	973	429	0 (1)	0
1969	103	1,030	492	0 (1)	0
1970	105	1,138	603	0 (1)	0
1971	105	1,271	665	0 (1)	0
1972	98	1,376	716	0 (1)	0
1973	101	1,536	681	(269)	100
1974	106	2,001	838	(520)	100
1975	113	2,602	1,012	(542)	200
1976	114	3,161	1,209	(730)	750
1977	114	3,797	1,446	(751)	1,250
1978	114	4,681	1,615	(539)	1,750
1979	114	5,935	1,879	(652)	2,250
1980	116	8,780	2,629	(499)	2,350
1981	118	11,493	3,311	(2,219)	3,830
1982	117	13,296	3,497	(2,433)	6,630
1983	116	15,840	4,311	(1,823)	8,930
1984	115	19,942	4,843	(2)	9,730
1985	115	21,718	5,685	0	10,984
1986	115	18,024	6,526	14	11,329
1987	114	19,996	6,749	134	11,329
1988	113	20,198	6,218	138	11,329

(1) Depreciation provision was adjusted in order to obtain the balance of income and expenditure.

Source: annual reports.

Fulvio Coltorti

SELECTED DATA ON THE LEADING
PRIVATE-SECTOR INDUSTRIAL GROUPS
FIAT

Year	No. of employees	Turnover	Capital exmpenditure in year	Profit or loss (1)	Share capital fund
	(thousands)		(billion lira)		
1968	158(2)	1,335(2)	115(3)	34(2)	115
1969	171(2)	1,425(2)	143(3)	13(2)	130
1970	185(2)	1,712(2)	164(3)	5(2)	150
1971	182(2)	1,810(2)	189(3)	16(2)	150
1972	278(4)	3,452(4)	204(3)	16(2)	150
1973	303(4)	4,201(4)	227(3)	0(2)	150
1974	309(4)	5,676(4)	354(3)	0(2)	150
1975	302(4)	7,198(4)	270(3)	0(2)	150
1976	329	9,270	185(3)	135(5)	150
1977	342	11,449	325(3)	114(5)	150
1978	348	13,135	393(3)	77(5)	165
1979	358	15,056	419(3)	76(5)	165
1980	343	18,138	404(3)	97(5)	165
1981	302	20,312(6)	818	90	338
1982	264	20,619	1,316	137	338
1983	244	21,985	1,452	253	338
1984	231	23,813	1,485	627	2,025
1985	226	27,102	1,433	1,326	2,025
1986	230	29,338	2,879	2,162	2,250
1987	271	38,435	3,437	2,373	2,340
1988	277	44,308	3,394	3,026	2,340

(1) Consolidated balance sheet data, net of profit or loss attributable to minorities, unless otherwise specified.
(2) Parent company only.
(3) Fiat, Fiat Auto and Fiat veicoli Industriali aggregated data.
(4) Main companies only.
(5) Parent company and Italian subsidiaries only.
(6) Restated data.
Source: R&S (various years), annual reports and *Il Sole/24 Ore* for selected 1968-70 items.

TABLE 5A *continued*

MONTEDISON

Year	No. of employees	Turnover	Capital exmpenditure in year	Profit or loss (1)	Share capital
	(thousands)		(billion lira)		
1968	142	1,447	78(2)	41 (2)	749
1969	153	1,633	107(2)	41 (2)	749
1970	176	1,868	157(2)	0 (2)	749
1971	178(3)	2,017(3)	376	(271)(4)	749
1972	171	2,100	224	(455)(4)	375
1973	159	2,590	167	27	375
1974	155	4,029	381	113	436
1975	149	3,535	619	(120)	436
1976	139	4,815	745	(161)	436
1977	135	5,472	732	(455)	436
1978	126	5,775	535	(265)	350
1979	115	6,833	378	19	356
1980	106	7,781	386	(448)	356
1981	94	8,927	372(3)	(619)	356
1982	88	9,019	405	(859)	996
1983	73	10,660	430	(322)	996
1984	71	12,382	467	(83)	996
1985	70	14,132	622	113	1,110
1986	67	12,834	809	320	2,568
1987	67	13,791	989	409	2,705
1988	47	14,122	1,056	630	2,705

(1) Consolidated balance sheet data, net of profit or loss attributable to minorities, unless otherwise specified.

(2) Parent company only.

(3) Fiat, Fiat Auto and Fiat veicoli Industriali aggregated data.

(4) Including profit or loss attributable to minorities.

Source: R&S (various years), annual reports and *Il Sole/24 Ore* for selected 1968-70 items.

Fulvio Coltorti

PIRELLI

Year	No. of employees	Turnover	Capital exmpenditure in year	Profit or loss (1)	Share capital
	(thousands)		(billion lira)		
1968	67	594	...	8 (2)	68
1969	73	687	...	(2)(2)	68
1970	77	767	...	1 (2)	68
1971	74	756(3)	...	(15)(4)	70
1972	72	805	21(4)	(35)(4)	70
1973	72	1,018	12(4)	(17)(4)	70
1974	74	1,384	15(4)	(11)(4)	70
1975	72	1,393	12(4)	(27)(4)	70
1976	72	1,905	13(4)	(2)(4)	70
1977	71	2,228	31(4)	(5)(4)	116
1978	73	2,580	39(4)	(2)(4)	116
1979	73	3,071	46(4)	(19)(4)	116
1980	77	4,104	55(4)	3 (4)	116
1981	73	4,711(3)	83(5)	8 (5)	196
1982	70	5,780	107(5)	(16)(5)	196
1983	64	5,932(3)	89(5)	17 (6)	231
1984	62	6,445	107(5)	105 (6)	292
1985	61	7,227	151(5)	166 (6)	419
1986	68	7,072	166(5)	180 (6)	447
1987	66	7,251	221(5)	195 (6)	840
1988	72	9,120	1,023	224	840

(1) Consolidated balance sheet data, net of profit or loss attributable to minorities, unless otherwise specified.

(2) Parent company only.

(3) Fiat, Fiat Auto and Fiat Veicoli Industriali aggregated data.

(4) Industrie Pirelli only (at end-1970 Pirelli industrial operations were concentrated in this firm).

(5) Figures relate to consolidated accounts of Italian subsidiaries controlled through Industrie Pirelli.

(6) Aggregated profit, excluding parent companies.

Source: R&S (various years), annual reports and *Il Sole/24 Ore* for selected 1968-70 items.

TABLE 5A *continued*

OLIVETTI

Year	No. of employees	Turnover	Capital exmpenditure in year	Profit or loss (1)	Share capital
	(thousands)		(billion lira)		
1968	61	370	11(2)	7 (2)	60
1969	68	400	19(2)	(1)(2)	60
1970	73	463	25(2)	6 (2)	60
1971	74	494	28(2)	4 (2)	60
1972	72	549	14(2)	4 (2)	60
1973	71	637	14(2)	4 (2)	60
1974	72	796	26(2)	4 (2)	60
1975	71	856	29(2)	(9)(2)	60
1976	69	1,126	28(2)	1 (2)	60
1977	66	1,365	34(2)	5 (2)	60
1978	62	1,556	36(2)	2 (2)	100
1979	56	1,853	40(2)	24 (2)	108
1980	53	2,180	60(2)	50 (2)	209
1981	53	2,888	208	96	291
1982	50	3,341	281	103	340
1983	48	3,736	330	295	344
1984	48	4,578	405	356	488
1985	49	6,140	403	504	494
1986	59	7,317	436	566	547
1987	58	7,375	549	402	550
1988	58	8,407	615	356	550

(1) Consolidated balance sheet data, net of profit or loss attributable to minorities, unless otherwise specified.

(2) Parent company only.

Source: R&S (various years), annual reports and *Il Sole/24 Ore* for selected 1968-70 items.

Fulvio Coltorti

TABLE 6*A*

PROFIT AND LOSS ACCOUNTS OF A SAMPLE
OF ITALIAN COMPANIES

Year	State-controlled companies				Private-sector companies			
	NOM (1)	Labour cost	Net financial charges (revenues)	Adjusted profit or loss (2)	NOM (1)	Labour cost	Net financial charges (revenues)	Adjusted profit or loss (2)
				in % of value added				
1974	13.0	68.8	20.0	(8.1	15.1	71.9	8.6	4.4
1975	6.5	73.1	25.2	(20.2)	8.9	78.4	11.5	(6.5)
1976	10.9	68.4	27.3	(17.1)	16.0	71.9	10.9	1.2
1977	12.4	66.2	28.1	(20.5)	16.7	71.3	10.9	(0.5)
1978	11.9	67.3	25.7	(17.7)	14.2	72.7	9.5	0.9
1979	10.8	66.8	22.4	(15.8)	16.0	71.6	8.8	4.0
1980	9.9	68.2	26.2	(21.5	)19.1	69.1	11.3	3.6
1981	11.5	66.4	32.0	(26.1)	19.7	68.0	12.9	0.6
1982	13.1	63.8	26.4	(22.0)	17.4	68.6	11.6	(2.2)
1983	13.8	62.9	21.7	(16.8)	17.6	67.6	8.7	2.1
1984	16.4	58.6	18.3	(9.5)	21.5	63.8	6.5	7.9
1985	17.7	57.1	14.8	(3.7)	22.2	63.6	3.6	13.0
1986	11.4	60.2	11.3	(4.2)	22.7	62.7	0.3	16.5
1987	12.9	58.6	11.3	(3.3)	21.7	63.5	(1.2)	17.1
1988	18.9	55.3	11,4	3.0	23.9	62.2	(1.1)	15.4

(1) Operating margin net of ordinary depreciation.
(2) Profit or loss adjusted for reserve movements, accelerated depreciation and financial charges capitalized.

Source: based on MEDIOBANCA figures (sample of 1,214 Italian companies).

GRAPH 1

INDEX ISTAT
OF ITALIAN INDUSTRIAL PRODUCTION

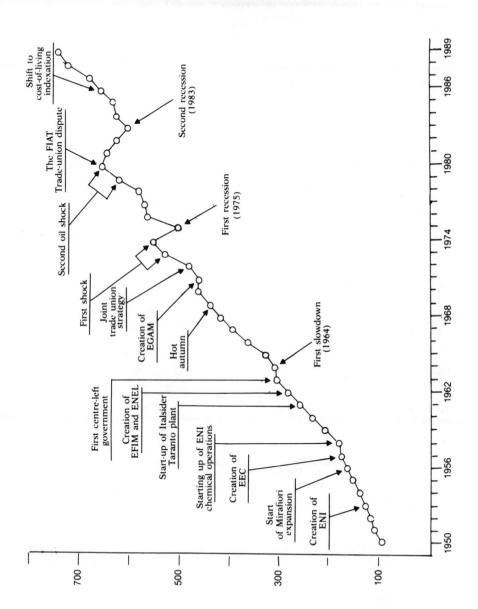

GRAPH 2

PRIVATE-SECTOR FIRMS
(labour costs, operating margin,
financial expenses, profit)

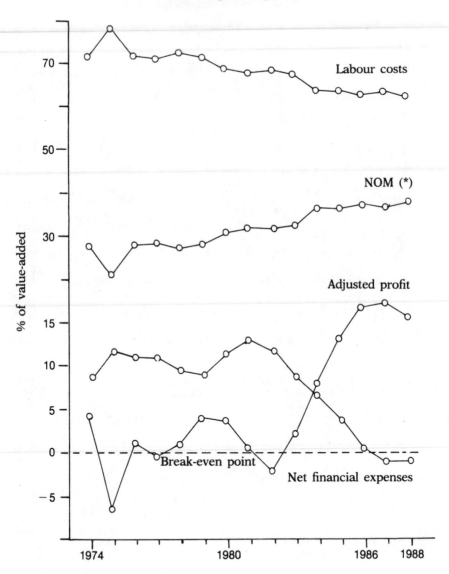

(*) Operating margin net of ordinary depreciation.

GRAPH 3

STATE CONTROLLED FIRMS
(Labour costs, operating margin,
financial expenses, profit)

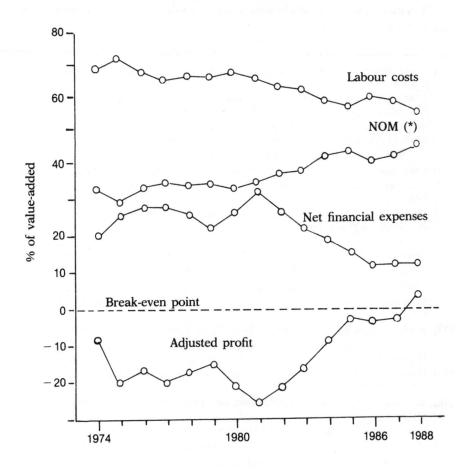

(*) Operating margin net of ordinary depreciation.

BIBLIOGRAPHY

[1] ALZONA G.: «Il caso Sir Rumianca», *L'impresa*, November-December 1971.

[2] BANCA D'ITALIA: *Relazione del Governatore per il 1964*, Roma, Banca d'Italia, 1965.

[3] —— : *Relazione del Governatore per il 1978*, Roma, Banca d'Italia, 1979.

[4] —— : *Ristrutturazione economica e finanziaria delle imprese*, Roma, Banca d'Italia, 1988.

[5] BANCA TOSCANA: «Le partecipazioni statali in Italia, Intervista di P. Barucci a Pasquale Saraceno», *Banca toscana studi e informazioni*, no. 1, 1981.

[6] BOTTIGLIERI B.: «Linee interpretative del dibattito sulle partecipazioni statali nel secondo dopoguerra», *Economia pubblica*, April-May 1984.

[7] CAIZZI B.: *Camillo e Adriano Olivetti*, Torino, Utet, 1962.

[8] CASTRONOVO V.: *L'industria italiana dall'ottocento a oggi*, Milano, Einaudi, 1980.

[9] CEEP: *Problemi di riorganizzazione delle partecipazioni statali*, Torino, Ceep, 1975.

[10] CENTRO STUDI F. CICOGNA: «Osservatorio sull'attività delle piccole e medie imprese», *Working Paper*, no. 1, January 1990.

[11] COMITATO INTERMINISTERIALE PER LA RICOSTRUZIONE: *Rapporto presentato dalla Delegazione del Governo italiano al V Consiglio generale dell'Unrra*, Roma 1946.

[12] CUZZI D.: *Breve storia dell'Eni*, Bari, De Donato, 1975.

[13] DALLA CHIESA N.: *Dopo la fabbrica: il caso Italtel*, Milano, «Il sole 24 ore», 1988.

[14] FRATIANNI M. - LA MALFA G. - TREZZA B.: *L'economia italiana 1974-1975*, Milano, F. Angeli, 1975.

[15] FUÀ G. (a cura di): *Lo sviluppo economico in Italia*, Milano, F. Angeli, 1969.

[16] FUÀ G. - ZACCHIA C. (a cura di): *Industrializzazione senza fratture*, Bologna, il Mulino, 1983.

[17] GRAZIANI A.: «L'industria italiana fra pubblico e privato», *Rassegna economica*, January-February 1984.

[18] IRI: *Relazione al bilancio 1968*, Roma, Iri, 1969.

[19] MAZZONI R.: «Localizzazione industriale e livelli occupazionali: un'analisi empirica 1951-1981», *L'industria*, October-December 1987.

[20] MEDIOBANCA: *Relazione al bilancio 1987*, Milano, Mediobanca, 1987.

[21] —— : *Dati cumulativi di 1710 società italiane*, Milano, Mediobanca, 1989.

[22] —— : *Indici e dati relativi ad investimenti in titoli quotati nelle borse italiane*, Milano, Mediobanca, 1989.

[23] MINISTERO DELL' INDUSTRIA E COMMERCIO: *L'istituto per la ricostruzione industriale*, Torino, Utet, 1955.

[24] MINISTERO DELLE PARTECIPAZIONI STATALI: *Rapporto sulle partecipazioni statali*, Venezia, Marsilio, 1980.

[25] OECD: *Italy 1988-1989*, Parigi, OECD, 1989.

[26] —— : *Italy 1989-1990*, Parigi, OECD, 1990.

[27] RICERCHE & STUDI: *L'industria chimica*, Milano, Ricerche e Studi, 1970.

[28] —— : *Le fibre chimiche*, Milano, Ricerche e Studi, 1972.

[29] — —: *La creazione di imprese*, Milano, Ricerche e Studi, 1989.

[30] UNITED NATIONS ECONOMIC COMMISSION FOR EUROPE: *Economic Survey of Europe in 1989-1990*, New York, 1990.

[31] VARIOUS AUTHORS: «Risanamento e riordino delle partecipazioni statali», Collana Ceep, *Industria pubblica e privata*, no. 5, Milano, F. Angeli, 1986.

[32] VILLARI L.: *Il capitalismo italiano del novecento*, Bari, Laterza, 1975.

[33] ZANETTI G. - FRAQUELLI G.: *Una nazionalizzazione al buio*, Bologna, il Mulino, 1979.

Public Enterprises and Industrial Policies

Paolo Leon
Università «La Sapienza», Roma

1. - Introduction

1.1 - The obverse of the theme, or the effects of industrial policies on Italian public enterprises, will not be dealt with here. My theme will be narrowed down — apart from a few generalizations — to the study of the role of industrial enterprises whose shares are owned by the State (1) as instruments of industrial policy. It is the presence of these firms that underscores the uniqueness of the Italian system, not that of public enterprises: though the effects on industry of the latter are clearly evident,they are usually created to achieve a purpose related to the specific goods and servicies they produce.

2. - Industrial Policies

2.1 - In the definition which will be used here, industrial policy is viewed from a microeconomic perspective, dealing with individal firms, individual markets and individual industries. The reason for this is not academic: a macroeconomic industrial policy certainly exists,

---

(1) These enterprises remain private, for the purpose of commercial law; they are, however, owned — wholly or partly — by public agencies (IRI, ENI, EFIM). They will be called herein after SP (State Participation) enterprises .

especially during the 1980s, but by its very nature (based entirely on general and automatic instruments, such as the interest rate and the exchange rate) it does not distinguish between the roles of public- and private-sector firms, not to mention that of SP enterprises (2). To be sure, they were used to further macroeconomic policies (as in the early eighties, when their recourse to the *Cassa integrazione guadagni speciale* was restricted), but this revealed the political, and not the industrial policy, use of these enterprises.

Although their sphere of operations is macroeconomic , industrial policies are only worthy of the name if their purpose is national in scope. A look ot the policies which are generally classified ad industrial provides sufficient evidence.

They include: *a)* financial and fiscal incentives policies; *b)* policies for the development of services to firms; *c)* policies to sustain the research and development of new process and products; *d)* antitrust policies; *e)* policies fostering the restructuring or conversion of firms; *f)* policies geared toward preserving the trademark or the firm in cases of bankruptcy or insolvency.

2.2 - That each of these policies has an underlying broad objective is clearly visible: *a)* financial and fiscal incentives (including parafiscal incentives, such as the reduction in social security contributions to be paid by the employers) are designed as a protective measure, both against international competition and to improve competitiveness of certain parts of the country vis-à-vis the rest; when they are extended to the entire nation and/or cover the goods/servicies not marketed abroad, their purpose is to redistribute income; *b)* services to firms can be protectionist measures capable of supplementing or substituting the ones described in *a)* above; they can also foster technology transfer, or innovation, benefiting the entire indus-

---

(2) At the end of the seventies, according to Law 675 on industrial restructuring, the CIPE (Interministerial Committee for Economic Planning) defined a series of industrial programmes designed to guide the application of incentives to industry. Large firms, and in particular state-owned, firms, played a key role in these programmes. In fact, each programme could be regarded as a sort of cartel involving private- and public-sector firms. This section of Law 675 was never enacted, and consequently the role of SP enterprises mentioned above never actually materialized.

try; however, services may not belong to either of these groups if they are offered by the publicly financed institutions that are not subject to market or customer scrutiny; *c)* the objective of promoting innovation is that of increasing productivity if enterprises cannot or will not develop new ideas. When such promotion is directed at a restricted group of firms, the objective becomes no less protectionist than that of financial and fisical incentives; *d)* the antitrust goal is to increase social welfare where the monopolistic market would reduce it. However, the legislation at present under review in Parliament defines antitrust measures as those that counteract the *abuse* of a dominant position, not the dominant position in itself. Thus, the spirit of the legislation aims only at forbidding unfair behaviour, not at minimizing welfare loss; *e)* fostering restructuring/conversion means limiting the waste of capital (labour and equipment) in cases where the market is unable to do so; *f)* the objective or relaxing insolvency procedures is similar to that discussed in *e)* above.

3. - The Role of SP Enterprises

3.1 - It is possible to divide such policies into two broad categories, according to their overall objectives: those that are protectionist in character, and those which aim at offsetting market failure. Clearly, the two categories are not equally broad. Even in a European context of lower trade barriers, the protectionist objective could be furthered by macroeconomic policies, as was the case in the seventies, when the exchange rate was linked closely to the pricing policies of large firms. Correcting market failure, on the other hand, has no macroeconomic substitute measures (3).

---

(3) Market failure is more a series of exceptions than a theoretical category. Only the "disequilibrium" school of thought generalizes this concept (see FITOUSSI J.P.: *Modern Macroeconomic Theory, an Overview*, Oxford, Oxford Blackwell, 1983), based on the assumption that markets exist which are incapable of exausting supply or of satisfying potential demand. When HICKS (in *Capital and Growth*) subdivides flex- and fixed-price sectors (markets), the presence of market failure is implied. Since this leads to the creation of a macroeconomic disequilibrium, macroeconomic disequilibrium policies may well be justified. Nowadays, however, it is difficult to distinguish between such policies and simple pragmatism.

3.2 - This reasoning helps us to place the potential role of SP enterprises into context. Since their role must be permanent, and must not vary with the terms of trade, these firms are principally instruments to correct market failure. Nonetheless, they may have many other objectives, and in the past, this type of enterprise played various roles. Of note is their importance during the postwar reconstruction period, when they were considered necessary to fill the entrepreneurial gap in the private sector. Shortly thereafter, SP enterprises were called upon to develop the heavy industrial sectors (steel, mechanics, shipbuilding, energy) with the purpose of the internalizing the production of intermediate goods for use by the private sector. Later, they were asigned the task of industrializing the Mezzogiorno. Still later, in the seventies, SP enterprises facilitated agreements with the trade unions, when their bargaining power became very strong. Viewed from this angle, these roles of SP enterprises fall into the two categories mentioned earlier. The production of intermediate goods is an example of non-tariff protection, especially when these goods are produced at a loss, or at lower productivity levels than those of the rest of industry. Postwar reconstruction, the Mezzogiorno and industrial relations are examples of remedies to market failures.

3.3 - To be sure, an over-abundance of objectives can undermine the effectiveness of an SP enterprise. The Tinbergen rule, which states that each objective must be linked to one instrument, should be observed also in this case. The past history of SP enterprises is actually less clear than the above outline would seem to indicate. For example, the objectives of restructuring troubled firms, reaching agreement with the trade unions and providing an industrial base co-existed throughout the seventies; industrialization of the South and trade-union consensus were pursued jointly from 1962 to 1975, as were reconstruction and the industrial base until the boom of 1958. These objectives were to be pursued together with yet another goal, that of enterprise profitability (which remained on paper, obviously, for long periods of time). This is why it was so difficult to rationalize, in retrospect, the behaviour of SP enterprises and to clarify the extent to which these firms can be considered instruments of industrial policy.

4. - Obstacles to Policies Remedying Failure

4.1 - If the principal role played by SP enterprises in industrial policy is that of offsetting market failure, let us turn now to the types of obstacles, implicit in the organizational framework of such firms, that tend to undermine it. The first obstacle is the profitability constraint of individual firms. Although the vast number of interpretations of this concept is matched only by the number of historical occasions on which it has been invoked (4) firms must at least obey some efficiency indicator, set at market prices. The least that can be done to achieve this objective is to minimize the input/output ratio. However, minimizing this ratio may lead to an accumulation of losses — and since profitability is a vague term, excessive losses are often attributed to low profitability. Conversely, the most that can be done to achieve this objective is to maximize the rate of profits of the firm. This concept is however unclear, both as an accounting concept and because of the theoretical difficulty in attaching value to capital. Of course, profits can always be based on the firm's market value, rather than the value of accumulated capital. Nonetheless, since SP enterprises are not usually available for sale on the capital market — a point which will be developed below — no market value can be established for them. Even when these firms issue shares on the stock exchange, control must remain in the hands of the State, their majority shareholder. It follows, then, that profitability is best achieved by maximizing the rate of return on new investment, or at least by ensuring a rate of return in line with that of the rest of the market. But is it possible to guarantee rates of return similar to market rates when investment in SP enterprises is made to offset market failure?

4.2 - The second obstacle is the fact that SP enterprises are grouped basically by industrial sector, while market failure need not necessarily result from sector causes. Whereas it is true that the sectorial division is not rigid and has often been bent out of shape, it is

---

(4) For a recent survey, see ARONICA A.: «La privatizzazione delle PP. SS.», in Di MAYO A. (ed.): *Le politiche di privatizzazione in Italia*, Bologna, il Mulino, 1989.

also true that no other criterion has ever been used to apportion firms into groups. One possible alternative to the sectorial criterion that has often been proposed is the use of the concept of integration, expected to justify the existence of different enterprise groupings. What is being referred to here is not vertical integration; otherwise, groups would not be subdivided by sector (Finsider-Finmeccanica, Agip-Snam). Horizontal integration — by commodity or by market — is conceivable, but it would lead to a sectoral composition of enterprises.

Integration, on the other hand, has not created specific organizational structures. In general, regardless of what it entails, the concept of integration clashes with the autonomy of individual firms — another organizational concept often invoked together with that of profitability: a term uncertain enough to permit the widest array and the most diverse forms of autonomy. On this subject, we must remember that entrepreneurial autonomy of an SP enterprise makes good sense if the company's shares can be sold on the market; although this is possible in theory, SP groups have never attached great importance to the mobility of ownership of individual companies. The SP groups are not investment or merchant bankers.

4.3 - A third obstacle is the lowering of tariff, exchange and tax barriers involved in the European integration process. Under these circumstances, an SP enterprise can only be used as an instrument to remedy market failure if the market failure ecompasses the European market, and not only the national one. Otherwise, the possible financial loss to publicly-owned companies, brought about by the correction of the failure, would be considered a subsidy and thus a hindrance to competition. Market failure and non-tariff protection would amount to the same thing if the former were limited to the national market.

A definition of market failure enlarged to take into consideration the whole European economic space would define SP enterprises in European terms. This theme is central to the future of these firms, whose status within the European Community is as yet uncertain, and whose legitimancy is constantly being questioned by EC Commissioners in Brussels.

5. - Market Failure and SP Enterprises

5.1 - Returning to industrial policies, let us examine those which offset market failure: research and development, services to firms, antitrust and restructuring. Historically, SP enterprises have probably done the most to further the latter policy. During the postwar years, in industries varying from metals to chemicals, from textiles/clothing to foods, from mining to glass, SP enterprises carried out many *salvage operations* and restructuring/conversion projects, often with impressive results. This function is justifiable under certain conditions: when the market failure can be traced to a single private entrepreneur; when the industrial sector is suffering a short-term crisis; when the recovered market share benefits the production of other goods/servicies supplied by the state-owned group, or lowers the cost of such productions (integration). These conditions are not of equal importance. If failure is the results of poor management, other public institutions (i.e. GEPI, Gestione partecipazione industriale) exist to tackle the problem. It many also be possible to regulate the market in such a way as to prevent entrepreneurial capital from being wasted (i.e. the Prodi law). A short-term crisis may be overcome by means of short-term subsides.

The benefits achieved through integration, which could not be felt in the marketplace, are therefore the justification for SP enterprises to act as instruments of industrial policy. Earlier, we observed that the organizational significance of integration is minimal. Integration is of no importance from an accounting perspective, either; SP managers are thus unable to calculate its costs and its benefits (5).

5.2 - SP enterprises may play a role in *research/development* if their cost-benefit calculation is not based on the same factors as those of private firms or the market in general. This means that the evaluation of risk, uncertainty and the rate of time preference must be lower for SP enterprises than for private-sector companies. This is an

---

(5) A recent case in point is the merger of the ENI and Montedison chemical firms: at the time, the "synergy" gains were given monetary values. As the bases of these calculations were not known, "synergies" were not really in the minds of those who drew up the agreements between the two companies.

important point. The risk factor of an SP enterprise is not dependent on the amount of accumulated capital, or on the market value of its share capital because, as mentioned earlier, these firms cannot be sold on the market; as a result, the risk factor calculated by the manager of an SP enterprise will be lower that that of a private-sector manager. Uncertainty, or future events which cannot be measured in terms of probability, is also lessened in the case of SP enterprises, since this, too, is tied to capital. The discount rate of an SP enterprises or of the owner-state, adjusted for risk, is inevitably lower than the market rate, the latter being influenced by the rate of time preference of individual owners and thus by individual life-cycles. For SP enterprises, the discount rate is based on an opportunity cost which is free of subjective considerations, while the owner-state may tailor opportunity cost to suit its own needs. This reasoning could be pushed more deeply: here however, it is sufficient that risk, uncertainty and the discount rate are lower, so that lower are the rates of yield considered adequate by SP enterprises vis-à-vis private ones, thus leading the former to an increased propensity toward research and development. For this reason, if policies providing Government subsides (the Istituto mobiliare italiano (IMI) fund; projects sponsored by the Consiglio nazionale delle ricerche (CNR); Law 46, and so on) are extended to all firms, then the ratio of company expenditure to subsides should be higher for SP enterprises than for private firms. The lack of sufficient data makes it impossible to draw conclusions, but it is certain that the Government has not given the matter serious consideration — an indication that this function of SP enterprises is not regarded as essential.

5.3 - As for *services to firms*, if the market were in short supply SP enterprises could well substitute or supplement private activity. A look at such services (consultancy, design, information) leaves some question whether such a shortage exists. If we were to say that there was a shortage in relation to potential demand, rather than to actual demand, we would find ourselves in a Popperian situation. It has been often said — in political statements — that SP enterprises should offer servicies to small- and medium-sized businesses — implying that SP enterprises have a responsibility toward enlarging the market of their small suppliers, thus increasing their autonomy and capacity for growth. The assumption that a market failure could occur among small business is not unfounded (6); the problem lies in deciding what can be done about it by an SP enterprise. A more favourable treatment of suppliers (perhaps by means of higher prices) does nothing to broaden their market, but jeopardizes their autonomy. Substituting the suppliers' marketing effort broadens their market, but reduces their autonomy. Limiting purchases increases their autonomy, but causes their market to shrink. There is no reasons why new SP enterprises cannot be created to perform this task: however, the fact that is has never been done (7) suggest that these enterprises do not consider themselves to be instruments of this particular industrial policy.

5.4 - *Antitrust* has always been considered a good reason for creating public enterprises, when the market structure undetermines social welfare and when insufficient legislation allows mono(oligo)polistic behaviour to continue unchecked. Of course, there is no reason not to create an SP enterprise rather than a nationalized one, with such an objective. For this measure to make sense, however, it is necessary for the SP enterprise — even though it remains a mono(oligo)poly — to avoid reducing social welfare. This implies that its price and quality-setting policies are dictated (controlled) from without, that is, by an authority capable of calculating which prices and qualities allow the firm to achieve its goal. This is apparently the case in various sectors (such as telecomunications, air transport, distributions of natural gas and petroleum products), but it has never been proven that the external body in charge of dictating (or controlling) prices was created to combat trusts. On the contrary: prices are based on average costs, quantities are unconstrained by public-sector objectives, the quality of the good/service produced is

---

(6) Pages 85-98 of the BANK OF ITALY: *Annual Report* (May 1990) clearly illustrate the slowdown in Italian small businesses during the eighties.

(7) Firms belonging to Istituto per la Ricostruzione Industriale (IRI) and Ente Nazionale Idrocarburi (ENI) are poised to create new enterprises (SPI, AGENI), but their objectives are social (broadly speaking, they are instances of job creation), not industrial.

not subject to standards and thus is not controlled. In the banking sector, where there is a high degree of monopoly by SP enterprises, prices and quantities are actually fixed by a cartel, with little or no interference from external authorities. When it comes to goods and services traded internationally, the degree of monopoly declines as liberalization spreads within the European Community, and the need for SP enterprises as an antitrust countermeasure is lessened (banks and air transport are good cases in point). Thus, if antitrust is not considered by the external authority to be a key role of SP enterprises and if this role overlaps that of freer international trade, then SP enterprises are not *in fact* an antitrust industrial policy measure. On the contrary, privatizing SP enterprises exhibiting a monopolistic behaviour could become an industrial policy, especially within a context of increased international competitiveness.

6. - SP Enterprises as Supply-Side Policy Instruments

6.1 - As is often the case, analysis manages to destroy rather than to create. Based on what has been said above, it would seem that even though SP enterprises appear to be instruments of industrial policy, they are in fact only partial instruments, the benefits of which cannot be assessed. However, one aspect of this analysis merits further discussion: the fact that the property of these enterprises cannot be sold on the market.

To be sure, recent years have witnessed a growing number of these firms on the stock market, trading a minority of their shares (8), while some of them have been privatized. What must be made clear is that SP enterprises are, in general, *separate* from the market: as a result, managers of these firms are not responsible for the value of the enterprises or for capital gains (losses), nor are they compelled to answer to their majority owner, the state. Arguably, the owner-state has no interest in maximizing (or in maintainig) the value of the firm's income statement. A similar observation was recently made concern-

---

(8) In fact, shares of firms belonging to IRI and ENI owned by the public account for approximately 26% of the total value of the market (June 1990).

ing public enterprises within a planned economy (9), but Italy's distinguishing feature is the fact that in most cases state-owned firms, like private companies, are compelled by law to issue asset-and-liability statements.

This discussion implies that, for some unknown reason, it is *necessary* to substract from the capital market a portion of the industrial wealth. Since this substraction does not benefit the financial market, the reasons for it clearly are not financial: in other words, the substraction does not remedy a market failure in the financial sphere. If this is true, then the substraction must be of organizational importance (10): it occurs because the managers of SP enterprises *must not* maximize capital value. The only rational explanation for this is a conflict between maximizing capital value and the objective of maximizing the rate of return on new investment mentioned earlier. An inordinate amount of literature on this subject deals with the existence (or the lack) of a single objective for the firm (which must maximize profits, rate of growth, value of the firm, etc.). Although every possible trade-off between the various objectives has been esamined, the results have nonetheless been inconclusive. For our purpose, we need only point out that the capital value and the rate of return on new investment may conflict: in environments where that value is of importance, new investments must overcome the constraint of maximizing it; in other words, it is necessary for new investments to raise, and not lower, this value. The owner of the firm may thus decide to reject more profitable projects if the value of the firms is not increased: a classic case in point is a profitable project which adds no value to the trademark of the firm. For SP enterprises, this constraint is relaxed, if not altogether absent; every new profitable project is carried out, even if it reduces the value of the firm. We could

---

(9) See LEON P.: «L'impresa sovietica e la perestroika» in *Note di ricerca Cles*, no. 2, March 1990.

(10) One school of thought links the subtraction to the "political" market. It suggest that SP enterprises exist because of their value as an expression of political rather than economic power. Although this suggestion is not scientifically well grounded, it results from observing real life. Its interpretation is that the political system can (or feels that it can) better control the economy with an instrument in the form of a company at its disposal. In this case, politically controlled, SP enterprises, would be part of an antitrust policy.

say that, at any given moment, the capital of an SP enterprise is viewed as a sunk cost in the eyes of its manager and therefore has no economic value. More specifically if the investment function of firms included the capital value, the expected return on a *project* would have to be compared with the interest rate and with the expected profit rate of the *enterprise*. In cases where the expected return of the project was higher than the rate of interest, but lower than the profit rate, the new project would be left by wayside. Further, maximing the market value of the firm, or making it appealing to potential buyers, means no longer selecting projects according to their return but according to the return which would be enjoyed by the future buyer (who purchases both the value of the firm and the value of the new project). An example might be useful here: if the buyer is interested in the market share held by the firm, and to him this represents the firm's value, then a project which taps a new market or launches a new product, or a project aimed at restructuring the technology or the organization of the firm, will not increase the value of the firm as far as the buyer is concerned. Generally, the higher the capital value in relation to the project, the more burdensome the constraint placed by the former, and the lower the propensity toward investment. This aspect can be viewed in a different light if a variable representing wealth is included in the investment function. It is common knowledge that the wealth of the economy as a whole is equal to zero: credits and debits, liabilities and assets always balance. Obviously, for single firms this is not the case. Each owner attempts to maximize the capital gains realized (or to minimize the losses suffered) on his property. It is also widely known that an owner looks to the capital gain as well as to the profits of firm, and that — within certain limits — he may establish a trade-off between the two: capital gains being viewed as current profits deferred over time. I wish to stress the expression "within certain limits": an owner cannot perfectly replace current profits with capital gains, since the latter also relies — as discussed earlier — on the market appraisal of the firm, and the market considers the firm to be a piece of wealth having different from that accruing to its owner. The capital gain of one owner must mean that, somewhere in the economy, another owner has suffered a corresponding capital shortfall; but the first owner neither knows nor cares about this. In any event, the individual makes his own choices without realizing that others will be compelled to make opposite choices — to an individual, maximizing one's own wealth is tantamount to maximizing wealth in general. This is why each individual owner has a telescopic defect which affects the investment of the firm.

If the interpretation were correct, then the entire system of SP enterprises would act like one giant industrial policy. Exempt from the constraint posed by wealth considerations, investment in these firms would only vary, in the Keynesian sense, with expectations, and the interest rate. This would set industrial investment (for two reasons: because the output of investment goods is largely industrial, and because input comes mainly from industry) at a higher rate than would otherwise be obtained.

Some may accuse me of belabouring the point in an effort to replace the golden rule according to which capital increases as the rate of profits declines — the law of dimishing returns. I will defend myself by noting that, on one hand, the law would be applied to all firms, regardless of their owners; and on the other hand, that it has never been proven. The simpler argument demonstrated above pre-supposes the existence of an additional constraint on private industry — which should suffice. Thus, SP enterprises, as regard their invest-ment, do not merely stimulate effective demand, but stimulate the demand for investment goods: they offset the market failure of private firms with a telescopic defect.

6.2 - Based on this argument, let us now observe what happens to SP enterprises when, after allowing their indebtedness to grow, an attempt is made to lower it. In Italy, the problem is real: after a sharp rise during the seventies, the indebtedness of SP enterprises declined (11) largely as a results of increased cost-effectiveness. Lowering indebtedness affects the wealth of the firm, since it is essentially a reduction of the debt-equity ratio. When this occurs, the investment function and the management of SP enterprises begin to look similar to those of the private sector.

---

(11) IRI-group net indebtedness fell from more than 11% of turnover in 1979 to 68% in 1987.

138 *Paolo Leon*

6.3 - What remains to be examined is why a policy that aims at keeping the share of industrial value added high should be (considered) necessary. If we rule out industrial fetishism (linked to culture, habits, or ideology), then such an objective is only justifiable if for the economy as a whole industrial growth has implications that differ from those of other sectors. After years of observation of post-industrial capitalism, this way of reasoning this cannot be accepted without question, nor is this an appropriate setting in which to pass judgement on neo-industrialism. It would probably suffice to compare rates of productivity increase during the past decade (Table 1): it becomes clear that the productivity growth of manufacturing is highest, and that total value added relies on the growth of industrial investment (12).

However, it also true that this function of SP enterprises is not truly recognized nowadays. We must remember that in Italy the

TABLE 1

VALUE ADDED AT FACTOR COST PER UNIT OF LABOUR
(1979 = 100)

	Industry	Manufacturing	Energy products	Construction	Services
1980	103.8	104.0	101.0	97.3	100.2
1981	105.7	106.0	98.7	95.0	98.8
1982	107.4	107.8	98.8	92.0	96.5
1983	112.3	124.0	96.1	90.8	94.8
1984	122.4	124.0	94.9	93.0	94.6
1985	127.6	129.5	95.2	93.0	94.7
1986	131.2	133.1	97.3	94.8	95.5
1987	137.6	139.8	98.7	97.3	96.9
1988	145.9	148.7	100.6	99.6	99.0
1989	149.8	152.6	105.2	102.6	101.8

Source: Based on data from BANK OF ITALY, May 1990

(12) The correlation between industrial investment and total value added is apparently a good one: during 1978-89, $R = 0,985$; $R^2 = 0,972$; R^2 adjusted = 0,968. I do not wish to join the debate on the Kaldor-Verdoorn law (see VAGLIO A.: «Fatti stilizzati ed interpretazione teorica: il caso della legge di Verdoorn», *L'industria*, Jannuary-March 1990). It would be more correct to prove the existence of ties between productivity growth in the manufacturing industry and growth in manufacturing value added, and subsequently demonstrate the link between the growth of the latter and the growth of total value added.

TABLE 2

INVESTMENT OF SP ENTERPRISES AND TOTAL INVESTMENT

	Ratio of investment in industrial SP enterprises to total industrial investment
1980	9.11
1981	10.64
1982	13.19
1983	11.02
1984	9.98
1985	11.37
1986	12.12
1987	10.79

Source: ISTITUTO CENTRALE DI STATISTICA (ISTAT): *Conti economici regionali,* new series, May 1990

privatization debate centered on the supposed strategic role of SP enterprises, and not on the significance of their investment as a stimulus to growth. A look at the ratio of investment by SP enterprises to gross fixed investment in industry during the eighties (Table 2) provides sufficient evidence: its unsteadiness cannot be considered a policy of any kind.

6.4 - We are thus left empty-handed: hardly suprising, given the fact that specific policies (those dealing with regional development, the industrial sector, the enterprise) carry little weight when compared with the great axes of macroeconomic policy. The most that can be said after this analysis is that SP enterprises, while having other functions not investigated here, are a potential instrument of industrial policy.

The Restructuring
of Large-Sized Industrial Groups

Gian Maria Gros-Pietro
Università di Torino

1. - Large-Sized Companies
and Public-Sector Involvement

In the early 1970s, Italian industry was judged the least developed of any industrialized country. Italy's place among the most developed nations never seemed entirely secure; it seemed that unfavourable future developments might be capable of jeopardizing this new-found status.

Two unsual traits were common to Italy and Japan: both were countries with industrial systems in which the concentration of small- and very small-sized firms was far higher than elsewhere in the industrialized world, and both nations' development indicators were less favorable than those of the other major economies. The two countries were considered likely to modify their behaviour so as to bring their development processes in line with those of the more experienced economies. During the two decades that followed, both countries did in fact attempt to do just that, with varying degrees of success.

What rendered the Italian situation unusual was the combination of rigidity and instability that weakened the industrial system. Rigidity could be found in the size structure of Italian industry, and in the way in which this structure had come into being. Unlike Japan, Italy was unable to add many large-sized firms to its mix of small- and medium-sized enterprises. The number of Italian companies mentioned in

Fortune's list of leading non-American firms, about ten each year, is lower than that of South Korea or Finland. On average, France and Germany have 50 companies each, and Great Britain hovers close to 70. The problem with the size of Italian firms is not only of inequality, but also of scarcity of large firms, in absolute terms. To a country ranked among the five most developed nations worldwide, an inadequate number of large-sized groups and companies means an asymmetrical division of industrial, financial and market power, and a lack of alternatives to the decisions of the few existing key players. This situation can jeopardize competition where the market is not completely open to international trade, and will surely cause industry to rely heavily on the behaviour of individual large-sized companies. In certain key sectors, the success of the market leader determines the success of national industry as a whole.

The weakness of the Italian industry had thus a structural origin. Moreover, the competitive behaviour of large-sized Italian firms had been rather risky, during those years. Until the second postwar period, Italian industry had outgrown the nation's economy, and the political climate had not encouraged firms to explore international markets in search of the large-scale operations unavailable in the domestic market. Indeed, the socio-political context had fostered the search for public-sector protection of industry, and, when that was considered insufficient, the public sector assumed direct responsibility for the management of a part of the industrial and financial system.

The creation of IRI during the first postwar period gave the public sector full control over the large-sized steel mills, a large portion of the metals industry, and most of the shipbuilding industry. In addition, the state held monopolies in telecommunications and radio broadcasting, a large share of the highway construction industry, and the major banks. The second postwar period saw the creation of ENI to manage the petrochemicals sector, ENEL for electricity, EFIM and other similar agencies. The state had almost complete control over the energy sector, played a major role in chemicals and aerospace, became the leading producer of aluminium and arms, and entered the glass industry. Large-scale public-sector involvement extended to seemingly non-strategic sectors, from food and restaurants to fashion houses, and included mining, clothing factories, agricultural agencies, shipping companies, insurance companies, film studios and publishers.

One evaluation of the impact of public-sector intervention is the time series data concerning a limited sample of firms, compiled by Mediobanca from 1968 on (Mediobanca [16] (*)). The portion of the sample included in the entire time series consists of 1,214 companies, and is principally made up of large-sized firms. During the first year, the number of state-controlled companies accounted for 29% of the sample and 45% of its gross assets, while in 1988 these figures had risen to 36% and 46% respectively. Also worthy of note is the fact that the sample excludes other types of state-owned industry, such as postal services, railways, production and distribution of electric power, and activities managed by local government agencies.

2. - The Lack of Public-Sector Industrial Strategy

Increased government intervention in large-sized enterprises could have been considered a strength rather than a weakness. In theory, assured central planning should be a boon to any country with a strategy designed to bring its development in line with other industrialized nations, and particularly so when there are few key players. Empirical evidence exists to support this view: for example, the presence of Italian industry in high-technology sectors, though somewhat limited compared with other developed countries, is for the most part the province of state-controlled companies. Without their involvement, planned and not market-driven, the situation would have been much worse.

Even during the postwar reconstruction and the so-called economic miracle, state-controlled industry served to rationalize and to guide by modernizing the steel industry and by setting up a state-owned firm to supply hydrocarbons. However, in the early 1970s, the effect of public-sector involvement in industry, rather than to spur production to new development objectives, was to rob the system of flexibility. A proper assessment of the long-term needs of

---

(*) Advise: the numbers in square brackets refer to the Bibliography.

industrial policy would have revealed the impossibility of a development model based on exports and low wages, which had been the driving force of the economic miracle. Because of its success, this model was no longer practicable. The conditions for a labour market in which wages were low no longer existed. The obvious alternative was to bring development in line with that of other countries, a major industrial undertaking for Italy; outmoded production methods would have to be abandoned, and incoming resources redirected toward forms of production with higher value-added. This need should already have been apparent since the 1963 crisis, which marked the end of the most active phase of development; nonetheless, it never became an industrial policy objective. The only major reconversion carried out during this period was that of the former power companies, which were compelled to seek new uses for the funds received in exchange for their newly nationalized utilities. Thus, the reconversion was essentially carried out by the private sector. Public-sector involvement was limited to promoting and encouraging investment, rather than guiding the latter in a given direction.

The absence of an explicit industrial policy was due to a lack of ideas rather than ideological choice. During that period, the Italian political climate was not at all opposed to public-sector intervention in the economy. Economic plans were enthusiastically thought out, drawn up, quantified and assigned deadlines. However, not much attention was paid to the real, organizational aspects of industry, whose objectives were largely described in aggregate terms. Qualitative content and its strategic implications sparked little interest.

The conservative management of state-controlled companies clearly revealed the public sector's disregard for competitivity, a factor vital to industry. Within the public sector, the basic management objectives included saving jobs, protecting wages and working conditions, and increasing the number of jobs in less-developed areas of the country. None of these goals could be considered an obstacle to a strategy aimed at matching the development of other countries, if such a strategy were explicitly defined. However, because of government neglect of the concrete aspects of industrial activity, protection of the concrete aspects of industrial activity, protection of the labour force became the only constraint imposed on production. Companies were compelled to protect existing jobs, even at times offsetting by financial means the negative ratio of labour productivity to cost. This behaviour was actually extended beyond the existing state-controlled companies with the creation of GEPI, whose role was to attempt to restore financial stability to troubled private-sector firms, or at least to make use of public funds to guarantee their survival.

Thus, rather than providing guidance, the unusually strong presence of the public sector in large-sized Italian firms introduced rigidity into the system and, in so doing, placed a major obstacle in the path of development strategy. During the same period, Japan's private sector firms were given a clear direction, the objective of continually renewing and expanding the industrial portfolio. This strategy was supported by government action and by gradual changes in financial policy, exchange rates and customs tariffs.

3. - The Competitive Position of Large-Sized Private-Sector Firms

Italy's large-sized private-sector firms were also affected by a lack of flexibility, caused by their past history, and accentuated by their competitive behaviour. Large-scale mass production was developed in Italy largely during the 1950s and 1960s in response to the first major rise in the demand for durable goods in the domestic market; exports, made possible by low wages, provided a further stimulus. Given the nature of their markets, large-sized Italian companies originally adopted a competitive market strategy aimed at low-priced, low-technology products.

When changing labour-market conditions made this type of competition less profitable, not even private-sector firms moved decisively toward a new market strategy. Instead, most firms opted for plant rationalization, or raising labour productivity by substituting this factor within the production equation, leaving markets essentially unchanged. This policy, followed consistently by large-sized firms in the private sector during the late 1960s, caused these companies to shoulder heavy burdens. The financial burdens brought about by high investment are a case in point: in the Mediobanca sample of private-

TABLE 1

PERCENTAGE OF INVESTMENT FLOWS AND OF DEPRECIATION
OVER FIXED CAPITAL STOCK (HISTORICAL VALUES), IN THE
PRIVATE-SECTOR COMPANIES IN THE MEDIOBANCA SAMPLE

Year	Investment/stock %	Depreciation/stock %
1969	11.50	6.84
1970	14.03	6.89
1971	13.96	6.63
1972	11.09	9.08
1973	10.60	7.68
1974	13.61	8.78
1975	13.07	7.91
1976	11.51	8.87
1977	11.63	8.66
1978	11.87	9.15
1979	11.52	9.16
1980	13.35	9.98
1981	14.58	11.03
1982	15.07	12.15
1983	11.32	10.44
1984	11.04	10.59
1985	12.22	10.55
1986	13.70	11.12
1987	13.94	11.67
1988	13.22	10.96

Source: CERIS-CNR [12].

sector large-sized firms, during the late 1960s and the early 1970s investment flows related to plant and equipment had reached levels ranging from 12% to 14% of stock, almost double the depreciation flows (Table 1).

The highest accumulation rate was reached in 1971 (Zanetti [18]), when investment in plant and equipment equalled 328% of the net self-financing of these private-sector firms. The imbalance between financial requirements and internal resources caused companies to turn to credit, the only readily available external resource. The ratio of financial debts to net capital, which in this group of firms stood at 0.93 in 1968, had doubled by 1972 and reached its highest level, 1.93, in 1975. Thus, the rationalization policy, applied to unchanged and no longer profitable productions, caused profit-and-loss statements to become very rigid. The rise of nominal rates beyond 20%, led many to a financial crisis which restricted the options available for strategic decisionmaking. Inflexible operations were another consequence of large-sized private-sector companies' hesitant approach toward new methods of production. The frenzied attempt to increase labour productivity was carried out in a general way by optimizing plants and production cycles. Almost invariably, this involved increasing plant size and abandoning low-volume production techniques. Rationalization was perceived as a process which further limited the possibility of market diversification and stymied productive capacity. In the mid-1970s, when violent market disturbances caused unexpected swings in demand and price, inflexible operations in many cases drove costs much higher than gains.

The decision to continue to invest in existing methods of production to enhance the production equation also had significant impact on employment. Since these production methods were not linked to rapidly rising demand, as in the case of new industrial sectors, the desired increases in labour productivity could only mean fewer jobs. However, this phenomenon was hidden by the favourable economic climate and by the reduced working hours of the early 1970s. By 1974, the number employed by the private-sector Mediobanca sample had risen by 17% in comparison with the 1968 figure, but the number of employees in state-controlled companies has seen a 47% increase. Both figures declined after 1974, albeit more rapidly in the private-sector firms. Labour disputes, coupled with the commitment of large-sized private-sector firms to boost productivity, had a negative impact on industrial relations. Conflict within the plants further emphasized the vulnerability of production processes: because of rationalization, any deviation from pre-set production levels was potentially a major disaster.

4. - Related Conditions

Broadly speaking, industrial relations were one of the factors of instability plaguing Italian industry. Unlike other industrialized countries, in Italy companies and workers were often divided on ideological grounds. If private-sector companies tended to maximize profits regardless of the effects on employment, the labour force, unwilling to bear the brunt of these companies' need to remain competitive, viewed each new technological innovation as a potential threat to the status quo. In the absence of a clear industrial policy direction, or rather, given the non-policy executed by many state-controlled companies, it was difficult to implement an industrial conversion based on technological development.

The inadequate capital market presented another obstacle to large-sized firms. In 1979, only 139 companies were listed on Italy's major stock ecxhange in Milan, compared with 223 in Denmark, 519 in Holland, 756 in France, and more than 3,000 quoted in London's City (Scognamiglio [7]). The limited scope of the Italian stock exchange was the result of a vicious circle: little recourse to a risky capital market had left the latter incapable of satisfying the needs of firms. It is true that the financial requirements of large-sized firms were met by means of the credit system, as mentioned earlier. This made the public sector even more important, since all of the major banks were state controlled. However, without a clearly defined industrial policy, this lever was not used to guide industry. As a consequence, operators faced the responsibility of acting independently and according to labour-related considerations. Even under these conditions, state-controlled banks were often used as intermediaries in the reconversion of the former electric power industry, the only major reconversion of the period. The petrochemicals industry was correctly identified as a major market, its low national supply being inable to satisfy growing demand. Over the years, banks became increasingly involved in the financing of this growth. Although the initial premises were well-founded, the industry had not yet generated enough entrepreneurial talent; as a result, already high financial requirements continued to rise. The financing of state-controlled companies by state-controlled banks provides another example. However, in this case, rather than acting on the basis of technical concerns, the banks believed that by extending credit to cover losses, they still managed to fulfill their mandate, since the responsibility for industrial management lay with the government, their principal shareholder. Moreover, depositors' savings were not placed at risk, because banks were convinced that the state would act as a debtor of last resort to guarantee the credit extended to firms under its control. Thus, the singular structure of the financial market was in itself a factor of instability, because banks had become a necessary part of all industrial projects, and because of the substantial loans amassed by these ventures in industrial sectors with little hope of being able to repay.

5. - Industrial Policy Requirements

Sweeping changes were needed to rectify the situation of large-sized Italian industry during the first half of the 1970s. The most important ones are listed below: 1) restoring financial health to most state-controlled companies, since most of these firms were involved in dead-end sectors, had inefficient production equations and were struggling with unmanageable debt loads; 2) redressing the disequilibria of certain industrial sectors, such as chemicals, in which both public- and private-sector firms were in difficulty; 3) encouraging large-sized private-sector firms to modify their competitive behaviour by targeting high-value products and more advanced technology; 4) freeing the major banks from the indebtedness incurred by certain large-sized firms, since this burden had begun to hamper the normal fuctioning of the credit system; 5) expanding the capital market, particularly the stock exchange, to satisfy the needs of Italian industry in a real way.

Unfortunately, the international economic climate and the situation of public finances did not permit these cumbersome but effective industrial policy objectives to be carried out. It would have been difficult to create a risk capital market, for example, at a time when the international economic climate had brought about a sharp decline in company profits. Within the Mediobanca sample group, in 1975 total revised losses climbed past 4% of turnover to settle at 2% for each subsequent fiscal year up to and including 1983. Since no real industrial policy had been put in place, financial management techniques helped firms to overcome that difficult period. A policy of preventive devaluations of the exchange rate was implemented to offset low productivity. This triggered a rise in inflation which companies were able to compensate, both on the international market because of lower parity and on the domestic market because prices could be adjusted so as to transfer wealth to firms. The effects of this type of inflation on interest rates, a potential threat to companies with heavy debt loads, were limited through control of credit management by the Central Bank. Consequently, nominal rates were prevented from completely offsetting inflation. Even though such management distanced the Italian financial system from the market and from the international scene, one of its effects was a sizeable profit over debt ratio, especially in heavily indebted industrial sectors. In this case, a hidden transfer of wealth was made from creditors to shareholders, leading to distortions in the allocation of resources. Indeed, controlled management of credit helped to find new loans for those most heavily in debt (Filippi and Sembenelli [14]). This situation resulted in a noticeable discrepancy between the profits recorded by accounting at historical cost, and the gains which could have been realized by giving due consideration to inflation-adjusted profit over net financial position, or conversely, the greater depreciation to be applied to duly

TABLE 2

PERCENTAGE OF REVISED FINANCIAL RESULTS OVER TURNOVER, EXPRESSED IN TIME SERIES VALUES AND CPP VALUES, OF THE 1,214 COMPANIES INCLUDED IN THE MEDIOBANCA SAMPLE

Year	Times series values	CPP values
1974	−0.56	8.22
1975	−4.06	2.45
1976	−2.18	4.93
1977	−2.97	−1.28
1978	−2.25	−1.06
1979	−1.39	2.07
1980	−1.92	0.55
1981	−2.77	0.55
1982	−2.93	−2.16
1983	−1.93	−2.12
1984	−0.39	−1.22
1985	0.90	0.01
1986	1.49	−0.12
1987	1.60	0.81
1988	1.93	1.38

Source: CERIS-CNR [12].

revalued plant and equipment. Comparison of time series data with inflation-adjusted figures using the CPP (Current Purchasing Power) method reveals that up to and including the 1982 fiscal year, the real profitability of companies was continually underestimated where time series data were used (Table 2); from 1983 on, real profitability was systematically overestimated, since phenomena linked to the re-stabilization of price levels were not taken into account (for a review of the methods and interpretation of these findings, see the CERIS [12] study referred to at the end of this paper).

6. - A Policy for Large-Sized Firms

Initially, it was the policies governing money supply, credit and exchange rates which temporarily eased the predicament of firms. This was especially true in the case of large-sized enterprises, which had incurred the largest debt burden. However, it was widely recognized that in the long run, these emergency measures could have worsened the plight of industry by distancing the Italian economy from the rest of Europe. As a result, 1977 and 1978 saw the approval of legislation geared toward the restructuring and reconversion of Italian industry. Clearly, the main objective of these regulations, though directed in principle at industry as a whole, was to assist large-sized firms. The major piece of legislation, Law 675 of 1977, targeted industrial sectors in which large-sized firms were present, such as steel, chemicals, electtronics, automobiles and aeronautics. To be sure, industrial sectors comprising small- and medium-sized enterprises such as tool machinery and fashion were also included, but the measures and procedures set out in Law 675 were such that the law applied almost exclusively to large-sized companies. Similarly, the other regulations which completed the array of measures geared toward restructuring Italian industry were also directed at large-sized firms: Law 787 of 1978 aimed at restructuring the financial system, and Law 95 of 1979 (the Prodi law) was approved to aid troubled large-sized enterprises. Together, these regulations made it possible to finance, partially with public funds, companies' investment, innovation and rationalization projects; further, the indebtedness of certain large-sized firms in dire financial straits could be removed from the normal credit of banks. This legislation was approved as a signal of government awareness that the troubles of industry lay within large-sized companies, and had had significant impact on the banking system. The situation of smaller businesses, not dealt with in this paper, was entirely different.

At the end of the 1970s, an explicit industrial policy focused on the recovery of large-sized firms had taken shape. In stark contrast to the permissive exchange-rate policy implemented in the past, this policy sternly reminded firms of the need to regain real competitivity. However, the various industrial policy instruments did not actually enter into force all at once. Measures aimed at stimulating active behaviour such as the promotion of innovations justifiably required more time to be put in place than instruments based purely on the granting of financial incentives. It does not seem farfetched to assert that it was this incentive-based intervention directed at state-controlled companies and at large-sized firms in difficulty that greatly influenced the spirit of the industrial legislation approved in the last part of the seventies. But later on, from 1978 to 1987, the composition of transfer payment flows from government to firms underwent a significant change. Consequently, the initial incentive-based intervention was gradually replaced by intervention aimed at stimulating new action or involving the amortization of the effects of reconversion and restructuring. Grants to the endowment funds of state-controlled companies, and amortization of their debt stock during 1978 accounted for 41% of total transfer payments, and in 1980 this amount rose to 44% (Carelli [8]). Bailouts, excluding state-controlled companies, respectively reached 12% and 23% in 1978 and 1979, and transfer payments to offset previous losses absorbed nearly half of all available funds during the earlier years of the period. In 1987, these types of assistance amounted to just over 6% of total transfer payments. Intervention policy aimed at state-controlled companies reached its highest level in 1983, at just over L7 trillion, or 1.1% of GDP (Table 3).

Not only were the industrial policy instruments approved in the late 1970s directed primarily at large-sized firms, but during the first five years of implementation, these policies also concentrated inter-

TABLE 3

ABSOLUTE VALUES, IN L BN AT CURRENT PRICES,
OF SELECTED TRANSFERS TO INDUSTRY
DURING 1978-1987

Year	Endowment funds of state-owned firms and debt stock repayments	Early retirement schemes and CIG	Other bailouts and reimbursements	Innovation, exports and other forms of promotion
1978	1.915	262	588	755
1979	—	353	892	977
1980	3.314	505	462	1.577
1981	2.046	1.256	863	1.572
1982	4.329	2.889	726	2.459
1983	7.081	3.922	1.812	3.391
1984	5.459	5.703	1.232	4.248
1985	3.777	6.262	1.968	4.175
1986	1.819	6.326	1.707	5.149
1987	843	6.161	557	5.148

Source: CER-IRS [11].

vention on the "great losers", first and foremost the state-controlled companies. Changes in this scenario ony occurred when the entrepreneurial objectives of these state-owned firms began to shift toward effective competitive strategy and a policy of doing away with non-strategic initiatives. During the same period, the total transfer payments absorbed by the *Cassa integrazione guadagni* (the state redundancy fund) and early retirement schemes was on the rise: from below 6% in 1979, this figure reached 36% in 1987 (Carelli [8]). Though legally available to all firms, this measure, too, was used more frequently by large-sized firms. The number of employees registered with the *Cassa integrazione guadagni* during 1981-1985 hovered near 3% for companies employing 20-100 workers, near 5% for those employing 100-500, and near 9% for firms with over 500 employed, peaking at over 10% in 1984 (Banca [4]). If firms controlled by the public sector are justified in arguing that a portion of the transfer payments received serves to offset the "extra burdens" incurred because of the management objectives imposed on them, then the *Cassa integrazione guadagni* and early retirement schemes should make a similar claim: that the direct transfer payments involved are not made to firms, but rather to employees no longer needed by industry, and retained on staff solely for social reasons. In any event, rather than guiding firms toward renewal, even these types of transfer payment served eventually to eliminate some obstacles to the change.

In conclusion, the types of transfer payment truly aimed at fostering changes in the industrial system (not including those with more specific objectives directed at the Mezzogiorno) were essentially geared toward technological innovations and exports. These transfer payments gradually began to increase, but only in 1984 did they break the 20% barrier, reaching levels near 27% of total transfer payments in 1986 and 1987, approximately 0.5% of GDP (Carelli [8]). The latter figure does not seem to follow the trends of industrial policy in place in other developed countries. The positive change of these transfer payments as a percentage of the total is worthy of note. Despite what was said earlier concerning the singular nature of transfer payments to state-controlled companies and to social stabilizers, it cannot be doubted that these payments played an essential role in the recovery of large-sized Italian firms. Policy designed to foster technological innovations particularly favoured large-sized firms as defined under Law 675 of 1977 (with a staff of over 300 or with net invested capital of over L50 mn at 1979 prices). The percentage of aid granted to large-sized enterprises by the Fund for Applied Research managed by IMI fluctuated between 70% and 80% during the 1970s, and rose gradually thereafter to 89% during 1986-1988 (Fraquelli [15]). The Fund for Technological Innovation managed by the Ministry of Industry contributed, under Law 46 of 1982, 83% of its grant to large-sized firms (Cardone, Cesaratto, De Marchi [7]).

7. - Independent Action of Large-Sized Firms

Even though the recovery of large-sized companies was accompanied by an explicit industrial policy, its presence can scarcely be considered the major cause. The available studies (Centrale dei bilanci [9], Barca [4], Barbetta and Silva [3]), cite the spontaneous action of companies and the collateral conditions created by a less permissive economic policy as the principal stimuli of the recovery. According to Barca, for exmaple, «during 1978-1980 the upturn in productivity was due firstly to the cyclical change in the international economic climate, in monetary policy and in exchange rates, and subsequently to a further rise in product in relation to the initial gains achieved» (Barca [4]). The recovery was both real, because of its rise in productivity, and financial, because of its easing of the financial burden on profit-and-loss statements. The general consensus seems to be that the second type of recovery was in part a consequence of the first, and not vice versa, though the decline of nominal interest rates undoubtedly provided a powerful and independent impetus for higher profitability.

The real recovery was made possible by the reorganization processes of large-sized firms concerning fixed capital technologies in use, management techniques and computerization. These changes did not occur simultaneously in each large-sized company. Barca and Magnani [5], define an initial phase, the two-year 1978-1989 period, when fixed capital was replaced in advance, with little or no effect on the rest of the company's structure; the subsequent phase involved changes in labour, brought about in a climate of good industrial relations.

Because of its links to technological progress and developments in competitive strategy, the entire process of change is steady and cohesive. By the early 1980s, large-sized Italian companies has finally begun to rethink technological and market strategy, a necessary step toward higher profitability. The many individual changes involved were cohesively linked to one another. As regards processes, the advent of automation increased labour productivity. Later, the large-scale automation and computerization of factories and of all logistical procedures achieved further gains in labour productivity and substantial savings of capital, especially circulating capital. The use of computers is essential if firms are to move toward improved market position, characterized by segmented and rapidly changing demand. For this reason, computerization proceeded apace with product renewal, which also requires computer-based planning and management techniques to ensure maximum effectiveness. The shift toward forms of competition based on innovation called for the reorganization of companies, and for the destruction of rigid organizational structures. In some respects, large-sized firms began to mirror their

Gian Maria Gros-Pietro

smaller counterparts, turning away from hierarchical structures in favour of self-contained operational and functional units. Legally, the development of the «network company» (Butera [6]) is often viewed as the division of the firm into its separate functioning entities. From an economic perspective, this deverticalization process differed greatly from old-style decentralization. Indeed, decisionmaking and resource management bodies were at times recentralized within the new framework.

The financial result of these changes on companies is clearly evident: the gross operating margin of Mediobanca sample firms rose from 31% in 1979 to some 40% during 1985-1988 (Table 4). At the same time, a marked improvement in the financial situation was observed, owing to the decline in interest rates and to the use of earnings to lower net indebtedness. Increased financial revenues of companies were not only the result of the accumulation of financial assets in the strict sense, but were also caused by the widespread use of group structures (Alzona [1]), Consolati and Riva [13]). New competitive strategies placed more emphasis on the internationaliz-ation and on the control of markets, hence the trend toward more complex organizations in which the financial bond was frequently the

TABLE 4

PERCENTAGE SHARE OVER VALUE ADDED OF SELECTED FLOWS
WITHIN THE MEDIOBANCA SAMPLE
OF 1,214 COMPANIES (TIME SERIES)

Year	Gross operating margin	Financial expenses	Financial revenues	Net financial expenses	Net self-financing
1979 ..	31.0	20.0	6.1	13.9	15.8
1980 ..	32.0	24.3	7.5	16.8	11.2
1981 ..	33.3	30.1	9.9	20.2	6.9
1982 ..	34.0	28.6	11.1	17.6	8.0
1983 ..	34.9	25.4	11.4	14.0	11.4
1984 ..	38.8	23.5	12.0	11.5	18.1
1985 ..	39.6	20.1	11.7	8.4	22.4
1986 ..	38.7	16.5	11.6	4.9	23.9
1987 ..	38.7	14.1	10.2	3.9	23.8
1988 ..	40.7	13.1	9.1	4.0	23.5

Source: ZANETTI, [18].

only legal constraint joining two entities within a "network company". Italy's large-sized firms were moving toward structures, behaviour, and results similar to those of the largest firms on the international market.

8. - Problems Yet to Be Solved

Although this brief outline of the restructuring of large-sized industrial groups in Italy may appear to be a story with a happy ending, it is nonetheless necessary to qualify such a conclusion.

Firstly, as mentioned earlier, the time series financial results do not take into account the substantial effects of inflation, both during its growth and downturn phases. The data included in the table examined here reveal that profits were overestimated from 1983 onward; data adjusted for inflation using the CPP method (Table 2) seem to correct the level of financial profits in absolute terms expressed as a ratio to turnover and its improvement over the last few years.

Secondly, a study conducted on the sample compiled by the Centrale dei bilanci [10] shows that the profitability of capital invested in the largest companies (63 firms with over L500 bn in turnover) saw a sharp decline from 1985-1988: in fact, the ROI of this aggregate fell

TABLE 5

ROI EXPRESSED AS A PERCENTAGE FOR A GROUP OF 10,070 PRIVATE-SECTOR COMPANIES

Year	All companies	Companies with over L 500 bn turnover
1982	10.98	6.72
1983	11.64	10.89
1984	13.17	14.16
1985	14.25	15.80
1986	14.41	15.67
1987	13.54	15.77
1988	12.11	11.32

Source: CENTRALE DEI BILANCI, [10].

during the same period from 15.80% to 11.32%, a dramatic decline
compared with the entire sample comprising over 10,000 firms (Table
5).

Thirdly, the structural weaknesses of Italian industry, in
comparison with other nations with comparable levels of industrial
development, have not yet been overcome. The lack of large-sized
enterprises and industrial groups, insufficient autonomy within the
financial market, and insufficient high-technology production are the
most serious offences. Though all of these problems may be alleviated
to some degree by Italy's integration into the European single market,
each factor is capable of hindering the development of Italian industry
in this direction.

BIBLIOGRAPHY

[1] ALZONA G.: «Diversificazione e controllo della grande industria italiana negli anni della ristrutturazione: principali mutamenti e schemi interpretativi», *L'industria*, 1986.

[2] ALZONA G. - PIETRO G.M.: *Strumenti e politiche per l'industria in Italia*, Torino, Genesi, 1989.

[3] BARBETTA G.P. - SILVA F.: *Trasformazioni strutturali delle imprese italiane*, Bologna, il Mulino, 1989.

[4] BARCA F.: «La dicotomia dell'industria italiana: le strategie delle piccole e delle grandi imprese in un quindicennio di sviluppo economico», in Atti del seminario *Ristrutturazione economica e finanziaria delle imprese*, Roma, Banca d'Italia, 1988.

[5] BARCA F.: - MAGNANI M.: *L'industria fra capitale e lavoro*, Bologna, il Mulino, 1989.

[6] BUTERA F.: *Strategie di automazione in un'ottica di impresa-rete*, Relazione al XXXIII Convegno nazionale annuale di automazione, Roma, Anipla, 1989.

[7] CARDONE A. - CESARATTO S. - DE MARCHI M.: *Strategie innovative, risultati tecnologici e competitività delle imprese italiane alla luce della politica industriale per l'innovazione tecnologica*, Roma, Mimeo, 1990.

[8] CARELLI M.T.: *I trasferimenti statali all'industria*, in ALZONA G. - GROS-PIETRO G.M. [2].

[9] CENTRALE DEI BILANCI: *Economia e finanza dell'industria italiana: 1982-1986*, Torino, 1988.

[10] —— : *Economia e finanza dell'industria italiana: 1982-1986*, Milano, Il sole-24 ore, 1990.

[11] CER-IRS: *Mercato e politica industriale*, Bologna, il Mulino, 1989.

[12] CERIS-CNR: *Rielaborazione per l'inflazione dei «Dati cumulativi Mediobanca 1989», analisi e commenti*, Torino, 1990.

[13] CONSOLATI L. - RIVA A.: «Crescita e riposizionamento della grande industria italiana negli '80 (1981-86)», in PADOAN P.C. - PEZZOLI A. - SILVA E.: *Concorrenza e concentrazione nell'industria italiana*, Bologna, il Mulino, 1989.

[14] FILIPPI E - SEMBENELLI A.: *Inflazione, disinflazione e fabbisogni finanziari delle imprese*, in CERIS-CNR [12].

[15] FRAQUELLI G.: *Attività di ricerca e sviluppo in Italia: ruolo finanziario del Fondo Imi*, Roma, Mimeo, 1990.

[16] MEDIOBANCA: *Dati cumulativi di 1710 società italiane*, Milano, 1989.

[17] SCOGNAMIGLIO C.: «Il profilo finanziario dell'industria metalmeccanica», in GROS-PIETRO G.M. - ONIDA F. - SCOGNAMIGLIO C.: *L'industria metalmeccanica italiana*, Bologna, il Mulino, 1986.

[18] ZANETTI G.: *Radici esplicative ed elementi di fragilità nei positivi andamenti reddituali delle imprese italiane*, in CERIS-CNR [12].

Industrial Policies
for Small and Medium Firms
and the New Direction of European
Community Policies

Patrizio Bianchi
University of Bologna

1. - Italian industrial Policies and the Contention with the EEC

The industrial policy concerning small and medium firms has to be evaluated taking into account the promotion of industry by government. This in turn has to be appreciated in the context of the European union process underwritten by means of the Treaty of Rome thirty years ago and restated and represented by the agreements on the Single Market completion by 1992.

As a a matter of fact, the subsidization policy to the firms performed by the Italian government has been subjected to heavy criticism by Community authorities (1). The reiterated Community criticisms and therefore the source of contention focuses on the decision making and execution of industrial policies in this country, as well as the amount of subsidization, which may be reduced by auditing or a more detailed analysis, but is indisputable relative to the other countries provisions. The Community blames Italy outright for the exclusive centralizing intervention as a support to structural imbalances rather than a means of creating an environment to overcome them. With reference to this the Graphs 1 and 2 show the Community census data.

---

(1) As well as Ecc [12] to verify sums and law reasons of the distributed subsidies, see Commissioner Brittanis strong position facing the Italian Parliament Industry Commission, SENATE [29] p. 241.
Advise: Numbers in square brackets refer to the Bibliography.

GRAPH 1

SUBSIDIES TO MANUFACTURING INDUSTRY

(thousand ECU)

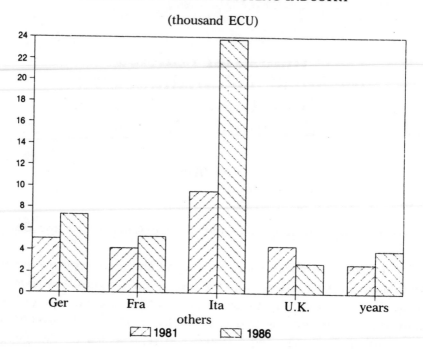

GRAPH 2

SUBSIDIES TO MANUFACTURING INDUSTRY

(thousand 1986 ECU)

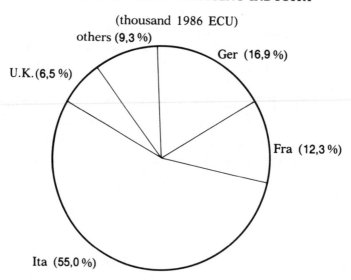

This contention dates back to a long time ago and concerns all major legislation on industrial policy. The Community categorically opposes laws which differ markedly from its guidelines (2). As a matter of fact, the Commission has modified or limited the enforcement of the Italian laws, because their terms clashed with the principles underlying the Treaty.

TABLE 1

MAIN ITALIAN INDUSTRIAL POLICY LAWS
SANCTIONED OR SUBJECT TO A PREVENTIVE CONTROL
BY THE EUROPEAN COMMUNITY COMMISSION

measures modified after the procedure began
(art. 93, p. 2 of the *Treaty*)

Law	1101 of 1971	textile law
dl.	431 of 1971	facilities inside the field of social security contributions (requested and obtained abolition) as the ones in art. 20 of Law 1101 of 1971
Law	464 of 1972	facilities in periods of employment crisis
Law	274 of 1973	IMI Fund refinancing to the intervention on behalf of firms in critical situation (no renewal at the expiry)
Law	319 of 1976	water safeguard
Law	675 of 1977	industrial rstructuration and reconversion (preventive notification and request to modify and abolish the sector programmes and relative application cases)
Law	63 of 1982	Rel

measures modified or limited
after a negotiation and without the procedure

Law	184 of 1971	Gepi
dpr.	902 of 1976	credit facilities according to geographic areas
Law	787 of 1978	bank pools to large firms in crisis

measures allowed with obligation
to notify the outstanding cases of application

Law	1089 of 1968	IMI Fund for applied research (preventive notification)
Law	46 of 1982	technology innovation fund (notification of the most relevant projects)

Source: Forti A. [16], Mariani - Ranci [8], p. 55.

---

(2) An analysis of the contention with the Community is in Cagli [10]; Bianchi and Giordani [9]; see Forti [16].

TABLE 2

CONTENTION BETWEEN ITALY AND EEC
OVER INDUSTRIAL POLICY RELATIVE
TO APPLICATION OF THE LAWS 675 OF 1977 AND 46 OF 1982

Fashion	
textile-cloting	(1)
footwear-leather	(1)
Electronics	
computers and microelectronics	(2)
appliances	(3)
steel	(5)
Chemicals	
man-made fibres	(1)
secondary	(3)
Mechanical engineering	(3)
Paper	
mass	(1)
special	(3)
Food and drink	(3)
Cars	(4)
Cars parts	(3)
Aerospace	(5)
Environment	(5)

(1) National subsidies forbidden
(2) National subsidies allowed
(3) National subsidies allowed, notification oblige to EEC
(4) National subsidies allowed only in situations stated by EEC
(5) National subsidies allowed only into Community plans

This stance has been rendered all the more critical in the last few years. In fact, after the industry was overcome and European integration process began with the signing of the agreement to create the single market, community resistance to the subsidization of individual firms has become increasingly pronounced. Indeed, the integration process is based on the abandonment of centralized public-sector intervention directed toward single enterprises. The ensuing plan aims at fostering industrial integration at various administrative levels, or with different degrees of authority.

On one hand, therefore, the Community encourages integrated intervention by focusing different structural subsidies on well defined areas, while on the other hand research programs for the creation of tight links between firms and institutions are promoted. In this regard, the reform of Community structural funds is a very clear signal of the new industrial policy pattern outlined by the Commission based on the agreements for the completion of the Single Market.

This reform can be narrowed down to five basic principles: 1) structural intervention focusing on regions and areas in the worst trouble and concerning the main questions; 2) cooperation among Community, national, regional and local agencies on working out plans, financing, managing, controlling and evaluating interventions; 3) consistency, and therefore integration, of the different agencies which interact, also by renegotiating incentives; 4) complementary action, including the granting of direct financial incentives in the form of subsidies and loans, to establish integrated programmes; 5) simplification and flexibility, that is intervention procedure standardization of the three structural funds and introduction of the intervention improvement opportunity already in progress. (EEC [13], pp. 13-23).

In other words, the industrial policy pattern entailed in the structural fund reform is characterized on one hand by financial incentive funds and rules linked to the aims and on the other hand by an accomplishment based on the means integration and of different local governments or agencies interested in their own advantages.

By taking stock of not only the reform of structural funds but also of the innovation policy supported by the Community and the strengthening of policies in favour of increased competition (and this the monitoring of national subsidies), we obtain a clear picture of an industrial policy whose aim is to create the necessary environment for the development of market forces; direct intervention is allowed on occasion to correct unusual imbalances and to promote the integration of firms, but only within a well-defined plan for integrated action.

To change the direction of the active intervention, represented by structural funds and aid to innovation, the Community has enforced the Treaty of Rome articles 92-94 more strictly. This has brought about the publishing of the *First census of governement subsidies in the European Community* (EEC [12]). Italy's situation was different from the rest of the Community, its subsidies to firms being double those granted in France and Germany and three times as much as those granted in Great Britain; these subsidies since 1981 to 1986 appear to have been on the average 5.7% of GDP and appear to have grown steadily in this period, while there had already been a reduction in all other countries since the early 1980s.

Italian authorities replied to these statements by means of a document worked out by the Bank of Italy, that — despite reformulating these values — had to confirm them. Its conclusion was that "the revision, even if using substantially the same method as the *White Paper*, has brought about a reduction of the overall subsidies to the firms to 1.4-2.9% of GDP. . . the difference between Italy and the other countries decreases, but it doesn't disappear" (Bank of Italy [3], p. 21) (3).

After pointing out that the subsidies sum began decreasing just since 1984, the Italian defence ends with these precise words: «The *EEC White Paper* analysis without the overvaluation for the 1981-1986 period and extended to 1987-1988 shows a decrease of the subsidies since 1984, but not enough to be equal to those of the other European countries. Even taking account of the social and productive feature characteristics and at the same time avoiding to incur the severe control Commission about competition defence, it appears to be necessary to go on with the subsidies reduction policy to align Italy to the average of the Community. This would allow it not to affect public finance and it would offer the opportunity to think over again the whole industrial policy, addressing it to more selective interventions than it was in the recent past» (Bank of Italy [3], pp. 22).

---

(3) In its 30th November 1989 hearing by the Senate Industry Commission into the cognitive survey and in a following 26th February letter to the Commission Chairman Cassola, the Competition Commissioner recalled the Bank of Italy revision as well accepted, but: 1) the data used by the Commission were Italian official data, source *Tesoro* and *Corte dei Conti*; 2) the Italian government had not given any collaboration to the Commisison, had neither requested debates about the Commission actions, nor answered officially to the Community asking formally since 1987 for a more large specifying; 3) finally the Bank of Italy revision confirmed both the Commission analysis outcome and its method (SENATE [29], p. 241, p. LIII).

2. - Subsidies Distribution to Industry

As a matter of fact, the Bank of Italy audit does not match the Community data and gives two different estimates, the first based on EEC data diminished by the sums that should not be at all included into the subsidies according to the Bank of Italy, the latter based on data that need further examination. Commissioner Brittan, faced with the maximum and minimum estimates, outlined that, though the Community data were inferred from already published Italian data and despite the non-cooperation of the Italian government, he was prepared to appreciate the Bank of Italy maximum estimate, while he considered the minimum one to be meaningless (*26th February 1990 Letter to the Chairman of the Senate Commission* [29], p. LVI).

Therefore, making allowances for the Bank of Italy maximum estimate, the annual average subsidies sum since 1981 to 1986 was 28,800 billion lira, that, as we can see, are not so different from the 31,550 billion lira estimate of the Commission (Brittan, as above) (4). Even taking account of the Bank of Italy audits, the amount of subsidies is far more than the other EEC big countries one. The

TABLE 3

SUBSIDIES DISTRIBUTED BY NATIONAL GOVERNMENTS, ESTIMATES REVISED BY BANK OF ITALY (*)

	Sum of subsidies		To manufact. industry		To manuf. ind. minus steel and shipyard	
	% of GDP	ECU per empl.	% of v.a.	ECU per empl.	% of v.a.	ECU per empl.
Italy (EEC est.)	5.66	1,357	16.72	6,226	15.8	5,951
Italy (B.I. est.)	4.26	1,022	10.97	4,086	10.1	3,084
France	2.68	792	4.93	1,649	3.6	1,223
Germany	2.53	761	3.03	982	2.9	940
UK	1.79	396	3.81	971	2.9	757

(*) Subsidies to manufacturing industry do not include contributions to agriculture, fishery, transports, coal where subsidies are given because of Community rules (see the following table).
Source: EEC [12], [13], [14]; BANK OF ITALY [3]

---

(4) The Bank of Italy least estimates themselves appear to be more than the subsidies distributed by every other country, see BANK OF ITALY [3].

following figures break down the Bank of Italy estimates and the Community census data. It results clear not only the higher amount of subsidies, but also the different way of distribution (Table 3).

While France first of all gives soft loans and Germany tax rebates, Italy and Great Britain support the firms activity by means of direct subsidies (Table 4). Moreover fewer incentives for innovation and environment are agranted, and current trands favour general investments and other not better identified interventions (Table 5); from the same figures France is inferred to have pursued an export promotion strategy, Germany a strategy to support innovation, Great Britain a mix of the two, while Italy's is less clear.

Besides we need to outline that, according to the Bank of Italy «in France, Germany and the United Kingdom, most of the subsidies are granted because of Community rules (agriculture, fishery, transports and coal)» while in Italy, according to the Community census, these decreased to only one third (augmented to 39% according to the Bank of Italy maximum estimates) (Bank of Italy [3], p. 20).

TABLE 4

DIFFERENT KIND OF SUBSIDIES IN % OF ALL THE SUBSIDIES TO MANUFACTURING INDUSTRY AND SERVICES
(average 1981-1986) (*)

	It. (EEC)	It. (B.I.)	France	Germany	UK
A) Transfers and tax facilities	79	72	24	86	71
A1) Transfers	68	50	20	35	69
A2) Tax facilities	11	22	4	51	2
B) Shareholding	18	26	26		18
C) Soft loans and deferred taxes	3	2	45	13	8
C1) Soft loans	3	2	38	6	6
C2) Deferred taxes	—	—	7	7	2
D) Guarantees	—		5	1	1
Total.......................	100	100	100	100	100

(*) Subsidies do not include contributions to agriculture, fishery, energy, transports.
Source: EUROPEAN COMMUNITY COMMISSION: [12], [13], [14]; BANCA D'ITALIA, [3]

TABLE 5

SUM OF SUBSIDIES PER GOALS/SECTORS
(average 1981-1986, million ECU)

		It. (EEC)	It. (B.I.)	France	Germany	UK
1.1	Agriculture (*)....	1,862	1,653	2,870	1,402	1,088
1.2	Fishery (*)	90	86	45	18	69
2.1	Industry/services goals	8,943	2,554	3,395	2,475	1,500
2.1.1	Innovation, R&D ..	733	206	221	1,384	543
2.1.2	Environment	0	0	5	86	0
2.1.3	Small medium firms	716	675	74	478	130
2.1.4	Trade/export	1,328	919	2,091	99	749
2.1.5	Energy saving......	101	101	82	168	16
2.1.6	General investments	1,234	108	921	98	139
2.1.7	Unemployment (1)	0	0	0	0	0
2.1.8	Training (1)........	0	0	0	0	0
2.1.9	Others	4,831	545	2	163	12
2.2	Industry/services secators	10,56	10,566	9,994	11,772	5,311
2.2.1	Steel	1,629	1,712	1,513	371	703
2.2.2	Shipyard	237	237	507	176	483
2.2.3	Transports (*)......	6,494	6,494	4,408	5,931	1,522
2.2.4	Coal (*)	0	0	2,286	5,003	2,069
2.2.5	Others					
2.2.5.1	Crisis sectors	934		616	0	469
2.2.5.2	Growing sectors....	416	2,123	318	157	42
2.2.5.3	Others	1,245		345	135	24
3.	Regional subsidies ..	5,855	6,020	383	3,447	1,372
3.1	Regions (2)	4,458	4,768	115	2,632	235
3.2	Others regions	1,397	1,252	269	815	1,137
	Total (billion ECU)	27.7	20.9	16.7	19.1	9.4

(*) Subsidies given mainly for Community rules.

(1) Training and unemployment measures are not included in the present report. However expenditures on identified measures, but not still taken into examination are the following: Italy 466, France 638, Germany 225, United Kingdom 1082.

(2) The south for Italy, oversea departments for France, Berlin for Germany, Northern Ireland for the United Kingdom.

Source: EUROPEAN COMMUNITY COMMISSION [12], [13]; BANK OF ITALY, [3].

Patrizio Bianchi

TABLE 5 *continued*

		It. (EEC)	It. (B.I.)	France	Germany	UK
1.1	Agriculture (*)....	7	8	17	7	12
1.2	Fishery (*)	0	0	0	0	1
2.1	Industry/services goals	32	12	20	13	17
2.1.1	Innovation, R&D ..	3	1	1	7	6
2.1.2	Environment	0	0	0	0	0
2.1.3	Small medium firms	3	3	0	2	1
2.1.4	Trade/export	5	4	13	1	8
2.1.5	Energy saving......	0	1	0	1	0
2.1.6	General investments	4	1	6	1	1
2.1.7	Unemployment (1)	0	0	0	0	0
2.1.8	Training (1)........	0	0	0	0	0
2.1.9	Others	17	3	0	1	0
2.2	Industry/services sec-tors	40	50	60	62	56
2.2.1	Steel	6	6	9	2	7
2.2.2	Shipyard	1	1	3	1	5
2.2.3	Transports (*)......	23	31	26	31	16
2.2.4	Coal (*)	0	0	13	26	23
2.2.5	Others					
2.2.5.1	Crisis sectors	3		4	0	5
2.2.5.2	Growing sectors....	2	10	2	1	0
2.2.5.3	Others	4		2	1	0
3.	Regional subsidies ..	21	29	2	18	15
3.1	Regions 92 (3) a (2)	16	23	1	14	2
3.2	Others regions	5	6	2	4	12
	Total (billion ECU)	100	100	100	100	100

(*) Subsidies given mainly for Community rules.

(1) Training unemployment measures are not include in the present report. However expenditures on identified measures, but not still taken into examination are the following: Italy 466, France 638, Germany 225, United Kingdom 1082.

(2) The south for Italy, oversea departments for Frane, Berlin for Germany, Northern Ireland for the United Kingdom.

Source: EUROPEAN COMMUNITY COMMISSION [12], [13]; BANK OF ITALY [3].

Regional subsidies appear to be even higher according to the Italian maximum estimate than according to the EEC data. The amount of per capita subsidies is extraordinarily higher in the subsidized areas than in the other countries taken into consideration, as shown in table 6.

The contention concerns industrial policymaking in our country as well as the amount of subsidies, that eventually one has to admit is higher than elsewhere. As a matter of fact, the Single Market is based on the idea of creating an European industrial entity are where the national differences do not disappear and are indeed made consitent with each other by accepting the same governments and legislative powers relative to the industrial development.

In this regard, the Italian authorities document itself has had to admit that "the Italian policy features themselves are bound to be subjected to contention" (Bank of Italy, [3], p. 3).

The Italian defence states, in fact (Bank of Italy [3], p. 4): «The interventions belong usually to the distribution kind, while the higher public administration efficiency in the other countries allows to put in action other means, as public demand, tax laws, etc.; moreover they

TABLE 6

REGIONAL SUBSIDIES
(billion ECU)

	Italy (EEC)	Italy (B.I.)	France	Germany	UK
Total	5,855	6,020	383	3,449	1,372
of which:					
Regions 92(3)a (1)	4,458	4,768	115	—	235
Regions 92(2)c and 92(3)c......	1,397	1,252	268	3,449 (2)	1,137
in % of GDP..................	1.2	1.2	0.1	0.5	0.3
% people in subsidized areas ..	48.9	48.9	38.7	47.3	44.1
per capita subsidies in the subsidized areas (ECU)	210.4	216.2	18.1	118.7	55.1

(1) Directory of subsidizable areas for the art. 92, subsection 3 letter *a)* of the EEC *Treaty*: Greece, Ireland and Portugal: the whole country; France: oversea departments; Italy: the South; Spain: Estremadura, Andalusia, Castilla-La Mancha, Galizia, Castilla-Leon, Murcia, Canary Isles, Ceuta-Melilla; United Kingdom: Northern Ireland.
(2) Berlin included with 2,632 million ECU.
Source: EUROPEAN COMMUNITY COMMISSION [12], [13]; BANK OF ITALY [3].

are centralized, that is to say stated by laws, beginning with the fund allocation because it simplifies the control, unlike the other countries using general guidelines and administrative acts».

The embodiment of this industrial policy pattern, as centralized, distributive, directed to individual firms, bureaucratic relative to the procedures action, is the entire policy in favour of small firms. It is a policy of offsetting imbalances regarded as incurable and therefore their outcome is to preserve rather than to remove non-competitive situations.

This policy is still more blameworthy since Italian small and medium firms innovative characteristic is precisely local integration. As a matter of fact, both national and international literature have shown how the typical and outstanding feature of Italian local development should lie in the agglomeration firms integrated on the basis of relative specializations. The Italian experience has led to a revision of the regional science literature about policies to create a local environment for development.

Even today, Italian intervention measures are aimed at subsidizing individual firms, providing assistance in the puchase of equipment and enacting policy centred on the granting of incentives, rather than easing constraints by means of coordinated, concerted administrative action and broader means of intervention in keeping with the behaviour of the other countries and with Commission requirements.

3. - The Role of Small Firms in the Italian Economy

Small-sized firms have always played a major role in Italy; firms emplaying less than 100 workers account for more than half of total postwar employment, and more than 80% of total jobs are provided by firms with staffs of less than 500. This situation is similar to the case of Japon, but differs greatly from than in France, the United States, Great Britain and West Germany, where firms employing less than 100 workers account for between one-third and one-fifth of total employment, and enterprises with less than 500 workers provide some 60%-50% of total jobs (Mussatti [23]).

Moreover, during the most critical years for the large firms the small ones assured a substantial employment increase between 1971 and 1981 (Barca-Magnani [4]; Giannola [17]). This employment contribution has been estimated at more than 700,000 workers by firms with less than 200 employees, unlike the employment decrease of 100,000 units and the recourse to the redundancy fund of larger ones. The most outstanding results were recorded in the 10-20 employec category, bringing about an industrial growth based on micro-firms (Mussati [23]). Besides, it corresponded to the employment growth a productivity one opposite to the firms size. (Mussatti [23]).

The success of smaller firms led to a critical review of theories directed all too easily toward stimulating economic development exclusively in large-sized firms, as shown in the United States. Actually, the success of Italian SMEs was due in large part to on extensive growth process, triagering the expansion of industrial activity over centire regions in a way that differed from the traditional patterns involving large-sized firms (5).

It is not by chance that the huge international interest in the Italian case has focused almost completely on the industrial districts. The emphasis has been put on the widespread organization of the firms at the local level. In other words, it has been put in fact on groups of small and medium firms where the efficiency of the single ones comes from the positive sum of economies of scale achieved at each stage of production and the economies of scale external to the firm, yet internal to the area (6).

The nature of these external economies of scale has been largely identified not only as know-how and market notions linked to particular methods of production, but also as the shared sense of belonging to a social context, meaning lower transaction area, as a result of the reciprocal trust among the firms of the district (7).

On the contrary, the 1980s represent an inversion and several

---

(5) It is not necessary of course to report here the huge literature developed in Italy on the spread economy and the industrial districts; see for example ALESSANDRINI [1]

(6) See for example PIORE and SABEL [25].

(7) See obviously BECATTINI [6]; relative to the analysis of the transaction costs into the district see also BIANCHI [8], GOBBO [18], pp. 47-59.

reasons for the success of smaller firms gave way to factors contributing to crisis. The latter reasons emerged because of a progressive reconquering dominant market position by large firms and the inability by single or local groups of firms to state autonomously strategies of acquisitions of dominant market position, relegating themselves to a "follower" position just as niches of specialization were becoming increasingly the domain of large-sized firms capable of managing flexible production systems, and thus a wide variety of goods, while making use of powerful instruments for directing and controlling the market (8).

4. - Intervention to Small Firms

Traditionally industrial policy to small firms has been directed at individual enterprises by law and performed by central authorities (9).

Since the second worldwar small firms have received incentives. This intervention were established already in 1952 by Law 949 bringing about subsidies to small firms whose activity was especially in central and northern underdeveloped areas, and reiterated in 1959 by Law 623. The same kind of intervention is established by DPR 902 of 1976 (Table 7) even now in force.

The rationale for these incentives was the necessity of giving aid to small and medium size firms, as the smallest firms were inferior by their nature because of technical diseconomies of scale, but especially of disadvantages in the relationships with the bank system. At the same time it was considered right to limit the intervention to the firms in central and northern underdeveloped areas, because the smallest firms in developed areas already enjoy a favourable context, since

---

(8) A large inspection of this thesis along with a detailed analysis of the crisis of the Prato economy regarded in the past as district industrial model is presented by Nomisma: *Laboratorio di politica industriale*, 1989.

(9) In particular, the responsibility is given by law to the Industry Ministry as far as all the laws providing subsidies are concerned, and to the Mediocredito Centrale as it happened with the Sabatini law in 1965, or to IMI as with Law 1470 of 1961; actually in all the intervention steps the firms applied to their own commercial bank that it was eventually the necessary means to receive the subsidy or the soft loan. The result was a local mix of commercial bank credit and soft loans.

TABLE 7

MAIN INDUSTRIAL POLICY LAWS

Year	Act	Content
1952	Law 949	small and medium firms development
1957	Law 634	southern regions industrialization
1960	Law 1061	credit to trading firms
1961	Law 1470	small and medium firms industrial reconversion
1965	Law 1329	new machines acquisition by small and medium firms
1967	Law 131	buyer credit
1968	Law 1089	applied research
1971	Law 184	creation of the public body to rescue firms in crisis - GEPI
	Law 1101	textile firms restructuration
1972	Law 464	small and medium firms restructuration
1975	Law 517	trading firms modernization
1976	Law 183	creation of the Fund for small and medium firms
	DPR 902	restructuration of northern small and medium firms
1977	Law 675	industrial restructuration; rearrangement of all the laws on industrial intervention
1979	Law 95	extraordinary commissars for the groups in crisis
1981	Law 240	small and medium firms export pools
1982	Law 46	national Fund Technological Innovation
	Law 63	consumer electronics restructuration
	Law 308	energy saving and new energy sources development
	dl 697	trading firms modernization
1983	Law 696	new machines acquisition by small and medium firms
1986	Law 64	extraordinary intervention in the South
1987	Law 399	machiners acquisition by small and medium firms

large-sized firms exist. Smaller firms in the South would receive more radical intervention managed by the *Cassa per il mezzogiorno* settled in 1952 by special laws as Law 634/1957 up to 651/1983 and the present Law 64/1986.

Intervention aimed at fostering the restructuring and innovation of smaller firms in specific cases is added to the general ones to small and medium firms directed to offset diseconomies regarded as structural. In 1961 bill 1470 of 1961 was passed to react to the coming into force of the early Community agreements to set up a industrial restructuration Fund mainly directed to finance the activity of firms without sufficient guarantee to obtain ordinary medium-term loans. This act had hardly any results in the early 1960's, but in the late 60s it was used more and more even for small size firms belonging to large industrial groups (Pontarollo [26], Silvestri [30], Ranci [27]).

After the industrial crisis deterioration this intervention was integrated by laws aimed at critical sectors, as Law 1101 of 1971 and Law 464 of 1972. By means of Law 183 of 1976 a special fund to the small and medium firms was set up and eventually, in the general reorganization of the restructuration and reconversion incentives legislation performed by Law 675 of 1977, a law restricted to small and medium firms, *ex* art. 10 was created (Bianchi [7]).

Moreover the restructuration process was supported also by means of subsidies to innovation, and more specifically to machinery acquisition: so it happened already in 1965, by Law 1329 the Sabatini, by the subsequent Law 696 of 1983 replaced by Law 399 of 1987. From a more general point of view the innovation activity has been promoted via the IMI Fund for Applied Research under Law 1089 of 1968 and Law 46 of 1982; intervention to the small and medium firms was established by a law restricted to them (art. 5 of the quoted Law 46 of 1982) (Momigliano [21]).

Add to these the laws fostering exports (Law 131 of 1967, Law 227 of 1977, Law 240 of 1981) and incentives to the modernization of commercial firms (Law 517 of 1975, DL. 697 of 1982).

Therefore the available legislative measures to the small firms are classifiable on one hand as explicitly and exclusively directed to small firms, on the other hand as general laws providing for special facilitations on behalf of the small firms. Law 399 of 1987 governs contribution to the high-tech machinery acquisition only for small and medium firms; it concerns credit facilitations and contributions without pay-back obligation to firms with less than 300 employees and less than 114 billion lira of invested capital; these contributions are at the most 350 million lira to central and northern firms, 600 million lira to the southern ones (10).

---

(10) It still is in force the Law 1329 of 1965 to the machine tools acquisition distributing interest contributions, according to which however precise size limits to get law benefits are not stated. However, it is necessary to notice that this law successed again in last years so that in 1987 the Mediocredito centrale allocated 3,957.2 billion lira, 89% to central and northern firms, in 1982-1987 period 8,287.2 billion were allocated, 81% (6,711.6) to central and northern firms (SCANAGATTA [28] in BATTAGLIA-VALCAMONICI [5], p. 299).

The DPR 902 1976 regulates financial incentives to whole invest-ment plans to new plants, enlargements and modernizations by small and medium firms. After such a slow beginning that in 1981 the distributed contributions did not equal 4 billion, it was a speed-up reaching its peak in 1988 (Scanagatta, in Battaglia and Valcamonici [5], p. 295).

Moreover article 4 of the Law 46 of 1982 directed to all national firms and to the innovation plans carrying-out support, stated special provisions to small firms, as repayment of outlays in applied research by external laboratories; article 5 of the same law resuming indeed article 10 of Law 675 of 1977 stated a law restricted to small firms allocating «at least 20% of applied research IMI fund availabilities to the research performed by small and medium firms». Therefore it concerns both interest and capital contributions.

In sum there are laws supporting the acquisition and moderniz-ation of generic tool machinery such as the "old" 1329 of 1965 directed implicity, but not explicitly at small and medium firms, and the DPR 902 of 1976. They do not concern the selective interventions projected in 1960s and 1970s but those represented just in the last years. Moreover, laws 696 and 399 have aimed more and more at addressing the small firms to accelerate their innovation trend, essen-tially inducing them to acquire machinery regarded as innovative. On the contrary, the 46 of 1982 tends to induce them to the innovation for applied research, design, experimenting, development and pre-in-dustrialization programs after establishing the major areas of interven-tion.

Old industrial policy issue arose regarding all of these laws: whether government intervention should be automatic or discre-tionary. The question about whether to define the subject to be subsidized, as small and medium firms or southern ones a related matter.

This last question appears to be an enlightening testimony to the way industrial policy action is considered. Assuming a structural state of small firms weakness, as is the case in other laws concerning southern firms, a constraint is placed on the use of public resources to protect these subjects; this constraint has been often subjected to criticism, since this restriction did not work bringing about not spent surplus sums. A legal restriction implies that the body that should manage the law is regarded as unreliable by the legislative authority which places constraints on the application of the law during its creation.

In fact, all of the legislation sets out detailed conditions for the concession of incentives by creating categories and requirements which are by necessity artful and restrictive; examples of these are the eligibility requirements based on sector and size which set empleyment and revenue levels that are only adequate for certain sectors.

What followed was the attribution of responsibility by government, limited to due acts, but at the same time a more bureaucratic approach was taken by which the only administration "power" amounted to the setting up of non-essential procedures to ascertain that applicants met the abstract eligibility requirements created under the law. The measure of administration efficacy appears to be biased: given the impossibility to measure the effects of the public intervention on the industrial structure, only the bureaucratically outstanding act is taken into consideration, that is to say the number of requests presented, the number accepted, and the processing time; in other words the subjects administrative access to the law benefits, but not their economic effects on the industrial structure (11).

In this regard, the debate concerning discretionary and automatic acts is inessential, since all the Italian legislation is directed to automatic acts enforced by law aimed at specifying bureaucratically the whole subsidy process. In conclusion, where the intervention is less than simple by necessity, there is the need of an agreement being nothing else than the formal acknowledgement of a veto right between parallel administrations.

5. - The Subsidies to Small Firms

All of these actions have however allowed the subsidies distribution to small firms, even if contradictory arguments in the judgement

----

(11) See BIANCHI and GIORDANI [9], presenting the research performed into the *Programma Finalizzato* CNR-Pubblica amministrazione, relative to the industry and foreign trade management.

of the government authority itself exist on their importance. The ministerial Commission to the study of issues concerning small and medium firms in fact states that «Looking over the data has revealed a growing availability of resources distributed to small firms by the Industry Ministry» (Mussatti [23], p. 21). Then a L.200 billion in 1984 distribution increasing to L.380 billion in 1985-1986 and L.250 billion in the following year is outlined. The intervention has been considered to have favoured an innovation speed-up due to financing of high-tech machinery acquisitions (*ex* Law 696 and 399).

Diametrically opposed to this conclusion is a more general analysis on the sharing between the interventions supporting small and large firms reported in the same book edited by the Industry Ministry itself on the Italian government industrial policy evaluation. Taking into consideration the 1971-1979 and 1980-1987 period the

TABLE 8

DISTRIBUTION OF INDUSTRIAL INCENTIVES
(1971-1987)

Periods		1971-1979			1980-1987		
Intervention areas	Size of firms benefited	Government contributions	Amount of financed projects	Number of actions	Governments contributions	Amount of financed projects	Number of actions
Centre-North ..	n.a.	9.2	9.1	2.6	3.5	4.3	12.4
	small	22.0	26.9	49.1	18.7	27.3	46.1
	large	7.5	9.1	4.3	27.4	32.7	6.0
	total	38.6	45.0	55.9	49.6	64.4	64.6
South	n.a.	1.3	1.5	0.9	1.8	1.8	6.7
	small	36.4	29.0	41.3	29.2	18.7	27.2
	large	23.6	24.4	1.8	19.4	15.1	1.5
	total	61.3	54.9	44.0	50.4	35.6	35.4
Total		100.0	100.0	100.0	100.0	100.0	100.0
Italy..........	n.a.	10.5	10.6	3.4	5.3	6.2	19.1
	small	58.4	55.9	90.4	47.9	46.1	73.3
	large	33.1	33.5	6.1	46.8	47.8	7.6
Total		100.0	100.0	100.0	100.0	100.0	100.0

Source: LA NOCE M. [19].

TABLE 9

LAW 46 OF 1982. TECHNOLOGICAL INNOVATION FUND DISTRIBUTION
(1984-1988) billion lira

	Mid-northern	Southern	Total
Small	595.1	18.7	613.8
Large	1,600.8	99.4	1,700.2
Total	2,195.9	118.1	2,314

TABLE 9*A*

1984-1988 (in %)

	Central-Northern	Southern	Total
Small	25.7	0.8	26.5
Large	69.2	4.3	73.5
Total	94.9	5.1	100

Source: elaborated data of INDUSTRY MINISTRY shown in BATTAGLIA and VALCAMONICI [5], p. 281 and following.

subsidy shift to the large firms is clear (tab. 8) (La Noce [19], p. 273) (12).

Both the rules to the machinery acquisitions (Law 696 and 399) and still more the Law 46 of 1982 have supported the central and northern firms, despite the restriction statement or the higher provisions to southern firms. Moreover the sectorial analysis confirms the interventions have first of all favoured the numerical control machines as essential to mechanical engineering industry in the Centre North (Tables 10-11) (Scanagatta [28] p. 283 and following). It was an obvious conclusion since the intervention way itself indeed gives a privilege to the autonomous action of firms to increase innovation rather than to create the innovation development conditions as shown by the Community.

These laws themselves have been a cause for contention with the Commission. As a matter of fact the Commission has blamed more

---

(12) The deferred distribution of the contributions *ex* Law 675 of 1977, started only in 1982, affected of course this subsidies speed-up in the early 1980s (BIANCHI [7], p. 147-8).

TABLE 10

LAW 46 OF 1982, TECHNOLOGICAL INNOVATION FUND DISTRIBUTION
TO SMALL AND MEDIUM FIRMS

	1984	1985	1986	1987	1988
Billion lira	42.7	115.2	126.0	182.1	147.4
% South	1.2	3.1	5.1	3.4	1.7
% Mechanical Engineering	60.2	64.9	68.6	67.0	69.6

Source: elaborated data of INDUSTRY MINISTRY shown in BATTAGLIA and VALCAMONICI [5], p. 281
and following.

TABLE 11

SUBSIDIES DISTRIBUTION BY MEANS OF LAWS 696 OF 1983
AND 399 OF 1987 (*)

	1984	1985	1986	1987	1987 (*)	1988 (*)
Billion lira	110.2	176.7	155.9	14.8	69.6	160.4
% South	1.3	3.9	3.5	9.6	0.1	0.5
% Mechanical Engineering	59.7	38.4	40.7	29.5	50.7	43.0

(*) Enforcement of Law 399 of 1987.

Source: elaborated data of INDUSTRY MINISTRY shown in BATTAGLIA and VALCAMONICI [5], p. 281
and following.

than once the Italian government about the creation and granting of
subsidies to machine tools acquisition. The law repeated refinancing,
the reiterated try to increase its size, the need to present documents in
accordance to the prevention of industrial accidents, not to be found
for Italian machines and therefore regarded by the Commission as a
real protectionist measure has prolonged a contention between the
Community and Italian government about the reform of the intervention to small and medium firms by means of mandatory, though not
fulfilled, invitations of the Community authorities to modify the policy
approach itself to small firms (13).

Therefore the overall action to small and medium firms has been
developed according to the opinion that the Italian ones suffered from
operative disadvantages essentially in the capital provision to the new

(13) The detailed report of this event is presented by CAGLI [10], p. 165 and
following.

machines acquisition. This opinion is based indeed on two assumptions, the first concerning the country financial structure, the latter the innovation process.

In the first case the subsidy is nothing else than a compensation to higher interest rates that small firms have to pay to the bank system to get loans to machineries acquisitions: in other words it does not become an extraordinary incentive to disdvantaged structural conditions but rather an aid to refund the banking systems ability to make price discrimination according to the customer size. Therefore, it is not an intervention to increase a firms competition, but a subsidy to support a situation not competitive enough in the banking system.

The customary and still recently represented statement Mussatti, p. 26) according to which the small firms suffer from higher interest rates than large firms do because of their lower contractual force is nothing else than a statement of inability to make more competitive the banking system and in particular the medium and long term assets; moreover just the existence of this subsidies whole distributed as both capital and interest contribution through the bank structere itself has created a mix between subsidized and medium-long term credit not favouring the competition conditions development in the credit market.

In the second case the innovation nature coming out from the legislation to small firms seems to be focussed first of all on the acquisition of machines, and in particular the electronic control ones. Therefore it is a innovation process by which the small firms acquires innovation *sub specie* of machines embodying the innovation itself. We can oppose a substantial criticism to this kind of action as intervention of technology transfer or innovation diffusion.

As well identified by Momigliano and Antoneli [22], p. 198) the technical progress embodied in the fixed capital represents only a part even if outstanding of an highly-structured process; emphasizing this side of the question can bring about problems in the firm if one does not act on the other aspects, as employees training and more in general the internal reorganization allowing to insert the new machines in a context effectively able to obtain advantages.

The innovation process both only acquiring externally the single innovations to then increasing them, and generating innovations, by which to affect the opponent and cooperating firm behaviour entails the identification of the innovative firm in the whole of the relationships characterizing its development. In this sense, as well testified by Momigliano and Antonelli [22]: «all of the foreign experiences confirm that when the objective to support the innovation introduction and diffusion in small and medium firms began to be inserted, it began also a regional operative structures creation» (Momigliano [21], p. 203).

However, just here is the essential point of the criticism to the Italian authorities policy to the small and medium firms. The provisions offered by the central authorities are "personal" interventions, that is to say actions to the single firm let alone the whole of its relationships and the relative externalities. It concerns interventions that tend to compensate structural or temporary weaknesses according to the opinion however that it is impossible to create market forces development conditions where the small frirms themselves can grow.

The State authority intervention is not to remove the market failures, but to compensate and so keep them. Just in this opinion that the industrial policy action as a personal, compensating, central event is the methodological contention between the Italian traditionally used approach and the one proposed by the Community.

6. - Community Policy to Small and Medium Firms

The Community has developed its own explicit policy to small and medium firms since the early 1980's, when it appears so clear that the industrial reorganization process following the large firms crisis would have taken again European economy towards full employment. The support policy to the small and artisan firms therefore is directed to strengthen into the European field firms usually strong only locally, but also to promote new firms; it concerns actions strengthening competition and so promoting the market forces development (14).

---

(14) It is necessary to remind that 1983 was stated as «year of the small firm» by the EEC and in March 1985 the European Council strongly outlined the smal firm role in the European recovery, forcing the Commission to act in order to promote this kind of firms (EEC [11]).

In June 1986 the Task Force "Small Firms" was set up by the Commission; it was up to this unit: *a)* to coordinate all the activities of the Commission concerning the small and medium firms; *b)* to promote a timely narraving of the gap between national legislation and Community policies; *c)* to settle links among all the organizations representing small enterpreneurship; *d)* to start new Community policies developing examples of integrated intervention in agreement with national and regional governements.

In August 1986 the Commission presented to the European Council a resolution concerning the action plan to small and medium firms (COM 86, 445 final) Council adopted in November of the same year. In the following years the Commission presented reports on the enforcement of these plans.

The goals of this plan are: 1) to create a legislative and adminis-trative context open enough to promote small and new firms; 2) to accelerate the small and medium firms modernization and growth

TABLE 12

APPLICATION STATE OF THE *WHITE BOOK*
ON THE COMPLETION OF THE SINGLE MARKET (March 1990)

	(1)	(2)	(3)	(4)	(5)
Belgium	53	22	12	0	3
Germany	75	11	1	0	3
Denmark	77	9	1	0	3
Spain	55	28	2	4	1
France	68	16	3	0	3
Greece	46	26	9	6	3
Italy	36	30	20	0	4
Ireland	67	13	5	1	4
Luxemburg	58	18	9	0	5
Nederland	63	20	4	0	5
Portugal	37	42	2	8	1
United Kingdom	77	7	2	1	1

(1) Notified measures.
(2) Not notified measures.
(3) Violation procedures.
(4) Derogation of the application date.
(5) Not applicable.
Source: Eec, 1990.

support process for: *a)* employees and management training; *b)* market, process and procuct information; *c)* export; *d)* new firms creation and innovation; *e)* cooperation among firms and regions; *f)* facilitations in the access to financing necessary to act into the European field.

The Community policy can therefore find its basis on four guidelines: *a)* small and medium firms activity promotion; *b)* development of the relationships among small and medium firms; *c)* financing by means of loans and subsidies; *d)* information about different aspects of the industrial and trading activities.

Therefore this policy bases on different tools that can be combined in various ways according to the specific needs of the single and still more agglomeration of single firms. The Community policy finds in fact its basis on the principle of the necessity not to limit the action to the single firms, but to act at the same time on the relationships among firms time and to create local development conditions.

This policy is therefore supported by various tools that have to be applied in the aggreement among local, national and Community authorities.

The Italian position however about the use of the Community provisions is extraordinarily frail, so that the Community funds national average utilization is about 40%. This is because regional governments themselves are not able to develop their own project capacities, so as to propose integrated plans as requested by the Community. Several regional experiences of promoting innovation through institutes of technology spreading and services to firms continue to uphold their local and sectorial interests and do not became a public good. As a matter of fact, the government keeps on perceiving them as marginal data relative to a policy centrally decreed and managed (Noel [24]) (15).

---

(15) It can be not by chance in fact that in the BATTAGLIA-VALCAMONICI book [5], regarded as reporting the industrial policy guidelines of the Minister in charge the different industrial policyt levels basis of the new Community approach are not evaluated. Moreover it is necessary to notice that every Italian region try to start a set of direct relationships with the Community has always been stopped by the central government.

The Italian position appears to be frail for the delay in carrying out the Community directives on the completion of the Single Market. The table 12 gives a good picture of the Italian situation characterized by the least of notified measures and by the most of violation procedures (EEC [15]). This delay shows itself as an industry and foreign trade management keeping on being regarded as an alternative approach relative to the one proposed by the european Community. That it is to say that industrial policy is still regarded as a law to be managed centrally to guide behaviours or to substitute some inefficiencies impossible to eliminate, to be managed through a central administration wishing to verify only conditions of eligibility for benefits distributed by the government authority.

The Community is absolutely contrary to non-selective incentives resulting biased subsidies essentially because they compensate and do not eliminate conditions of low competition, but it is not contrary to tax concessions directed to favour innovation and supports and promotes local development and cooperation.

Even now Italy seems to be unable to follow this guideline, facing seriously the local agencies and regions role in the territorial exploitation, the central and local administrative agencies reform, starting with bureaucratic control bodies moving towards task forces able to promote development planning. Last but not least, the longest delays involve in the laws on competition and consumer protection.

The creation of a policy to small firms can request perhaps specific provisions to innovation to be justified in front of EEC, but it needs first of all a legal context able to support their growth; this is possible if conditions of competition in the credit system are created, infrastructures are made available, services are provided and relationships with research and training institutes are developed, the local and international cooperation is favoured. All of this can be aided by the enforcement of a specific law, but it can not be limited to one single law.

BIBLIOGRAPHY

[1] ALESSANDRINI P.: «Mutamenti strutturali e sistemi di piccole e medie imprese: problemi e prospettive», *Economia Marche*, vol. VIII, no. 3, December 1989, pp. 239-58.

[2] BALLONI V.: *Esperienze di ristrutturazione industriale*, Bologna, il Mulino, 1985.

[3] BANCA D'ITALIA: *Analisi del Libro bianco della Cee sugli aiuti di Stato*, Mimeo, January 1990.

[4] BARCA F. - MAGNANI: *L'industria tra capitale e lavoro: piccole e medie imprese dall'autunno caldo al risanamento*, Bologna, il Mulino, 1988.

[5] BATTAGLIA A. - VALCAMONICI R. (a cura di): *Nella competizione globale. Una politica industriale verso il 2000*, Bari, Laterza, 1989.

[6] BECATTINI G. (eds.): *Mercato e forze locali: il distretto industriale*, Bologna, il Mulino, 1987.

[7] BIANCHI P.: *Politiche industriali di settore*, in BALLONI [2], 1985.

[8] — · — : *Concorrenza dinamica, distretti industriali e interventi locali*, in GOBBO [18], 1989.

[9] BIANCHI P. - GIORDANI M.G.: *L'amministrazione dell'industria e del commercio estero*, Bologna, il Mulino, 1990.

[10] CAGLI A.: *La politica industriale italiana tra sovranità nazionale e vincoli comunitari*, in BIANCHI - GIORDANI [9], 1990, pp. 145-72.

[11] EEC: *Operations of the European Community Concerning Small and Medium-sized Enterprises*, Bruxelles, Practical Handbook 1988.

[12] — · — : *Primo censimento degli aiuti di Stato nella Comunità europea*, Bruxelles, EEC, 1989.

[13] — · — : *Vademecum sulla riforma dei fondi strutturali comunitari*, Bruxelles, EEC, 1989.

[14] — · — : *Quadro comunitario di sostegno, 1989-1993 per lo sviluppo e l'adeguamento strutturale delle regioni in ritardo di sviluppo*, Italia, Bruxelles, EEC, 1989.

[15] — · — : *Quinto rapporto della Commissione al consiglio e al Parlamento europeo sull'attuazione del Libro bianco della Commissione relativo al completamento del mercato interno*, Bruxelles, EEC, May 1990.

[16] FORTI A.: *Gli aiuti statali alle imprese e la politica per la concorrenza nella Comunità europea*, in MARIANI - RANCI [20], 1988.

[17] GIANNOLA A.: «Il ruolo delle piccole e medie imprese nel recente sviluppo industriale italiano», *Economia Marche*, vol. VIII, no. 3, dic. 1989, pp. 215-38.

[18] GOBBO F. (eds.): *Distretti e sistemi produttivi alla soglia degli anni '90*, Milano, F. Angeli, 1989.

[19] LA NOCE M.: *Linee di intervento delle politiche di incentivazione industriale dal 1970 al 1987*, in BATTAGLIA A. - VALCAMONICI R. [5], 1989, pp. 251-80.

[20] MARIANI M. - RANCI P. (a cura di): *Il mercato interno europeo*, Bologna, il Mulino, 1988.

[21] MOMIGLIANO F.: *Le leggi della politica industriale*, Bologna, il Mulino, 1986

[22] MOMIGLIANO F. - ANTONELLI C.: *Politiche per la ricerca applicata, l'innovazione, l'ammodernamento e il trasferimento tecnologico*, in MOMIGLIANO [21], 1986, pp. 103-213.

[23] MUSSATTI G.: *Rapporto della Commissione per lo studio della problematica della piccola e media impresa*, Roma, Ministero dell'industria del commercio e dell'artigianato, 1988.

[24] NOEL E.: *Presence de l'Italie Dans la Communaute*, Convegno Ispi, Mimeo, Milano, 12 December 1989.

[25] PIORE M. - SABEL C.: *The Second Industrial Divide*, New York, Basic Books, 1984.

[26] PONTAROLLO E.: «Le politiche di ristrutturazione industriale in Italia dal 1961 al 1977», *L'industria*, vol. I, no. 3, 1980, pp.369-94.

[27] RANCI P.: *I trasferimenti dello Stato alle imprese industriali negli anni settanta*, Bologna, il Mulino, 1983.

[28] SCANAGATTA G.: *L'attuazione degli interventi di politica industriale per le piccole e medie imprese*, in BATTAGLIA A. - VALCAMONICI R. [5], 1989, pp. 281-301.

[29] SENATO DELLA REPUBBLICA: *La politica degli aiuti alle imprese, indagine conoscitiva svolta dalla Commissione industria e dalla Giunta per gli affari delle Comunità europee, introduzione del senatore R. Cassola*, Roma, 1990.

[30] SILVESTRI P.: *Agevolazioni sul credito e contributi in conto capitale*, in RANCI [27], 1983, pp. 35-82.

The Tortuous Road of Industry Through the Mezzogiorno

Mariano D'Antonio
Università di Napoli

1. - During the 1980s, the rate of growth of the economy in southern Italy — the Mezzogiorno — slowed considerably compared with the north-central region. As a result, the distance between the "two Italies", rather than narrowing, has widened. The sluggishness of industry in the South is one of the determinant factors causing the Mezzogiorno to lag behind the more economically developed areas of Italy.

The figures in Tables 1-3 below, which speak for themselves, are nonetheless worthy of comment. The gap between per capita gross domestic product (GDP) and per capita consumption in the Mezzogiorno is readily apparent: in the period 1980-1987, the former figure slowed by four-and-a-half percentage points with respect to the north-central region, while per capita consumption in the South rose approximately one point higher than it did in the North. Net imports, which reached 24.4% of production, underscore the disparity betweeen per capita consumption and production: in some regions (such as Basilicata and Calabria), net imports equalled or exceeded half of 1987 local production. In short, during the last decade the subsystem known as the Italian Mezzogiorno has become increasingly dependent on the production surpluses of Italy's stronger regions.

One sign of stagnation, or the slower speed of development in this area is the rate of unemployment in the Mezzogiorno. Calculated as the ratio of job seekers to the labour force, in recent years this rate has risen as high as 20%, and even higher in regions such as Campania.

TABLE 1

DEVELOPMENT INDICATORS AND UNEMPLOYMENT RATES
(in thousand lira at 1980 prices)

Region and territory	Per capita GDP			Per capita consumption			Net imports to GDP		Unemployment rate	
	1980	1987	Rate of change	1980	1987	Rate of change	1980	1987	1980	1987
Abruzzo	5,741.0	6,442.0	12.2	5,050.2	6,046.6	19.7	20.7	21.3	8.6	10.8
Molise	4,884.8	5,413.6	10.8	4,528.6	5,295.5	16.9	41.7	35.4	9.8	11.9
Campania	4,587.5	5,021.1	9.5	4,587.5	5,021.1	9.5	18.7	23.1	11.9	23.0
Apulia	4,928.4	5,423.7	10.1	4,278.0	5,026.6	17.5	14.7	16.0	8.0	16.5
Basilicata	4,522.8	4,464.0	− 1.3	4,231.0	4,966.5	17.4	33.3	48.0	12.4	20.1
Calabria	3,842.1	4,211.1	9.6	4,138.5	5,046.4	21.9	40.1	53.4	14.6	21.8
Sicilia	4,640.4	5,106.9	10.1	4,521.3	5,259.9	16.3	25.0	28.2	9.7	18.3
Sardegna	5,044.2	5,621.6	11.4	4,383.4	5,437.9	24.1	20.4	25.6	15.1	20.1
Mezzogiorno . .	4,698.6	5,159.5	9.8	4,370.3	5,154.1	17.9	22.3	26.4	10.9	19.2
Centre-North (*)	8,059.7	9,208.4	14.3	5,818.4	6,806.1	17.0	− 1.6	− 3.4	5.6	8.4

(*) Net imports for the Centre-North are in effect net exports.

Source: Based on I STAT (Central Institute for Statistics) data

The weakness of industry (especially the manufacturing industry, shown in Table 2) is confirmed by various indicators such as the amount of investment, which remained unchanged during the first half of the decade while north-central investment declined, but was similarly unaffected by the subsequent concentration of industry in the more developed regions, as shown by the figures in Table 3 and Graph 1.

TABLE 2

BREAKDOWN OF VALUE-ADDED

	Centre-North		Mezzogiorno	
	1980-1982	1985-1987	1980-1982	1985-1987
Market goods and services	89.6	90.0	82.3	82.5
Agriculture, forests, fisheries	4.7	4.6	10.4	9.9
Industry	39.9	38.5	27.2	26.2
Industry	33.3	33.2	17.5	17.6
— Energy products	1.8	1.6	2.8	2.7
— Manufactures	31.5	31.6	14.8	14.9
Building and public works	6.6	5.4	9.7	8.5
Services	44.9	46.9	44.7	46.4
Non market services	10.4	10.0	17.7	17.5
Total gross of imputed bank services	*100.0*	*100.0*	*100.0*	*100.0*

Source: based on ISTAT data

The downturn of industry-sector employment experienced in the north-central regions (Table 4) was adequately compensated by the creation of jobs in the service sector; however, in the Mezzogiorno the service sector — already over-represented, particularly as regards non-market services — was unable to absorb the entire labour force which could no longer be employed by industry or agriculture. At the end of the decade, the number employed in the manufacturing industry (manufactures) in the South did not exceed 16% of the total.

The weakest area of southern industry, given the imminence of European unification, is brought to the fore by the gross productivity per standard labour unit: the disparity between South and North continued to grow throughout the 1980s (Table 5 and Graph 2).

TABLE 3

GROSS FIXED INVESTMENT
(billion lira at 1980 prices)

	1980	1981	1982	1983	1984	1985	1986	1987
Centre-North								
Industry	23,737.9	21,706.1	19,485.0	18,374.5	19,171.7	19,506.5	20,347.5	22,257.1
Industry	21,346.9	19,533.6	17,583.6	16,636.8	17,359.5	17,412.1	18,478.6	20,391.7
— Energy products	3,407.5	3,680.8	3,501.5	3,504.9	3,394.5	3,703.8	4,061.3	3,938.9
— Manufactures	17,939.4	15,852.8	14,082.1	13,131.9	13,965.0	13,708.3	14,417.3	16,452.8
Building and public works	2,391.0	2,172.5	1,901.4	1,737.7	1,812.2	2,094.4	1,868.9	1,865.4
Mezzogiorno								
Industry	6,771.1	6,309.9	6,297.0	6,141.5	6,453.3	6,178.5	6,328.5	6,607.9
Industry	5,575.1	5,051.4	5,269.4	5,164.2	5,428.5	5,105.9	5,439.4	5,660.3
— Energy products	1,795.5	1,786.2	1,798.5	1,834.1	1,967.5	2,081.2	2,600.7	2,476.1
— Manufactures	3,779.6	3,265.2	3,470.9	3,330.1	3,461.0	3,024.7	2,838.7	3,184.2
Building and public works	1,196.0	1,258.5	1,027.6	977.3	1,024.8	1,072.6	889.1	947.6

Source: based on ISTAT data

GRAPH 1

GROSS FIXED INVESTMENT IN INDUSTRY

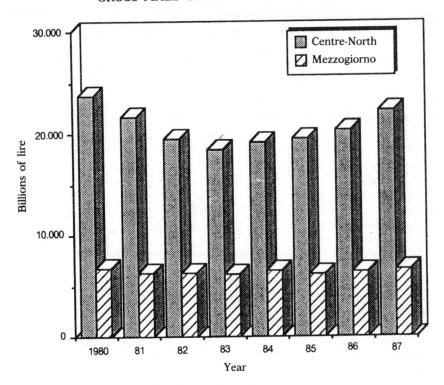

The social security charge reductions granted to enterprises in the Mezzogiorno through special legislation prevent the productivity gap between the two areas from carrying over to the cost of labour per unit of production which in the South has not yet reached north-central levels, as shown in Tables 6 and 7.

In conclusion, the 1980s were a period of low industrialization in the Mezzogiorno. The industrial progress shown in certain areas (such as Abruzzi, Molise, and to some degree, Apulia) and the dynamism of small local enterpreneurs did little to offset the net effect, which fell dismally short of satisfying the needs of a rapidly growing number of (especially female) job seekers

The reasons for the industrial slowdown experienced in the Mezzogiorno during the last decade are manifold.

　　　　　　　Mariano D'Antonio

TABLE 4

STANDARD LABOUR UNITS
(absolute values in thousands)

	Centre-North			Mezzogiorno		
	1980	1984	1987	1980	1984	1987
(absolute values)						
Market and goods services..	8,589.1	8,073.3	8,276.2	3,173.7	3,154.9	3,122.5
Agriculture, forests, fisheries	259.0	222.0	203.6	677.5	570.4	545.2
Industry	5,231.7	4,415.3	4,299.9	1,352.5	1,283.6	1,200.3
— Industry	4,492.3	3,777.3	3,691.4	833.3	755.9	719.7
— Energy products	132.8	131.0	136.3	56.3	58.9	63.0
— Manufactures	4,359.5	3,646.3	3,555.1	777.0	697.0	656.7
Building and public works ..	739.4	638.0	608.5	519.2	527.7	480.6
Services	3,098.4	3,436.0	3,772.7	1,143.7	1,300.9	1,377.0
Non-market services	2,439.4	2,620.2	2,717.8	1,206.9	1,339.6	1,411.6
Total	*11,028.5*	*10,693.5*	*10,994.0*	*4,380.6*	*4,494.5*	*4,534.1*
(percentages)						
Markets goods and services	77.9	75.5	75.3	72.4	70.2	68.9
Agriculture, forests, fisheries	2.3	2.1	1.9	15.5	12.7	12.0
Industry	47.4	41.3	39.1	30.9	28.6	26.5
Industry	40.7	35.3	33.6	19.0	16.8	15.9
— Energy products	1.2	1.2	1.2	1.3	1.3	1.4
— Manufactures	39.5	34.1	32.3	17.7	15.5	14.5
Building and public works ..	6.7	6.0	5.5	11.9	11.7	10.6
Services	28.1	32.1	34.3	26.1	28.9	30.4
Non-market services	22.1	24.5	24.7	27.6	29.8	31.1
Total	*100.0*	*100.0*	*100.0*	*100.0*	*100.0*	*100.0*

Source: based on ISTAT data

Firstly, the critical progress of north-central industry and the structure of southern industry were decidedly out of phase. International factors (the adjustment of industry in wealthier nations to the second oil shock, to restrictive monetary policy, to the public budget crisis and the resultant, disproportionate rise in the public debt) and national ones (such as the discipline imposed on Italy upon entering the European Monetary System) compelled north-central enterprises

TABLE 5

GDP PER STANDARD UNIT OF LABOUR
(thousand lira)

	1980-1982 average	1985-1987 average
Centre-North		
Industry	*23,183.1*	*28,590.6*
Industry	22,575.0	28,727.2
— Energy products	39,866.9	38,317.6
— Manufactures	22,020.1	28,365.7
Building and public works	26,814.5	27,774.5
Mezzogiorno		
Industry	*18,522.6*	*21,947.1*
Industry	19,761.5	24,795.1
— Energy products	45,723.4	45,367.5
— Manufactures	17,860.5	22,916.5
Building and public works	16,668.0	17,742.9

Source: based on ISTAT data

GRAPH 2

MEZZOGIORNO:
RELATIVE PRODUCTIVITY OF INDUSTRY

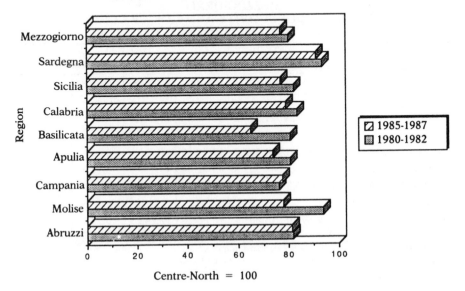

Centre-North = 100

Mariano D'Antonio

TABLE 6

CENTRE-NORTH:
WAGE RATES, PRODUCTIVITY AND LABOUR COSTS(*)
(absolute values in thousand lira)

	Wage rates		Labour productivity		Unit cost of labour	
	1980-1982	1985-1986	1980-1982	1985-1986	1980-1982	1985-1986
Industry	*15,125.9*	*28,328.5*	*23,183.1*	*28,590.6*	*0.652*	*0.991*
Industry	15,310.7	28,931.5	22,575.0	28,727.2	0.678	1.007
— Energy products ..	23,956.6	44,746.8	39,866.9	38,317.6	0.601	1.168
— Manufactures	15,030.5	28,334.4	22,020.1	28,365.7	0.683	0.999
Building and public works	14,020.8	24,728.0	26,814.5	27,774.5	0.523	0.890

(*) Wage rate refers to income per standard unit of labour, at current prices; productivity refers to gross product, at 1980 prices, per unit of labour employed.
Source: based on ISTAT data

TABLE 7

MEZZOGIORNO
WAGE RATES, PRODUCTIVITY AND LABOUR COSTS (*)
(absolute values in thousand lira)

	Wage rates		Labour productivity		Unit cost of labour	
	1980-1982	1985-1986	1980-1982	1985-1986	1980-1982	1985-1986
Industry	*11,538.6*	*21,310.5*	*18,522.6*	*21,947.1*	*0.623*	*0.671*
Industry	12,620.8	24,362.7	19,761.5	24,795.6	0.639	0.983
— Energy products ..	23,886.2	44,352.3	45,723.4	45,367.5	0.522	0.978
— Manufactures	11,795.3	22,533.9	17,860.5	22,916.5	0.660	0.983
Building and public works	9,897.0	16,802.1	16,668.0	17,742.9	0.594	0.947

(*) Wage rate refers to income per standard unit of labour, at current prices; productivity refers to gross product, at 1980 prices, per unit of labour employed.
Source: based on ISTAT data

to modify their programmes in favour of intensive investments and assistance for the restructuring and reorganization of factories, and to place less emphasis on extensive investments, many of which could be easily located throughout the country. These changes brought decentralization of industry from North to South to a standstill.

Secondly, the public polices aimed at industrializing the Mezzogiorno were either altogether ineffective or incapable of offsetting the tendency of private and public resources to concentrate in regions where the industrial base was more solid and where firms pressed for incentives to restructure and to rationalize their production cycles. Some of the instruments designed as a buoy for southern industry were shown to be outdated or difficult to put in place; others went down with the decline of pro-Mezzogiorno policy. This decline is clearly reflected in Law 183 of 1976 for special intervention in the Mezzogiorno. After its expiry at the beginning of the 1980s, Law 183 of 1976 was extended on a case-by-case basis for very brief periods (six months, one year) before being replaced by Law 64 of 1986, the result of an arduous journey through Parliament, only five years later.

It is on the industrial policies of the Mezzogiorno that our attention will be focused: we will examine the seemingly vast store of measures geared toward the industrialization of southern Italy with a view to selecting those which succeeded and those which failed.

2. - Traditionally, the two pillars of industrial policy in the South have been the investment of state-owned firms and the availability of incentives, especially financial incentives (capital account contributions and soft loans). Both of these pillars were reduced during the 1980s and attempts by public authorities to replace them with other measures, or to give southern enterprises priority using instruments of a more general nature — for example, a reserve of allocated funds made available to southern enterprises — proved to be ineffectual.

Let us begin by examining the role of state-owned firms in the region during the 1980s, bearing in mind that since 1957 these firms have been compelled by law (a law which, as questionable as it may seem, has never been repealed) to invest at least 40% of new investment, and to place at least 60% of capital stock, in the South.

According to our calculations (Graph 3 and Table 8), state-owned

GRAPH 3

INVESTMENT OF STATE-OWNED FIRMS: 1980-89

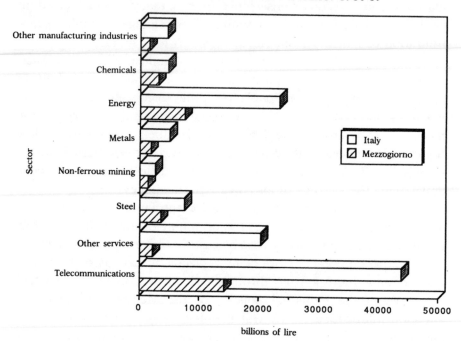

billions of lire

firms invested just over L35 trillion in the Mezzogiorno from 1980-1989, or 31% of approximately L112 trillion invested throughout Italy. However, if the average investment levels of the five-year periods 1980-1984 and 1985-1989 are considered separately, it becomes clear that state-owned investment in manufacturing in the South declined over time. In addition, Table 8 reveals that state-owned firms gradually began to increase their presence as providers of services (mainly telephone service) rather than manufacturers in southern Italy as well. The reduced involvement of state-owned firms in Mezzogiorno industry is clearly shown in Graph 4: here we see that during the second half of the 1980s the disparity between levels of involvement in the north-central regions and in the Mezzogiorno continued to widen.

Public firms are unlikely to change their outlook toward the South — the golden years, as it were, of state-owned firms in the

TABLE 8

INVESTMENT MADE BY STATE-OWNED FIRMS
(billion lira)

Average years	1980-1984 average				1985-1989 average			
	Italy		Mezzogiorno		Italy		Mezzogiorno	
Services	Abs. values	%	Abs. values	%	Abs. values	%	Abs. values	%
Telecommunications	3,118	39.0	923	34.3	5,645	39.2	1,889	43.5
Radio and television	112	1.4	24	0.9	284	2.0	53	1.2
Sea transport	70	0.9	2	0.1	315	2.2	19	0.4
Air transport	395	4.9	0	0.0	505	3.5	4	0.1
Building and public works	329	4.1	36	1.3	1,304	9.1	188	4.3
Other	119	1.5	33	1.2	615	4.3	80	1.8
Total	*4,145*	*51.8*	*1,018*	*37.8*	*8,668*	*60.2*	*2,233*	*51.4*
Manufacturing industries								
Steel and related activity	642	8.0	336	12.5	851	5.9	369	8.5
Non-ferrous mining	257	3.2	130	4.8	272	1.9	143	3.3
Cement	13	0.2	9	0.3	16	0.1	8	0.2
Metals	465	5.8	204	7.6	542	3.8	173	4.0
Electronics	140	1.7	44	1.6	301	2.1	87	2.0
Shipbuilding	48	0.6	5	0.2	81	0.6	13	0.3
Energy	1,879	23.5	720	26.8	2,784	19.3	780	18.0
Chemicals	237	3.0	149	5.6	723	5.0	474	10.9
Textiles	20	0.3	5	0.2	4	-	-	-
Food	87	1.1	35	1.3	80	0.6	29	0.7
Other	62	0.8	36	1.4	71	0.5	36	0.8
Total	*3,849*	*48.2*	*1,674*	*62.2*	*5,725*	*39.8*	*2,113*	*48.6*
Nationwide investment	7,994	100.0	2,692	100.0	14,393	100.0	4,346	100.0

Source: based on data from the *Relazione generale sulla situazione economica del paese.* Roma, various years.

GRAPH 4

INVESTMENT OF STATE-OWNED FIRMS IN INDUSTRY

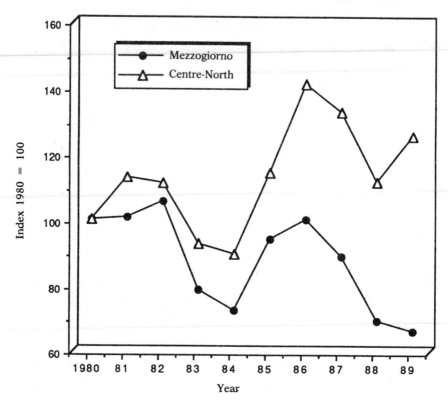

Mezzogiorno were 1966-1975, the upswing of a cycle of investment in petrochemicals, steel and automobiles. The wait-and-see attitude taken by the management of state-owned firms, that is, its policy of waiting for better days, has caused enormous amounts of government resources to be frittered away in company losses. Recent attempts to involve state-owned firms in "nobler" causes — offering services to firms, promoting small industrial initiatives, training employees, or cleaning up the environment — in the Mezzogiorno have not yet produced concrete results and may never do so, given the prevailing organizational framework of public firms and their management's selection criteria, which are all too insistent on institutional equilibria.

Let us now turn to the policy instruments designed to stimulate industry in southern Italy, and in particular to the financial incentives to investment which cover sizeable portions of the cost of building or enlarging a productive enterprise. A Svimez [7] (*) (Association for the Development of Southern Italy) estimate sets total incentives to industrial investment during the 1980s, on average, at 60% of investment costs.

Under Law 64 of 1986 on special intervention in the Mezzogiorno region (which to a large extent confirms the system put in place by the previous legislation), projects involving new production initiatives in the Mezzogiorno or improvements on existing plants (modernization, enlargement, restoration, reconversion, restructuring) may benefit from two types of incentives : a) a capital account contribution, whose percentage varies with each additional share of fixed investment (40% for investments up to L7.5 bn; 30% for the remaining share of investment beyond L7.5 bn to L32 bn; 15% for the share exceeding L32 bn); and b) subsidised financing of eligible expenses. Under the latter financing scheme, which requires the signing of a contract by the bank and the firm requesting the financing, and the setting up of an amortization schedule for repayment, the government, through the Agenzia per il Mezzogiorno (Agency for the Development of Southern Italy) provides assistance by repaying a part of the interest. The firm requesting the financing is responsible for the repayment of 36% of the reference interest rate for eligible projects with up to L32 bn of fixed investment, and 60% of the reference interest rate for more than L32 bn of fixed investment.

The amount of financing varies with the share of fixed investment (30% up to L7.5 bn and 40% on the remaining share beyond L7.5 bn). The maximum financing term is fixed at 15 years for new initiatives and 10 years for existing plants. In both cases, a preamortization period (of a maximum of 5 and 3 years, respectively) exists during which the applicant firm repays only the interest.

As for inventories, 40% of the quota eligibile for financing (which must not exceed 40% of fixed investment) may be subsidized. The ceiling for the financing of inventories is thus set at 16% of fixed investment.

(*) *Advise:* the numbers in square brackets refer to the Bibliography.

The grant may be increased by one-fifth if the initiative involves a priority sector and by another fifth in one of the provinces considered to be below average development levels according to certain socioeconomic indicators (income, industrial progress, unemployment, emigration). For the purposes of these increases, the provinces are divided into the following three groups: 1) provinces below the average development level, which are entitled, to both supplements (Group *A*); 2) provinces with average development, eligible only for the supplement involving subsidized sectors (Group *B*); provinces above average development levels, which receive no supplements (Group *C*).

Total financial incentives, limited to a maximum of 70% of fixed investment, may be increased to 75% when combined with subsidies offered under other national, regional or Community legislation, provided that the supplements to the basic contribution according to sector or province remain unchanged.

Entrepreneurs may ask for and receive the financial incentives guaranteed by law for the Mezzogiorno by means of subsidized leasing. This type of subsidy may involve the purchase of a complete plant or the purchase of machinery alone for enlargement or modernization (plant leasing), or for the purchase of individual machines used in industry or in scientific and technoogical research (equipment leasing). The term of a subsidized leasing transaction is fixed at 5 years for equipment and 8-9 years for initiatives involving the leasing of an entire plant.

In this case, incentives consist of capital account and interest account contributions which include the supplement for priority areas and sectors. The subsidies are received by the leasing company which owns the goods, and passed on in turn to the applicant firm in the form of reduced rental payments.

Table 9 and Graph 5 below clearly show the slowdown in special intervention and particularly in contributions to productive sectors, over the last decade.

As well as the general factors (mentioned earlier) which played a major role in lowering the tendency toward investing in the South, particularly in the case of companies with head offices located elsewhere, until 1986, at least, the poor preformance of policies

TABLE 9

SPECIAL INTERVENTION
ALLOCATED FUNDS AND EXPENDITURE
(billion lira at 1989 prices)

Year	Infrastructure			Aid to industry sectors			Other intervention			Total		
	allocated funds	exp.	all./exp. in %	allocated funds	exp.	all./exp. in %	allocated funds	exp.	all./exp. in %	allocated funds	exp.	all./exp. in %
1976	6,394	5,418	118.0	2,198	2,408	91.3	705	495	142.4	9,297	8,321	111.7
1977	11,651	5,875	198.3	3,042	2,176	139.8	205	362	56.6	14,898	8,413	177.1
1978	7,287	5,682	128.2	4,057	2,194	184.9	317	297	106.7	11,661	8,173	142.7
1979	6,771	4,689	144.4	1,966	2,104	93.4	425	341	124.6	9,162	7,134	128.4
1980	10,287	4,646	221.4	1,506	1,501	100.3	344	312	110.3	12,137	6,459	187.9
1981	7,275	4,699	154.8	1,781	1,362	130.8	168	280	60.0	9,224	6,341	145.5
1982	6,550	4,311	151.9	2,397	1,196	200.4	244	309	79.0	9,191	5,186	158.0
1983	5,339	6,499	82.2	2,330	1,199	194.3	277	125	221.6	7,946	7,823	101.6
1984	2,309	5,429	42.5	1,067	1,289	82.8	88	188	46.8	3,464	6,906	50.2
1985	6,502	4,308	150.9	2,321	1,294	179.4	501	385	130.1	9,324	5,987	155.7
1986	2,862	3,623	79.0	1,186	1,463	81.1	67	219	30.6	4,115	5,305	77.6
1987	5,509	2,959	186.2	1,562	1,357	115.1	178	151	117.9	7,249	4,467	162.3
1988	7,501	2,982	251.5	2,188	1,500	145.9	1,525	209	729.7	11,214	4,961	239.1
1989	6,694	3,365	198.9	5,901	1,883	313.4	2,047	413	495.6	14,642	5,661	258.6

Source: based on SVIMEZ data

GRAPH 5

SPECIAL INTERVENTION, BY TYPE OF EXPENDITURE

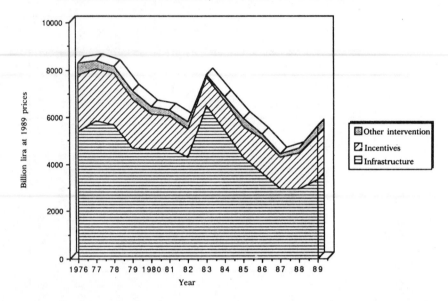

designed to stimulate industry in the Mezzogiorno could also be attributed to more specific factors. One of these, uncertainty about the future of special intervention, was due to the lack of teeth in Italian legislation, also mentioned earlier. Others included the increasingly muddled administration of incentives, under attack by entrepreneurs for being excessively bureaucratic; the binding nature of legislation (this greatly influences sector-by-sector planning since under law 183 of 1976 and later under Law 64 of 1986, industry in the Mezzogiorno must be divided into eligible sectors, non-eligible sectors, and sectors whose eligibility is under review. The eligible sectors are in turn divided into two groups, only one of which is entitled to the one-fifth supplement); and the inefficient system of payment to entrepreneurs.

This model of industrial policy, involving special intervention in the Mezzogiorno, is thus an example of economic planning. It is common knowledge that economic planning has had its day, having fallen into disgrace during the 1980s not only in the eyes of market participants, but also in the more collective view of the general public.

From 1986 on, the number of incentives granted — largely in an effort to sway the decisions of enterpreneurs — rose appreciably, as shown by the data in Table 10.

In ten years the number of subsidized initiatives more than doubled after slowing considerably by amount of investment during the first half of the decade. The number of capital account contributions surpassed by far the number of interest account contributions; the increase in the number employed (a forecast figure which, as it appears in the investment schedule, is usually overestimated) declined over the years.

Industries which received the incentives have shifted their focus over time away from investments in new plants and toward enlargements (Table 11), following the trend established approximately five years earlier in the Centre and in the North.

The distribution of subsidized investment according to size of firm reveals a decrease in the amount of investment subsidized for firms with over L30 bn in fixed investment, whereas subsidized investment for firms with up to L2 bn in fixed investment is on the rise, as shown in Graph 6.

Graphs 7 and 8 show the distribution of subsidized investment by sector and by Mezzogiorno region. Of note is the impressive increase in subsidized investment in the Abruzzo region.

Two recent developments have brought about changes in industrial policy involving special intervention funds: the first involves the signing of programme contracts by large industrial groups (Fiat, Olivetti, IRI, Texas Instruments, Bull) with the Ministry for the Mezzogiorno; the second is the incentives to young entrepreneurs granted under a law approved specifically for this purpose (Law 44 of 1986).

Companies entering into programme contracts are offered the advantages of an attractive incentive package (which often reaches the maximum percentage permitted by law), of submitting non-material investments (research and development, employee training) for financial aid, and of receiving, preferential treatment for the review process for each project in its investment schedule.

The contracts in force until 1990 cover some L8.3 trillion in investment, a sign of big industry's rekindled interest in creating new

TABLE 10

SPECIAL INTERVENTION: INDUSTRY SUBSIDES, BY YEAR
(from 1980 to 31/3/1990; in billion lira)

Year	No. granted	Subsidized	Capital acct.	Subsidized	Int. acct.	Rise in no.	Average investment	No. employed per L bn of investment
			billion lira at current prices					
1980	1,202	1,012.4	340.1	319.0	220.7	22,454	0.84	22.2
1981	1,667	1,558.6	546.6	435.7	341.9	24,710	0.93	15.9
1982	2,202	2,053.7	712.8	664.4	528.5	29,461	0.93	14.3
1983	2,594	2,100.0	759.8	681.9	507.9	23,842	0.81	11.4
1984	1,355	1,229.7	433.3	399.9	285.8	10,904	0.91	8.9
1985	3,533	3,029.1	1,031.3	934.7	662.7	17,221	0.86	5.7
1986	1,625	1,833.2	612.0	573.4	381.2	11,529	1.13	6.3
1987	2,048	2,407.6	921.1	827.2	414.0	10,513	1.18	4.4
1988	2,263	4,742.1	1,554.2	1,032.2	538.0	11,545	2.10	2.4
1989	2,962	5,413.8	1,896.8	1,535.8	799.6	16,266	1.83	3.0
1990	842	2,099.1	723.3	663.6	358.3	4,857	2.49	2.3
total	22,293	27,479.6	9,531.3	8,067.8	5,038.4	183,302	1.23	6.7
			index numbers at costant prices					
1980	100.0	100.0	100.0	100.0	100.0	100.0	100.0	100.0
1981	138.7	120.9	126.2	107.3	121.7	110.0	87.2	91.0
1982	183.2	136.2	140.7	139.8	160.7	131.2	74.3	96.3
1983	215.8	126.5	136.2	130.3	140.3	106.2	58.6	84.0
1984	112.7	70.6	74.1	72.9	75.3	48.6	62.7	68.8
1985	293.9	147.7	149.7	144.6	148.2	76.7	50.2	51.9
1986	135.2	87.6	87.1	87.0	83.6	51.3	64.8	58.6
1987	170.4	110.3	125.6	120.3	87.0	46.8	64.7	42.2
1988	188.3	205.4	200.4	141.9	106.9	51.4	109.1	25.0
1989	246.4	222.9	232.5	200.7	151.0	72.4	90.5	32.5

Source: based on AGENZIA data (from the Agency for the Development of the Mezzogiorno)

TABLE 11

SPECIAL INTERVENTION:
DISTRIBUTION OF SUBSIDIZED INVESTMENT
BY TYPE OF INITIATIVE

Type of initiative	1980-1983 average		1984-1987 average		1988		1989	
	No	% of subsidized investment	No	% of subsidized investment	No	% of subsidized investment	No	% of subsidized investment
New plan and equipment	736	46.5	563	32.8	539	23.7	715	24.1
Enlargement	868	44.7	1,139	50.1	1,573	69.2	2,075	70.1
Modernization	56	8.8	119	17.1	160	7.0	172	5.8
Other	1,660	100.0	1,821	100.0	2,272	100.0	2,962	100.0

Source: based on SVIMEZ and AGENZIA data

GRAPH 6

DISTRIBUTION OF SUBSIDIZED INVESTMENT
BY SIZE OF FIRM

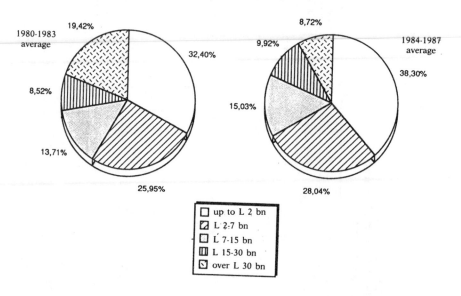

initiatives, or, better yet, in maintaining existing activity in the Mezzogiorno. Nonetheless, it is still too early to judge the effects of this experiment, as the programmes have only recently been started; first signs suggest no loosening of the tightly woven net of protocol to be observed by companies wishing to receive their incentives.

The results of the law governing the activity of young entrepreneurs have been more encouraging. As of May 1990, 574 projects have been approved (of a total of 2,493 proposed), with total investment at approximately L 1.6 trillion, expected to generate some 12,000 new jobs. As well as financial incentives for investment, Law 44 of 1986 also permits contributions deferred over time (up to three years) toward the management costs of the new firm.

The law for young entrepreneurs provided a good opportunity to foster a new generation of market participants, not all of whom belong to entrepreneurial families. Here, too, given the newness of this experiment, an assessment of the extent to which this measure has helped or hurt young entrepreneurs must be made at a later stage.

GRAPH 7

MEZZOGIORNO:
SUBSIDIZED INVESTMENT, BY SECTOR

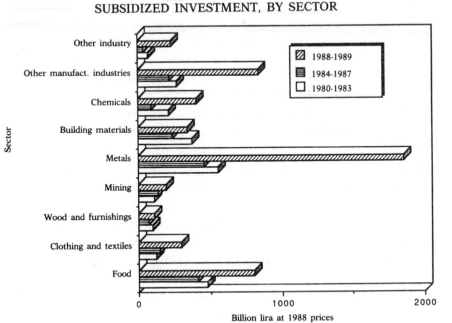

GRAPH 8

MEZZOGIORNO:
SUBSIDIZED INVESTMENT, BY REGION

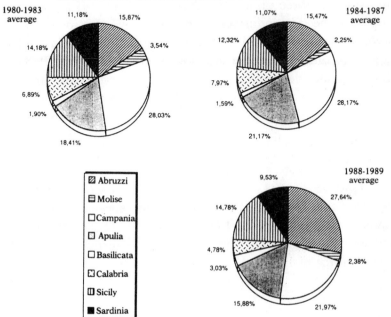

3. - During the 1980s, several incentives geared toward stimulating industry were made available to firms throughout Italy, while reserving a percentage of financial assistance for the southern region. Industrial policy during the last decade placed considerable emphasis on technological innovation, modernization and rationalization of firms, and comprised a series of measures aimed at helping entrepreneurs to purchase high-level production equipment, to carry out research and development projects, and to introduce new technology.

More specifically, the intervention considered to be most significant in recent years has fostered both research and development programmes and the purchase of high-level production equipment so as to allow technology to be transferred to small- and medium-sized enterprises. The former objective was governed by Law 46 of 1982, while the latter was pursued under Law 396 of 1983, amended by Laws 399 of 1987 and 185 of 1989, which worked together to tighten the standards set for the selection of firms under the previous legislation, Law 1329 of 1965.

Apart from incentives to innovation, the other driving force of industrial policy in recent years (despite a downturn, particularly in north-central industry) has been direct intervention as a means of offsetting failure of the market or of individual firms.

This objective is dealt with under Law 675 of 1977, which remained in force until 1982, and Laws 193 of 194 (for the restructuring of the steel industry), 63 of 1982 (civil electronics), and 808 of 1985 (civil aeronautics). Other key legislation in this area includes Law 184 of 1971 for the creation of GEPI (Gestione Partecipazioni Italiane), an agency that has continued to rationalize enterprises in recent years, and parts of Law 46 of 1985 for cooperation.

3.1 Fostering Technological Innovation and Research: Law 46 of 1982

Law 46 of 1982 created the IMI (Istituto mobiliare italiano) Special Fund for Applied Research (Fondo speciale IMI per la ricerca applicata) and the Special Rotative Fund for Technological Innovation (Fondo speciale rotativo per l'innovazione tecnologica) managed by the Ministry of Industry.

The Fund for Applied Research (set up under Law 1089 of 1968 and modified various times prior to the enactment of Law 46) encourages the process of product innovation from the supply side. Incentives take three different forms: *a)* Investment in the capital of research firms. This form of intervention generally applies to research and development programmes of national or industry-wide scope, affecting a large number of enterprises. The Fund must have a majority of shares, and its involvement is understood to be a vehicle for the promotion of research and development; *b)* the granting of subsidized credits to be used for research projects. Subsidized financing may not exceed 80% of the project's cost, and the rate of interest is set by Treasury decree. Financing is awarded to government economic agencies operating in sectors producing goods and services, to productive firms or consortia, and to the research enterprises mentioned in *a)* above. The amortization period may vary from 3 to 10 years beyond the expected date of payment. The entire term cannot exceed 15 years; *c)* cash grants, awarded only to applied research projects of particular technological importance or involving high industrual risk, for up to 50% of research costs to a limit of L200 mn per applicant per year.

Law 46 also provides for a 40% share of the Fund to be reserved for use in the Mezzogiorno, and for a further 20% reserved for small- and medium-sized enterprises (SMEs), including cooperatives. Overall, the Fund for Applied Research reserves a 12% share for central or northern SMEs, and 8% for those in the south of Italy.

The Special Rotative Fund for Technological Innovation (established by Article 14 of Law 46 of 1982 and rendered fully operational only in 1984) provides state financial assistance at subsidized rates to firms whose programmes, which satisfy the conditions concerning industrial sector and objective set out in the directives of the Interministerial Committee for the Coordination of Industrial Policy (CIPI), lead to new technology yielding new products and new production processes. These programmes may be executed by firms producing goods and services, by consortia of productive firms, by special offices of local agencies, and by agricultural enterprises or consortia whose primary activity is of an industrial nature.

Expenditures eligible for subsidies include design, testing, development and pre-manufacturing. Incentives provided by this Fund should therefore cover the stages of the development process which follow those financed by the Fund for Applied Research. Each firm's application must include fairly detailed documentation evaluating the market opportunities and analyzing the causes and possible consequences of an innovation programme from economic and industrial perspectives.

The percentage of programme expenditure eligible for financial aid is based on the economic and technological significance of the expense. Aid is provided at two different rates, 35% and 55% of the registered cost of technological innovation programmes; the rate awarded is commensurate with the level of innovation created.

Shares of this Fund are also reserved for initiatives in the Mezzogiorno and for small- and medium-sized enterprises, at percentages equalling those of the Fund for Applied Research.

Overall, the result obtained by Law 46 by means of the IMI Fund and the Fund for Technological Innovation has been a large concentration of this measure's benefits, both geographically and with regard to the size of the firm.

In the period 1982-1988 (the last year for which data on the Fund for Applied Research were available), large industry in the north-central region received between 65% and 70% on average of all financing granted by the IMI Fund (Table 12).

During the time period studied, over L5 trillion in financial aid was granted; a very unsteady trend was followed by a sharp decline in 1988, the result of modifications introduced in Law 346 of the same year that shifted the responsibility for a portion of the financing associated with the Fund to the Ministry for Scientific Research. The share allocated to small- and medium-sized enterprises, particularly in the South, seems to have diminished considerably.

Relief provided by the Fund for Technological Innovation is more concentrated geographically, though it is perhaps more widespread among firms of different sizes, at least in the north-central region; Tables 13 and 14 show the financing granted from 1984-1989 in absolute terms and as percentages. Together the regions of Piedmont and Lombardy received 77.8% of incentives destined for large enterprises and 59.2% of funding for small- and medium-sized firms.

TABLE 12

LAW 46 OF 1982 INITIATIVES GRANTED BY
THE MINISTRY FOR SCIENTIFIC RESEARCH THROUGH THE IMI FUND
(1982-1988, billion lira)

Year	Mezzogiorno			Centre-North			Italy		
	small firms	large firms	total	small firms	large firms	total	small firms	large firms	total
A) absolute values									
1982	4.7	133.0	137.7	32.7	466.3	499.0	37.4	599.3	636.7
1983	11.6	78.6	89.6	62.9	243.1	306.0	74.5	321.1	395.6
1984	11.8	69.1	80.9	55.6	206.9	262.5	67.4	276.0	343.4
1985	5.3	210.7	216.0	86.7	636.6	723.3	92.0	847.3	939.3
1986	12.5	461.7	474.2	70.8	766.4	837.2	83.3	1,228.1	1,311.4
1987	15.5	233.9	249.4	109.1	778.6	887.7	124.6	1,012.5	1,137.1
1988	5.7	109.4	115.1	75.1	425.1	500.2	80.8	534.5	615.3
B) percentages									
1982	0.7	20.9	21.6	5.1	73.2	78.4	5.9	94.1	100.0
1983	2.9	19.7	22.6	15.9	61.5	77.4	18.8	81.2	100.0
1984	3.4	20.1	23.6	16.2	60.3	76.4	19.6	80.4	100.0
1985	0.6	22.4	23.0	9.2	67.8	77.0	9.8	90.2	100.0
1986	1.0	35.2	36.2	5.4	58.4	63.8	6.4	93.6	100.0
1987	1.4	20.6	21.9	9.6	68.5	78.1	11.0	89.0	100.0
1988	0.9	17.8	18.7	12.2	69.1	81.3	13.1	86.9	100.0

Source: IMI

TABLE 13

LAW 46 OF 1982
DISTRIBUTION, BY REGION AND SIZE OF FIRM,
OF FUND FOR TECHNOLOGICAL INNOVATION SUBSIDIES
TO 31/12/1989 (billion lira)

Region	Large enterprises				Small- and medium-sized enterprises				total			
	no.	financ.	contr.	total	no.	financ.	contr.	total	no.	financ.	contr.	total
Piemonte	64	701.4	152.2	853.7	176	137.6	12.3	149.9	240	839.0	164.6	1,003.6
Valle d'Aosta	0	0.0	0.0	0.0	2	1.6	0.0	1.6	2	1.6	0.0	1.6
Liguria	15	38.7	7.5	46.2	8	2.0	0.4	2.4	23	40.7	7.9	48.6
Lombardia	117	577.8	147.0	724.8	306	274.8	25.7	300.6	423	852.7	172.7	1,025.4
Trentino Alto Adige	1	0.2	0.0	0.2	6	5.1	0.0	5.1	7	5.3	0.0	5.3
Veneto	18	35.8	2.2	38.1	58	52.9	4.0	56.9	76	88.8	6.2	95.0
Friuli Venezia Giulia	6	17.8	0.0	17.8	13	15.4	0.1	15.5	19	33.2	0.1	33.3
Emilia Romagna	29	72.4	6.2	78.7	154	132.1	14.8	147.0	183	204.6	21.1	225.7
Marche	4	6.4	0.3	6.5	11	5.2	0.5	5.7	15	11.3	0.8	12.1
Toscana	16	74.6	3.7	78.2	30	21.0	1.2	22.2	46	95.5	4.9	100.4
Umbria	2	2.8	0.5	3.3	5	3.5	0.1	3.5	7	6.2	0.6	6.8
Lazio	14	43.8	12.2	56.0	22	26.7	1.9	28.6	36	70.4	14.1	84.5
total Centre-North	*286*	*1,571.5*	*331.9*	*1,903.4*	*791*	*677.9*	*61.0*	*738.9*	*1,077*	*2,249.5*	*392.9*	*2,642.4*
Campania	12	51.6	16.3	67.9	9	6.0	1.0	6.9	21	57.6	17.2	74.8
Abruzzo	4	13.1	2.9	16.0	7	5.7	0.1	5.8	11	18.8	3.0	21.8
Molise	0	0.0	0.0	0.0	1	0.3	0.0	0.3	1	0.3	0.0	0.3
Apulia	4	3.4	0.0	3.4	2	3.7	0.1	3.7	6	7.1	0.0	7.1
Basilicata	0	0.0	0.0	0.0	1	0.2	0.1	0.3	1	0.2	0.1	0.3
Calabria	0	0.0	0.0	0.0	1	0.5	0.3	0.8	1	0.5	0.3	0.8
Sicilia	2	19.2	12.3	31.5	4	4.8	0.1	4.9	6	24.0	12.4	36.4
Sardegna	2	6.0	0.0	6.0	0	0.0	0.0	0.0	2	6.0	0.0	6.0
total Mezzogiorno	*24*	*93.3*	*31.5*	*124.8*	*25*	*21.1*	*1.6*	*22.7*	*49*	*114.5*	*33.1*	*147.5*
total Italy	*310*	*1,664.9*	*363.4*	*2,028.3*	*816*	*699.0*	*62.6*	*761.6*	*1,126*	*2,363.9*	*426.0*	*2,789.9*

Source: Ministry of Industry

TABLE 14

LAW 46 OF 1982 DISTRIBUTION, BY REGION
AND SIZE OF FIRM, OF FUND FOR TECHNOLOGICAL INNOVATION SUBSIDIES
TO 31/12/1989
(percentages)

Region	Large enterprises				Small- and medium-sized enterprise				total			
	no.	financ.	contr.	total	no.	financ.	contr.	total	no.	financ.	contr.	total
Piemonte	20.6	42.1	41.9	42.1	21.6	19.7	19.7	19.7	21.3	35.5	38.6	36.0
Valle d'Aosta	0.0	0.0	0.0	0.0	0.2	0.2	0.0	0.2	0.2	0.1	0.0	0.1
Liguria	4.8	2.3	2.1	2.3	1.0	0.3	0.6	0.3	2.0	1.7	1.9	1.7
Lombardia	37.7	34.7	40.4	35.7	37.5	39.3	41.1	39.5	37.6	36.1	40.5	36.8
Trentino Alto Adige	0.3	0.0	0.0	0.0	0.7	0.7	0.0	0.7	0.6	0.2	0.0	0.2
Veneto	5.8	2.2	0.6	1.9	7.1	7.6	6.4	7.5	6.7	3.8	1.5	3.4
Friuli Venezia Giulia	1.9	1.1	0.0	0.9	1.6	2.2	0.1	2.0	1.7	1.4	0.0	1.2
Emilia Romagna	9.4	4.4	1.7	3.9	18.9	18.9	23.7	19.3	16.3	8.7	4.9	8.1
Marche	1.3	0.4	0.1	0.3	1.3	0.7	0.8	0.7	1.3	0.5	0.2	0.4
Toscana	5.2	4.5	1.0	3.9	3.7	3.0	2.0	2.9	4.1	4.0	1.2	3.6
Umbria	0.6	0.2	0.1	0.2	0.6	0.5	0.1	0.5	0.6	0.3	0.1	0.2
Lazio	4.5	2.6	3.4	2.8	2.7	3.8	3.1	3.8	3.2	3.0	3.3	3.0
total Centre-North	*92.3*	*94.4*	*91.3*	*93.8*	*96.9*	*97.0*	*97.5*	*97.0*	*95.6*	*95.2*	*92.2*	*94.7*
Campania	3.9	3.1	4.5	3.3	1.1	0.9	1.5	0.9	1.9	2.4	4.0	2.7
Abruzzo	1.3	0.8	0.8	0.8	0.9	0.8	0.2	0.8	1.0	0.8	0.7	0.8
Molise	0.0	0.0	0.0	0.0	0.1	0.0	0.0	0.0	0.1	0.0	0.0	0.0
Apulia	1.3	0.2	0.0	0.2	0.2	0.5	0.0	0.5	0.5	0.3	0.0	0.3
Basilicata	0.0	0.0	0.0	0.0	0.1	0.0	0.2	0.0	0.1	0.0	0.0	0.0
Calabria	0.0	0.0	0.0	0.0	0.1	0.1	0.5	0.1	0.1	0.0	0.1	0.0
Sicilia	0.6	1.2	3.4	1.6	0.5	0.7	0.1	0.6	0.5	1.0	2.9	1.3
Sardegna	0.6	0.4	0.0	0.3	0.0	0.0	0.0	0.0	0.2	0.3	0.0	0.2
total Mezzogiorno	*7.7*	*5.6*	*8.7*	*6.2*	*3.1*	*3.0*	*2.5*	*3.0*	*4.4*	*4.8*	*7.8*	*5.3*
total Italy	100.0	100.0	100.0	100.0	100.0	100.0	100.0	100.0	100.0	100.0	100.0	100.0

Source: based on Ministry of Industry data

In total, 95.2% of subsidized financing and 92.2% of contributions
flowed to central and northern Italy; the only fairly consistent flows
toward southern Italian industry involved a handful of large firms in
Campania and, to a lesser degree, in Sicily. However, within multi-
regional programmes that apply to both areas, funds are allocated
according to "preponderance" of industrial activity; in some cases, the
influence of the Mezzogiorno may be underestimated, especially with
regard to big industry. Small- and medium-sized enterprises in the
South, which accounted for 0.8% of financing received, trail far
behind their central and northern counterparts. This figure seems
even more negative given the ability of smaller enterprises in central
and northern Italy to find their way through legislation that is
definitely not in their favour. In fact, Italian SMEs outside the
Mezzogiorno hold 26.5% of total financing granted.

Overall, L2.8 trillion in financing had been granted by the Fund
for Technological Innovation until 1989, as against L4.9 trillion
committed and L10.7 trillion in programme costs. In this case, the
noticeable downturn over the last few years (Table 15) is linked to the
supplements and amendments to industrial policy legislation effected
recently.

TABLE 15

LAW 46 OF 1982
DISTRIBUTION, BY REGION AND BY YEAR,
OF FUND FOR TECHNOLOGICAL INNOVATION SUBSIDIES
(billion lira)

Region	1984	1985	1986	1987	1988	1989	total
Centre-North	209.8	341.0	591.9	632.2	424.6	442.9	2,642.4
Campania	9.3	5.2	19.2	18.5	14.2	8.5	74.8
Abruzzi	0.0	1.1	3.2	5.1	1.0	11.4	21.8
Molise	0.0	0.3	0.0	0.0	0.0	0.0	0.3
Apulia	0.0	1.7	1.0	1.1	2.3	1.0	7.1
Basilicata	0.0	0.0	0.0	0.0	0.0	0.3	0.3
Calabria	0.0	0.0	0.0	0.0	0.0	0.8	0.8
Sicily	0.5	10.5	4.0	16.9	0.1	4.5	36.4
Sardinia	0.0	0.0	0.0	1.1	0.4	4.6	6.0
Mezzogiorno	9.8	18.7	27.3	42.7	17.9	31.2	147.5
total Italy	219.6	359.7	619.2	674.9	442.5	474.1	2,789.9

Source: MINISTRY OF INDUSTRY

Tables 16 and 17 outline the participation of firms in the Fund by year and according to size as regards cost of programmes and funds committed. A study of these data reveals the advantageous position enjoyed by larger firms compared with smaller firms: their share of subsidies on the cost of programmes is higher (48.0% compared with 41.2%), as is their average cost per programme (L14.4 bn as against L3.1 bn).

These results may be considered a consequence of increased productivity linked to processes of information purchase and management, namely the information imbalance among firms, and of the high cost of the application: the cost of writing, gathering information from specialized offices, presentation and support range from L50 mn to L100 mn. Thus a situation of differentiated access over time is created, in which economies of scale enable large firms to receive financial benefits in a shorter time. Poised on the brink of technological change, large enterprises are also able to present financing proposals for programmes that are more consistent and objectively superior to those of SMEs.

The Rotative Fund experiment seems to indicate the need for industrial policy to take into account, when developing its measures, the characteristics of its beneficiaries, of their imperfect knowledge and of their heterogeneity of structure.

If intervention is viewed according to the type of innovation pursued in subsidized programmes, both Funds place more emphasis on product rather than production process or other innovation.

3.2 Fostering the Use of High-Level Equipment in Small- and Medium-Sized Enterprises

As mentioned earlier, the transfer and diffusion of technologies, or fostering the use of innovative processes developed outside the small enterprise, was the province of Law 1329 of 1965 (the Sabatini law), of Presidential Decree 902 of 1976, and of Law 696 of 1983, amended by Laws 399 of 1987 and 185 of 1989. Each piece of legislation refers specifically to small- and medium-sized enterprises.

Presidental Decree 902 of 1976 and Law 1329 of 1965 do not

TABLE 16

LAW 46 OF 1982
FUND FOR TECHNOLOGICAL INNOVATION ASSISTANCE, BY TERRITORY AND SIZE OF FIRM
(1983-1989, billion lira)

Year	Small- and medium-sized enterprises					Large enterprises					total				
	no.	program cost	financ.	contr.	Total	no.	program cost	financ.	contr.	total	no.	program cost	financ.	contr.	total
Mezzogiorno															
1983	8	19.0	7.8	0.5	8.3	10	264.6	94.6	42.6	137.2	18	283.6	102.4	43.1	145.5
1984	7	16.1	7.4	0.2	7.6	2	7.1	3.3	0.2	3.5	9	23.2	10.7	0.4	11.1
1985	7	14.9	5.8	0.9	6.7	6	41.3	17.3	2.7	20.0	13	56.2	23.1	3.6	26.7
1986	9	24.8	10.1	0.7	10.8	9	189.7	58.5	34.3	92.8	18	214.5	68.6	35.0	103.6
1987	1	1.6	0.9	0.0	0.9	5	67.6	32.9	1.5	34.4	6	69.2	33.8	1.5	35.3
1988	3	8.2	1.5	1.1	2.6	7	51.2	17.8	3.4	21.2	10	59.4	19.3	4.5	23.8
1989	2	4.5	1.1	0.3	1.4	4	80.3	16.8	8.2	25.0	6	84.8	17.9	8.5	26.4
Centre-North															
1983	177	709.3	338.1	12.4	350.5	86	2,456.4	1,061.0	242.9	1,303.9	263	3,165.7	1,399.1	255.3	1,654.4
1984	162	350.4	145.1	13.8	158.9	55	448.9	236.9	6.6	243.5	217	799.3	382.0	20.4	402.4
1985	114	286.2	112.9	12.7	125.6	36	702.5	239.4	72.3	311.7	150	988.7	352.3	85.0	437.3
1986	211	638.5	238.4	27.3	265.7	82	1,032.2	367.5	97.6	465.1	293	1,670.7	605.9	124.9	730.8
1987	135	353.1	123.5	21.1	144.7	61	588.3	227.8	35.0	262.8	196	941.4	351.3	56.2	407.3
1988	148	554.5	139.8	25.7	165.7	58	592.4	186.3	51.3	237.6	206	1,146.9	326.1	77.2	403.3
1989	161	543.9	176.5	27.4	203.9	76	623.0	218.8	49.0	267.8	237	1,166.9	395.3	76.4	471.7
Italy															
1983	185	728.3	345.9	12.9	358.8	96	2,721.0	1,155.6	285.5	1,441.1	281	3,449.3	1,501.5	298.4	1,799.9
1984	169	399.5	152.5	14.0	166.5	57	456.0	240.2	6.8	247.0	226	822.5	392.7	20.8	413.5
1985	121	366.5	118.7	13.6	132.3	42	743.8	256.7	75.0	331.7	163	1,044.9	375.4	88.6	464.0
1986	220	663.3	248.5	28.0	276.5	91	1,221.9	426.0	131.9	557.9	311	1,885.2	674.5	159.9	834.4
1987	136	354.7	124.4	21.1	145.6	66	655.9	260.7	36.5	297.2	202	1,010.6	385.1	57.7	442.8
1988	151	562.7	141.3	27.0	168.3	65	643.6	204.1	54.7	258.8	216	1,206.3	345.4	81.7	427.1
1989	163	548.4	177.6	27.7	205.3	80	703.3	235.6	57.2	292.8	243	1,251.7	413.2	84.9	498.1

Source: MINISTRY OF INDUSTRY

LAW 46 OF 1982
PERCENTAGE DISTRIBUTION BY TERRITORY
OF FUND FOR TECHNOLOGICAL INNOVATION SUBSIDIES
BY TERRITORY AND SIZE OF FIRM
(1983-89)

Year	Small- and medium-sized enterprises					Large enterprises					Total				
	no.	program cost	financ.	contr.	total	no.	program cost	financ.	contr.	totale	no.	program cost	financ.	contr.	total
A) Mezzogiorno															
1983	4.3	2.6	2.3	3.9	2.3	10.4	9.7	8.2	14.9	9.5	6.4	8.2	6.8	14.4	8.1
1984	4.1	4.4	4.9	1.4	4.6	3.5	1.6	1.4	2.9	1.4	4.0	2.8	2.7	1.9	2.7
1985	5.8	4.9	4.9	6.6	5.1	14.3	5.6	6.7	3.6	6.0	8.0	5.4	6.2	4.1	5.8
1986	4.1	3.7	4.1	2.5	3.9	9.9	15.5	13.7	26.0	16.6	5.8	11.4	10.2	21.9	12.4
1987	0.7	0.5	0.7	0.0	0.6	7.6	10.3	12.6	4.1	11.6	3.0	6.8	8.8	2.6	8.0
1988	2.0	1.5	1.1	4.1	1.5	10.8	8.0	8.7	6.2	8.2	4.6	4.9	5.6	5.5	5.6
1989	1.2	0.8	0.6	1.1	0.7	5.0	11.4	7.1	14.3	8.5	2.5	6.8	4.3	10.0	5.3
B) Centre-North															
1983	95.7	97.4	97.7	96.1	97.7	89.6	90.3	91.8	85.1	90.5	93.6	91.8	93.2	85.6	91.9
1984	95.9	95.6	95.1	98.6	95.4	96.5	98.4	98.6	97.1	98.6	96.0	97.2	97.3	98.1	97.3
1985	94.2	95.1	95.1	93.4	94.9	85.7	94.4	93.3	96.4	94.0	92.0	94.6	93.8	95.9	94.9
1986	95.9	96.3	95.9	97.5	96.1	90.1	84.5	86.3	74.0	83.4	94.2	88.6	89.8	78.1	87.6
1987	99.3	99.5	99.3	100.0	99.4	92.4	89.7	87.4	95.9	88.4	97.0	93.2	91.2	97.4	92.0
1988	98.0	98.5	98.9	95.9	98.5	89.2	92.0	91.3	93.8	91.8	95.4	95.1	94.4	94.5	94.4
1989	98.8	99.2	99.4	98.9	99.3	95.0	88.6	92.9	85.7	91.5	97.5	93.2	95.7	90.0	94.7

Source: based on MINISTRY OF INDUSTRY data

specifically promote technological innovation; rather, they foster overall investment by granting interest account contributions.

More specifically, Presidental Decree 902 of 1976 regulates the granting of short- and medium-term credit at subsidized rates for investment in programmes involving new plant and equipment, enlargement or modernization effected by small- and medium-sized enterprises in the north-central region. Eligible programmes, the ceiling for financing and the percentage of eligible expense are geographically defined.

Among the measures aimed at promoting the diffusion of new techonologies by subsidizing purchases of machinery, the oldest piece of legislation, Law 1329 of 1965 (the Sabatini law) should be examined first. Originally conceived to provide relief to tool machinery producers, the law provides for the purchase of machinery within certain categories by means of bills of exchange, discounted at the appropriate medium-term special credit institutions and re-discounted at the Bank of Italy or at the Central Institute for Medium-Term credit (Mediocredito centrale).

The re-discounting of bills is coupled with another incentive granted by the Mediocredito centrale: an interest account contribution equal to the cost of the discount transaction is paid by this Insitute to lower the interest rate applied to the installment payment of the firm requesting the aid. This contribution, paid in advance in one lump sum, covers the difference between revenues calculated at the reference rate and at the subsidized rate. The latter is equal to 35% of the reference rate (in effect on the day the bill is discounted) for machinery purchased in order to be used in the Mezzogiorno, and 45% of the reference rate for machinery purchased to be used in the rest of the country.

Law 1329 sets no limits on the size of enterprises eligible for financial assistance.

Law 696 of 1983, amended by Law 399 of 1987 (which raised the level of machinery technology) and by Law 185 of 1989, creates a system to subsidize the purchase or rental of high-level production equipment by artisan firms and SMEs.

The instrument used is the cash grant, originally commensurate with the geographical location of the firm, and, more recently under

Law 185 of 1989, with size in the case of north-central firms. The latter enterprises are entitled to a contribution equalling 25% of the cost of machinery net of VAT for enterprises with up to 99 employees; those with staff of 100-199 and 200-300 employees are eligible for grants of 20% and 10% respectively.

The maximum contribution, initially set at L245 mn by Law 696 of 1983, has been raised by Law 399 of 1987 to L350 mn for companies located in central or nothern Italy. Southern Italian firms are entitled to 32% of the investment cost, up to L600 mn. Each company may apply for the subsidized purchase of no more than two machines; moreover, Law 399 of 1987 forbids financing of investments below L50 mn in total.

Whereas Law 399 of 1987 sets a threshold for Law 696 of 1983 by restricting the level of eligible investment, the Sabatini law, which had no threshold, was modified so as to simplify the procedure involved in granting incentives to small enterprise. These modifications caused a drop in the average amount of financing subsidized under the Sabatini law and brought about a year-over-year rise (still unnoticable in the available figures) in the amount of assistance provided under Law 696 of 1983.

Thus the two laws increasingly satisfy needs that are differentiated quantitatively and qualitatively. The former law aims primarily at providing smaller amounts of financing to smaller firms in need of relatively unsophisticated equipment.

The latter is directed at purchases of more costly high-technology equipment.

The differentiation between the innovation incentives of small- and medium-sized enterprises probably has repercussions pertaining to geographical area. During the 1980s southern Italian enterprises increased their share of transactions and amount funded under Law 1329, which in recent years has witnessed an overall rise in the number of transactions and in the amount funded (Table 18).

Whereas the number of southern Italian firms requesting aid is on the rise, average investment has fallen sharply (especially if values are measured at constant prices rather than at current prices). Requests by enterprises in the Mezzogiorno for the benefits provided for under more recent legislation is generally quite low.

TABLE 18

LAW 1329 OF 1965
NUMBER AND AMOUNT OF OPERATIONS
SUBSIDIZED BY MEDIOCREDITO CENTRALE
(1980-1988)

Year	Mezzogiorno			Centre-North			Italy		
	number	amount	average amount	number	amount	average amount	number	amount	average amount
A) absolute values									
1980	361	24.9	0.069	3,452	304.5	0.088	3,813	329.4	0.086
1981	473	34.9	0.074	5,088	487.5	0.096	5,561	522.4	0.094
1982	478	37.7	0.079	5,400	537.7	0.106	5,878	611.4	0.104
1983	383	41.1	0.107	3,570	546.5	0.153	3,953	587.6	0.149
1984	370	52.3	0.141	2,833	598.4	0.211	3,203	650.7	0.203
1985	825	91.7	0.111	4,983	816.3	0.164	5,808	908.0	0.156
1986	1,458	147.6	0.101	7,661	1,424.7	0.186	9,119	1,572.3	0.172
1987	5,628	439.2	0.078	24,632	3,518.0	0.143	30,260	3,957.2	0.131
1988	4,487	385.4	0.086	20,863	3,216.9	0.154	25,350	3,602.3	0.142
B) percentages									
1980	9.5	7.6		90.5	92.4		100.0	100.0	
1981	8.5	6.7		91.5	93.3		100.0	100.0	
1982	8.1	6.2		91.9	93.8		100.0	100.0	
1983	9.7	7.0		90.3	93.0		100.0	100.0	
1984	11.6	8.0		88.4	92.0		100.0	100.0	
1985	14.2	10.1		85.8	89.9		100.0	100.0	
1986	16.0	9.4		84.0	90.6		100.0	100.0	
1987	18.6	11.1		81.4	88.9		100.0	100.0	
1988	17.7	10.7		82.3	89.3		100.0	100.0	

Source: MEDIOCREDITO CENTRALE

TABLE 19

LAW 696 OF 1983
NUMBER OF APPROVED REQUESTS AND AMOUNT OF ALLOCATED FUNDS
(billion lira)

A) absolute values

Territory	Year	Industry			Artisan firms			Total		
		no.	invest.	contrib. granted	no.	invest.	contrib. granted	no.	invest.	contrib. granted
Mezzogiorno........	1984	19	3.2	1.0	2	0.3	0.1	21	3.5	1.1
	1985	106	24.0	7.7	28	2.2	0.7	134	26.2	8.4
	1986	189	40.9	13.1	43	2.7	0.9	232	453.6	14.0
	1987	213	44.0	14.1	46	2.9	0.9	259	47.0	15.0
Centre-North......	1984	1,833	348.4	86.7	787	69.8	17.4	2,620	418.2	104.1
	1985	5,132	881.6	219.9	2,262	184.9	46.2	7,394	1,066.5	266.1
	1986	8,021	1,347.2	336.1	3,368	277.4	69.3	11,389	1,624.6	405.4
	1987	8,284	1,386.4	345.9	3,488	284.2	71.0	11,772	1,670.6	416.9
Italy.............	1984	1,852	351.5	87.7	789	70.1	17.5	2,641	421.7	105.2
	1985	5,238	905.6	227.6	2,290	187.1	46.9	7,528	1,092.8	274.5
	1986	8,210	1,388.1	349.2	3,411	280.1	70.2	11,621	1,668.2	419.3
	1987	8,497	1,430.4	360.0	3,534	287.1	71.9	12,031	1,717.5	431.9

B) percentages

Territory	Year	Industry			Artisan firms			Total		
		no.	invest.	contrib. granted	no.	invest.	contrib. granted	no.	invest.	contrib. granted
Mezzogiorno........	1984	1.0	0.9	1.2	0.3	0.4	0.6	0.8	0.8	1.1
	1985	2.0	2.7	3.4	1.2	1.2	1.5	1.8	2.4	3.1
	1986	2.3	2.9	3.7	1.3	1.0	1.2	2.0	2.6	3.3
	1987	2.5	3.1	3.9	1.3	1.0	1.3	2.2	2.7	3.5
Centre-North......	1984	99.0	99.1	98.8	99.7	99.6	99.4	99.2	99.2	98.9
	1985	98.0	97.3	96.6	98.8	98.8	98.5	98.2	97.6	96.9
	1986	97.7	97.1	96.3	98.7	99.0	98.8	98.0	97.4	96.7
	1987	97.5	96.9	96.1	98.7	99.0	98.7	97.8	97.3	96.5
Italy.............	1984	100.0	100.0	100.0	100.0	100.0	100.0	100.0	100.0	100.0
	1985	100.0	100.0	100.0	100.0	100.0	100.0	100.0	100.0	100.0
	1986	100.0	100.0	100.0	100.0	100.0	100.0	100.0	100.0	100.0
	1987	100.0	100.0	100.0	100.0	100.0	100.0	100.0	100.0	100.0

Source: based on MINISTRY OF INDUSTRY data

As shown in Table 19, the quota of financing subsidized in the Mezzogiorno under Law 696 from 1984 to 1987 is extremely low, at approximately 2% of applications, 2.5% of investment and 3% of total contributions granted. Very few artisan enterprises in the South receive aid, while a significant number of central and northern artisan enterprises apply for intervention (this number appears to be all the more significant, given the technological content standards set by the law). Average values of investment and contributions are provided in table 20.

TABLE 20

LAW 696 OF 1983
NUMBER OF APPROVED REQUESTS AND AMOUNT OF
ALLOCATED FUNDS
(billion lira)

Territory	Year	Industry		Artisan firms		Total	
		avg. invest.	avg. contrib.	avg. invest.	avg. contrib.	avg. invest.	avg. contrib.
Mezzogiorno	1984	0.167	0.053	0.155	0.050	0.166	0.053
	1985	0.227	0.073	0.079	0.025	0.196	0.063
	1986	0.216	0.069	0.064	0.020	0.188	0.060
	1987	0.207	0.066	0.063	0.020	0.181	0.058
Centre-North	1984	0.190	0.047	0.089	0.022	0.160	0.040
	1985	0.172	0.043	0.082	0.020	0.144	0.036
	1986	0.168	0.042	0.082	0.021	0.143	0.036
	1987	0.167	0.042	0.081	0.020	0.142	0.035
Italy........	1984	0.190	0.047	0.089	0.022	0.160	0.040
	1985	0.173	0.043	0.082	0.020	0.145	0.036
	1986	0.169	0.043	0.082	0.021	0.144	0.036
	1987	0.168	0.042	0.081	0.020	0.143	0.036

Source: based on MINISTRY OF INDUSTRY data

Aid requested by southern Italian compaines under laws 399 of 1987 and 185 of 1989 is virtually non-existent, as shown in Tables 21 and 22.

TABLE 21

LAWS 399 OF 1987 AND 185 OF 1989
NUMBER OF APPROVED REQUESTS AND AMOUNT OF
ALLOCATED FUNDS
(billion lira)

A) absolute values

Territory	Year	Industry			Artisan firms			Total		
		no.	invest.	contrib. granted	no.	invest.	contrib. granted	no.	invest.	contrib. granted
Mezzogiorno	1987	0	0.0	0.0	1	0.2	0.1	1	0.2	0.1
	1988	9	3.8	1.2	1	0.2	0.1	10	4.0	1.3
	1989	16	4.8	1.5	3	0.4	0.1	19	5.2	1.7
Centre-North	1987	652	227.6	56.9	265	48.7	12.2	917	276.4	69.1
	1988	2,350	737.4	183.4	1,054	176.9	44.2	3,404	914.3	227.6
	1989	3,058	932.8	230.2	1,592	254.0	63.4	4,650	1,186.8	293.6
Italy	1987	652	227.6	56.9	266	48.9	12.2	918	276.6	69.1
	1988	2,359	741.2	184.6	1,055	177.1	44.2	3,414	918.3	228.8
	1989	3,074	937.6	231.7	1,595	254.4	63.6	4,669	1,192.0	295.3

B) percentages

Territory	Year	Industry			Artisan firms			Total		
		no.	invest.	contrib. granted	no.	invest.	contrib. granted	no.	invest.	contrib. granted
Mezzogiorno	1987	0.0	0.0	0.0	0.4	0.5	0.6	0.1	0.1	0.1
	1988	0.4	0.5	0.7	0.1	0.1	0.2	0.3	0.4	0.6
	1989	0.5	0.5	0.7	0.2	0.1	0.2	0.4	0.4	0.6
Centre-North	1987	100.0	100.0	100.0	99.6	99.5	99.4	99.9	99.9	99.9
	1988	99.6	99.5	99.3	99.9	99.9	99.8	99.7	99.6	99.4
	1989	99.5	99.5	99.3	99.8	99.9	99.8	99.6	99.6	99.4
Italy	1987	100.0	100.0	100.0	100.0	100.0	100.0	100.0	100.0	100.0
	1988	100.0	100.0	100.0	100.0	100.0	100.0	100.0	100.0	100.0
	1989	100.0	100.0	100.0	100.0	100.0	100.0	100.0	100.0	100.0

Source: based on MINISTRY OF INDUSTRY data

TABLE 22

LAWS 399 OF 1987 AND 185 OF 1989
NUMBER OF APPROVED REQUESTS AND AMOUNT OF
ALLOCATED FUNDS
(billion lira)

Territory	Year	Industry		Artisan firms		Total	
		avg. invest.	avg. contrib.	avg. invest.	avg. contrib.	avg. invest.	avg. contrib.
Mezzogiorno	1987	-	-	0.225	0.072	0.225	0.072
	1988	0.424	0.136	0.225	0.072	0.404	0.129
	1989	0.302	0.096	0.121	0.039	0.273	0.087
Centre-North	1987	0.349	0.087	0.184	0.046	0.301	0.075
	1988	0.314	0.078	0.168	0.042	0.269	0.067
	1989	0.305	0.075	0.160	0.040	0.255	0.063
Italy........	1987	0.349	0.087	0.184	0.046	0.301	0.075
	1988	0.314	0.078	0.168	0.042	0.269	0.067
	1989	0.305	0.075	0.159	0.040	0.255	0.063

Source: based on MINISTRY OF INDUSTRY data

3.3 Intervention by Sector, Industrial Restructuring and Salvage Measures

As mentioned earlier, the other driving force of industrial policy during the '80s was the need to offset the failure of the market or of individual firms by promoting the reconversion and restructuring of industry.

The first case of intervention by industry for review is the rationalization of the steel industry under Law 193 of 1984. This law provided incentives for the reduction of productive capacity, for the modernization of production cycles and for industrial development in other sectors. Grants were the instrument used to further this objective. Assistance received in the Mezzogiorno was extremely limited (approximately 5% of the total); the law tended to favour the private-sector steel industry, concentrated mainly in the Centre and in the North.

Law 63 of 1982 is a temporary measure of intervention by sector for the transformation of the civil electronic industry. This law aims at concentrating and rationalizing production in order to increase productivity, to benefit from economies of scale and to regain market share nationally and internationally using the available trademarks. The instrument created to achieve these objectives is a finance company for electronic restructuring known as the REL (Ristrutturazions Elettronica SpA), of which the Ministry of Industry and IRI own 95% and 5% respectively. Its purpose is to coordinate the five-year transformation programmes of enterprises which receive assistance.

Available incentives take two forms: the setting up, by the REL and the enterprises in this sector, of at least one operating firm; and the finance company's holding a minority interest in the capital increase of existing enterprises. At the end of the five-year period, the shares, or stock previously held by the public finance company may be redeemed at par by the private shareholders. From 1983-1987, assistance provided in the Mezzogiorno stood at 10% of the national figure.

Law 808 of 1985 concerning the aeronautic industry provides for three types of incentives; state loans for the development of programmes and studies, and for participation in international programme aimed at designing or developing new aeronautic products; interest account contributions for aeronautic products, developed internationally, at the series production stage; or interest account contributions on installment payments made by end-users of aeronautic products developed in international programmes. At over 70% of the national total, relief provided to the Mezzogiorno has been substantial.

Law 675 fo 1977 was created to foster industrial restructuring and reconversion. This law provided for the creation by the Ministry of Industry of a fund whose four-year term was extended to 1982, to grant financial subsidies to manufacturing, mining and quarrying enterprises involved in restructuring and reconversion projects in accordance with the law.

Under this scheme, three types of intervention were available: interest contributions on medium-term credit and on bond issues; low-cost loans from the Ministry of Industry; and capital account contributions reserved for initiatives in the Mezzogiorno. A total of 40% of the fund's initial grant was reserved for southern Italian enterprises. At the end of the Restructuring and Reconversion Fund experiment, residual funds were allocated under Law 46 of 1982 for technological innovation.

Projects taken on by southern Italian firms received an impressive share of financing, as shown in Table 23; the large number of requests received from sectors present in the Mezzogiorno (steel, transport, chemicals) was a determinant factor.

The institution which offers incentives to failed enterprises is known as GEPI. Created by Law 184 of 1971, GEPI is a joint-stock company whose shareholders include IMI (50%) and the state-owned enterprise boldings (EFIM, ENI, and IRI). Its purpose, to contribute toward maintaining and increasing levels of employment jeopardized by short-term diffuculties of productive enterprises, is achieved by providing assistance in the form of restructuring or reconversion plans enabling troubled firms to re-enter the market.

The instruments used to pursue these objectives are as follows: the purchase of shares in individual firms; the setting up of a company to manage or transfer ownership of industrial firms; and the financing, even ta subsidized rates, of public compaines.

The two types of intervention governed by Law 49 of 1985 (the Marcora law) take the form of two funds. The first, a rotative fund for development and cooperation, is managed by the special section for cooperation credit (Sezione speciale per il credito alla cooperazione) of the Banca nazionale del lavoro; however, in this case it is the Minister of Industry who grants the subsidies on the basis of recommendations made by the interministerial committee concerned (CIPI). Production and labour cooperatives are eligible if their members are employees of enterprises which have reduce or ceased activity wishing to renew plant and equipment or to begin new productive acivity in an effort to save jobs. The instrument used is a cash grant aimed at increasing the capital of these cooperatives. The amount of aid received is commensurate, within the limits set by the fund, with assistance provided by the Cassa Integrazione (State-Financed Redundancy Fund).

4. - A few conclusions on the policies to stimulate industry in southern Italy would be appropriate. Earlier, we observed that special

TABLE 23

LAW 675 OF 1977
ELIGIBLE INVESTMENTS AND SUBSIDIES
(amounts in billion lira and number employed in thousands)

A) absolute values

Territory	Year	No. of programmes	Fixed inv.	Inventories	Total inv.	Eligible financing	Subs. loans	Cap. acct. contr.	No. Employed (before)	No. Employed (after)
Centre-North..	1980	14	62.9	9.2	72.1	33.6	—	—	4,756	4,729
	1981	30	401.0	29.0	430.0	177.7	31.4	—	22,017	20,299
	1982	31	1,329.4	136.2	1,465.6	488.7	200.3	34.2	48,937	55,315
	1983	39	1,163.3	42.1	1,205.4	342.7	107.4	2.1	43,015	36,896
	1984	53	1,988.2	31.5	2,019.6	751.4	214.7	23.4	64,894	62,633
	1985	6	65.9	3.0	69.0	26.3	6.1	0.0	9,214	6,648
Mezzogiorno ..	1980	0	0.0	0.0	0.0	0.0	0.0	0.0	0	0
	1981	13	1,529.3	166.2	1,695.5	584.7	286.7	299.6	41,716	35,811
	1982	13	233.3	20.6	253.9	92.1	32.0	46.2	1,544	3,611
	1983	25	392.3	133.0	525.3	214.3	183.0	144.6	27,074	23,953
	1984	14	1,227.9	15.0	1,242.9	227.8	291.4	251.7	12,096	11,498
	1985	3	41.4	0.0	41.4	14.8	5.8	8.4	2,682	1,122
Italy..........	1980	14	62.9	9.2	72.1	33.6	0.0	0.0	4,756	4,729
	1981	43	1,930.3	195.2	2,125.6	762.4	318.0	299.6	63,733	56,110
	1982	44	1,562.7	156.8	1,719.5	580.8	232.3	80.4	50,481	58,926
	1983	64	1,555.6	175.1	1,730.7	557.0	290.4	146.6	70,089	60,849
	1984	67	3,216.0	46.5	3,262.5	979.2	506.1	275.1	76,990	74,131
	1985	9	107.3	3.0	110.4	41.1	11.9	8.4	11,896	7,770

Source: based on MINISTRY OF INDUSTRY data

TABLE 23 cont.

B) percentages

Territory	Year	No. of programmes	Fixed inv.	Inventories	Total inv.	Eligible financing	Subs. loans	Cap. acct. contr.	No. Employed (before)	No. Employed (after)
Centre-North ..	1980	100.0	100.0	100.0	100.0	100.0	0.0	0.0	100.0	100.0
	1981	69.8	20.8	14.9	20.2	23.3	9.9	0.0	34.5	36.2
	1982	70.5	85.1	86.8	85.2	84.1	86.2	42.6	96.9	93.9
	1983	60.9	74.8	24.0	69.6	61.5	37.0	1.4	61.4	60.6
	1984	79.1	61.8	67.7	61.9	76.7	42.4	8.5	84.3	84.5
	1985	66.7	61.4	100.0	62.5	64.1	51.5	0.0	77.5	85.6
Mezzogiorno ..	1980	0.0	0.0	0.0	0.0	0.0	0.0	0.0	0.0	0.0
	1981	30.2	79.2	85.1	79.8	76.7	90.1	100.0	65.5	63.8
	1982	29.5	14.9	13.2	14.8	15.9	13.8	57.4	3.1	6.1
	1983	39.1	25.2	76.0	30.4	38.5	63.0	98.6	38.6	39.4
	1984	20.9	38.2	32.3	38.1	23.3	57.6	91.5	15.7	15.5
	1985	33.3	38.6	0.0	37.5	35.9	48.5	100.0	22.5	14.4

Source: based on MINISTRY OF INDUSTRY data

intervention and national legislation that held funds in reserve did little to speed up industrialization in the Mezzogiorno during the 1980s. Neither type of instrument succeeded in offsetting the tendency of the market toward the concentration of capital in north-central industry, buoyed by international stimuli and by the macro-economic policies (on money supply, public debt and exchange rate) adopted in Italy.

Further, incentive policies — with much administrative latitude, often unclear an unfailignly complex procedures, and burdensome

TABLE 24

TRENDS IN ALLOCATED FUNDS AND PAYMENTS OF SOCIAL SECURITY REDUCTIONS

Year	Chapter 3589 (1)	Chapter 3612 (2)	Chapter 3614 (3)	Chapter 3620 (4)	Total
allocated funds					
1981 ..	500.0	174.5	2,588.6	3,758.0	7,021.1
1982 ..	0.0	0.0	0.0	0.0	0.0
1983 ..	2,921.8	596.1	3,422.6	4,475.0	11,415.5
1984 ..	0	0.0	0.0	0.0	0.0
1985 ..	2,600.0	600.0	3,640.0	4,634.0	11,524.0
1986 ..	3,275.0	950.0	7,077.9	0.0	11,302.9
1987 ..	3,202.9	1,107.7	7,140.0	0.0	11,450.6
1988 ..	3,785.0	1,287.7	8,387.0	0.0	13,459.7
1989 (*)	4,081.0	1,481.7	348.0	0.0	5,910.7
payments					
1981 ..	0.0	0.0	1,017.8	1,300.0	2,317.8
1982 ..	1,327.0	174.5	5,446.0	6,261.3	13,208.8
1983 ..	3,421.8	0.0	3,080.3	4,027.5	10,529.6
1984 ..	2,200.0	1,630.0	3,645.8	4,670.9	12,146.7
1985 ..	2,600.0	650.0	3,618.2	4,618.0	11,486.2
1986 ..	3,241.6	950.0	7,113.0	0.0	11,304.6
1987 ..	4,236.3	1,107.7	7,221.7	0.0	11,565.7
1988 ..	3,113.2	1,287.7	7,563.3	0.0	11,964.2
1989 ..	0.0	1,481.7	1,062.0	0.0	2,543.7

(1) Contributions to the state to lower southern firms social security payments.
(2) Reductions in the contributions of industrial, artisan and hotelkeeping enterprises.
(3) Reductions in the social security contributions due under Art. 1 of law 782.
(4) Reductions in social security contributions due under other articles of Law 782.
(*) Provisory data.
Source: based on data of the *Relazione generale sulla situazione economica del Paese,* BANK OF ITALY, 1990

requests addressed to enteprises — by their very nature have led
potential beneficiaries, notably smaller firms located in the South, to
regard the few incentives made available to southern Italian enterprises as unattractive or inaccessible.

Given the circumstances, it should come as no surprise that
southern Italian entrepreneurs are highly appreciative of automatic
benefits such as reductions in social security contributions; as shown
in Table 24, payments of this type of incentive surpass by far all other
means of financing made available to industry in this region.

Industrialization policies in the South have suffered not only from
the unfavourable climate for the decentralization of production
throughout Italy, from bureaucratic delays or from the high cost of
applications for smaller entrepreneurs. Fitted into a larger framework,
namely the growing internationalization of the Italian economy,
industrial policies for the South seem to have devoted little attention
to the areas of weakness of southern industry, such as competition in
international markets, or the ability to export.

All available indicators reveal an exceptionally low capacity for
export in the Mezzogiorno; moreover, export flows from the South
stem primarily from large industry (Table 25 and Graph 9).

The big question concerning the southern Italian industrial
apparatus is how to create, ove the next few years, a steady flow of
exports and how to include small enterprises in this flow. Incentive
polices must either find a suitable answer to this question, or risk
being accused or suspected of acting as a curtain to southern Italian
entrepreneurs, shutting out not only foreign competition but also
international markets.

DISTRIBUTION OF EXPORTING FIRMS AND EXPORT REVENUES

Export turnover	Mezzogiorno exporting firms		Centre-North exporting firms		Mezzogiorno export revenues		Centre-North export revenues	
	no.	%	no.	%	no.	%	no.	%
L. 0 - 50 mn	5,375	53.6	28,373	39.3	108	1.1	634	0.6
50 - 100 mn	1,214	12.1	8,139	11.3	98	1.0	671	0.6
100 - 500 mn	1,915	19.1	17,006	23.6	514	5.1	4,690	4.4
L. 500 - 1 bn	592	5.9	6,261	8.7	480	4.7	5,091	4.8
1 - 5 bn	735	7.3	9,192	12.7	1,751	17.3	23,139	21.8
5 - 10 bn	97	1.0	1,763	2.4	779	7.7	13,937	13.2
10 - 50 bn	76	0.8	1,215	1.7	1,578	15.6	26,389	24.9
50 - 100 bn	16	0.2	85	0.1	686	6.8	6,502	6.1
over 100 bn	16	0.2	75	0.1	4,123	40.8	24,907	23.5
Total	10,029	100.0	72,109	100.0	10,117	100.0	105,960	100.0

Source: based on ICE (Institute for Foreign Trade) data

GRAPH 9

EXPORTS, RANKED BY TURNOVER

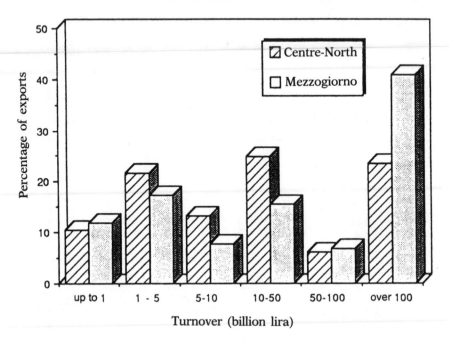

BIBLIOGRAPHY

[1] Brancati R.: «Gli incentivi alle attività produttive», *Delta*, Jan.-Feb. no. 40, 1990.

[2] D'Antonio M.: *Il mezzogiorno nella struttura dell'economia italiana*, Milano, 1990.

[3] Monitor: *Il commercio con l'estero dell'industria meridionale*, Mimeo, Napoli, January. 1990.

[4] Monitor: *Il sostegno all'industria del mezzogiorno. Un bilancio critico*, Mimeo, Napoli, June, 1990.

[5] Nisticò A. - Prosperetti L.: «I divari nord-sud di produttività industriale», *Rivista economica del mezzogiorno*, no. 1, 1989.

[6] Scanagatta G.: «Le leggi nazionali di incentivazione per le piccole e medie imprese industriali e il mezzogiorno», *Rivista economica del mezzogiorno*, no. 1, 1989.

[7] Svimez: *Rapporti 1989 e 1990 sull'economia del mezzogiorno*, Bologna, Svimez, 1989 e 1990.

Industrial Policies and Territorial Development in Northern and Central Regions of Italy

Maurizio Tenenbaum (*)
Università «La Sapienza», Roma

1. - Introduction

The literature on the Italian industrial policy in the 1980s has recently been given a new boost which seems to be stronger than would have been legitimately expected at the end of the decade.

With reference to the previous decade it is useful to remember that at that time the debate took place in a context in which, despite the recovery in 1976-1979, the difficulties of private and public firms were such as to induce the entrepreneurs to make a proposal for an industrial policy that was defined "factor-oriented industrial policy" (1), as opposed to the sector-oriented one on which the pre-existing legislation was based, referring only to the problems of the industrial reorganization or reconversion and to the related rescue of trouble enterprises. In other words, the idea characterizing the proposal by the entrepreneurs was to request industrial policy interventions of a horizontal type, i.e. usable by all firms, instead of vertical interventions typical of the sector plans started in the second half of the 1970s (law 675 of 1977) (2).

(*) Special thanks are owed to Dr. G. Rotino for the supply of full data on the Sabatini Law, and to Dr. A. Ranieri and Dr. G. Galli for their help in the statistical processings.
(1) See CONFINDUSTRIA [16], pp. 1086-93. Numbers in square brackets refer to the Bibliography.
(2) This proposal was partially accepted through the Law 46 of 1982 (Art. 1-19) with the revolving fund for technological innovation, which appears aimed at all enterprises involved in innovation, processing and production programmes.

The current debate is taking place in a totally different context. The 1980s witnessed the reorganization of the large industrial firms, both in real and financial terms, while small and medium-sized enterprises (SMEs) seemed less competitive, hence the questioning of the validity of the model of "flexible specialization" which was considered to have originated the successes of the 1970s. The problems considered "critical" for the SMEs (mainly for the small ones) are today brought back to two phenomena, technological and organizational adjustment, and the growth of the services sector, which seem more and more connected with the too limited operational size of the firm (3). Additionally, the progressive internationalization process of the Italian economy in the 1980s must be considered together with the acceleration that will be recorded starting from 1993 with the completion of the European single market and the consequent need for a better resource allocation to be achieved through a higher efficiency of the market.

Within this frame of dynamic growth it seems even more "peculiar" that in the areas where the manufacturing sector is more widespread the economic policy debate pays very little attention to the territorial aspects of the industrial policy. As a matter of fact, the debate seems to focus almost exclusively on the problems of the North-South territorial reequilibrium, actually neglecting to thoroughly investigate themes concerning the relation existing between the development in northern and central areas and the industrial policy.

In the official documents, and also in the proposals put forward at a legislative level and in the more authoritative literature, all analyses seem to be focused on the inadequacies of the industrial policy carried out with regard to the following aspects: obsolescence of the instruments used, diversion of the employed resources towards targets which differ from the planned ones, replacement of the legislative instrument with the administrative one, scattering of competences, insufficient facilities to SMEs (4).

The little attention paid to the problems of territorial reequili-

---

(3) See BARCA F. - FRASCA F.M. [7], pp. 224-80.
(4) See CER [11], pp. 253-97.

brium is obviously due to the fact that no legislative interventions addressed to the reequilibrium were carried out, but only initiatives aiming at supporting the productive apparatus in its industrial localization: specific *ad hoc* rescue interventions started for instance through GEPI or, more recently, the reindustrialization plan prepared by IRI in front of the crisis of the iron and steel domestic industry.

In the few instances in which a territorial analysis of the industrial policy grants was carried out, a mere description of the distribution by region of the transfer payments (5) was given, or, in other cases, emphasis was placed once more on the growing gap between Centre-North and South of Italy (6). The North-South gap certainly represents the historical problem of the Italian economic development, but in our opinion the failure to analyse the relationship existing in the 1980s between the Italian industrial policy and the productive evolution in northern and central regions is a serious shortcoming of the current debate.

Naturally, one of the reasons why analyses at a territorial level were not carried out is to be found in the scarcity of available infracensus data, and in the high "risk" of interpretations based on estimated data, especially in the imminence of the new census-taking. However, the very recent availability of the new series of regional accounting reelaborated by ISTAT allows a better estimate of the industrial value added at a sectorial level and a verification of the existing link between the transfer payment flows relative to the main industrial policy laws and the sectorial dynamics of regional production. In addition, in one case it was possible to make a full regions-sectors cross section in a sufficiently wide time series as to be explanatory of the medium-term trends (Sabatini Law).

Another group of industrial policy interventions which was neglected by the more authoritative literature concerns the legislative interventions of territorial reequilibrium carried out by the regions following the delegation in the field of equipped industrial areas and industrial syndicates (Law 382 of 1975 and DPR 616 of 1977). Such intervention, though limited as to financial resources, seem to supply

---

(5) See SCANAGATTA G. [37], 281-301.
(6) See LA NOCE M. [27], pp. 251-80.

very interesting elements for the industrial policy, as they represent the most direct link with the perculiarities of each industrial area, and therefore any indicate, case by case, the local characteristics of the problems of the industrial sector (7). The lack of a connection between the industrial policy as expressed by the national legislation and the requirements codified in the regional interventions is further proof of the previously mentioned little interest in the territorial reequilibrium of the firms.

Finally, there are some recent studies on specific industrial areas with different charactristics (industrial districts, industrial areas, industrial territories) which in their peculiarity give — on the basis of thorough sample surveys at the firms — precise indications on the needs of the same firms and on the shortcomings of the Italian industrial policies (Massa Carrara, Terni, Valdarno, Piombino). The analyses and the operational proposals resulting from area studies, discussed from time at a local level in "economic conferences" promoted by the Regions and/or by other local Authorities, are in our opinion a rich source of elements and indications for reinterpreting some deindustrialization processes in progress, and for defining better the strategy of national industrial policy.

2. - Industrial Policies and Industrial Development at Regional Level: the Obviousness of a Diversion

Analysing the dynamics of the industrial incentive schemes carried out during the 1980s in their territorial and sectorial distribution, the interpretative difficulties are clearly evident for those wishing to verify at an empirical level not only some theoretical approach, but also a simple cause and effect relation between the public transfer payments to the firms and the dynamics of the productive sectors at a regional level. The prevailing opinion in literature, however, is that the available theoretical models are inadequate to interpret industrial policies not only in Italy, but also in other industrialized countries. This inadequacy derives both from reasons of social targets (employ-

---

(7) Lee REGIONE LOMBARDIA, [35], i.e. [36].

ment instead of productive efficiency of the industrial policies) and, in many cases, from the exploitation of the same interventions in order to justify in economic terms a purely political target (8).

Being this the approach, which may be shared, it seems necessary to reduce the interpretative ambition and to limit the analysis of the quantitative evidences to the research of the main connections between the public incentives and the sectorial and territorial development of production.

An industrial policy incentive represents an advantage for the entrepreneur, that consists in the reduction of the charges on interest accounts, or, in case of financings with no repayment, of the amount of invested capital.

In both cases the effects are a support of the industrial production: in the first case, if the investment goes to increase the productive basis and the market penetration, the industrial policy may cause an increase in the production of the firm receiving the financing; in the second case the industrial policy through the improvement of the productive efficiency should allow to keep the industrial production at higher levels than those obtainable in the absence of incentives. The final result should in any case consist in the increase in the percent weight of the industrial production in those sectors and geographic areas where the incentive flow was more considerable.

Should the industrial policy target include also a territorial reequilibrium, we would record a diversion of the incentive flow towards those areas and sectors one wishes to boost, and the corresponding modification of their relative weight as compared to the *ex-ante* situation.

A first appraisal of the main national incentive laws may be effected by comparing the distribution of financed investments by region with the value of industrial production.

As data clearly show (Table 1), in the considered period the total of activated investments does not follow, or better, is not synchronous with, the production amount of the northern and central regions. The simple concentration ratio used (difference between territorial distribution of the financed investments and territorial

---

(8) This is for instance A. Gerschenkron's position, referred to and supported by M. Grillo and F. Silva, see GRILLO M. - SILVA F. [21].

TABLE 1

INVESTMENTS FINANCED THROUGH THE MAIN LAWS
ON INDUSTRIAL INCENTIVES
IN THE PERIOD 1980-1987, INCLUDING THE SABATINI LAW (*)
(billion lira at 1980 prices)

Region	Financed investments (a)	% (b)	Industrial value added total 1980-1987 (c)	% (d)	Concentration index (b)-(d)
Piemonte-Val d'Aosta ..	4,658	20.20	136,067	14.30	5.90
Liguria	281	1.22	31,254	3.28	− 2.07
Lombardia	3,234	14.02	307,453	32.30	−18.28
Trentino Alto Adige	5,020	21.77	17,121	1.80	19.97
Veneto	658	2.86	112,886	11.86	− 9.01
Friuli Venezia Giulia ..	1,115	4.84	27,075	2.84	1.99
Emilia Romagna	2,186	9.48	110,611	11.62	− 2.14
Marche	971	4.21	32,056	3.37	0.84
Toscana	779	3.38	91,123	9.57	− 6.20
Umbria	1,394	6.04	16,822	1.77	4.28
Lazio	2,763	11.98	69,276	7.28	4.71
Centre North territory..	23,059	100.00	951,744	100.00	

(*) The data of the Sabatini law refer to the 1982-1987 period.
Source: Based on data by Istat and La Noce M. [27].

distribution of production) shows the absence of apparent distributive logics: Lombardia seems to be more or less as much disadvantaged as Trentino Alto Adige is disadvantaged, Veneto receives 9% less than the weight of its regional value added over the total for the Centre-North, and also Toscana, Emilia and Romagna, and Liguria receive in the period 1980-1987 less incentives than the relative weight of their industrial production.

At first glance, therefore, it is possible to exclude the "neutral" hypotesis that at a territorial level the incentives were directed where the corresponding productive activites were located. Even examining the appropriation data instead of the financed investments (9), the

(9) The financed investment aggregate is a multiple of the appropriations forming the real disbursement of the incentives. The ratio between the two aggregates obviously depends on the amount of the credit granted under credit facilities and of the tranfer payments with no repayment, compared to the total investment. The laws taken into account are those applied by the Ministry of Industry, IMI, and by the Fund for the Development of the South of Italy.

results remain unchanged as to the sign and size of the diversion, while the differences are partly modified (Table 2).

The fact that the incentives did not follow the regional distribution of production is obviously not sufficient to express a judgement into the merits of the following: *a)* the industrial policies seem partly

TABLE 2

APPROPRIATIONS FOR THE MAIN LAWS ON INDUSTRIAL INCENTIVES IN THE PERIOD 1980-1987, EXCLUDING THE SABATINI LAW
(billion lira at 1980 prices)

Region	Appropria-tions (a)	% (b)	Industrial value added 1980-1987 total (c)	% (d)	Concentration index (b)-(d)
Piemonte-Val d'Aosta ..	1,284	21.06	136,067	14.30	6.76
Liguria	122	2.00	31,254	3.28	− 1.29
Lombardia	879	14.42	307,453	32.30	−17.88
Trentino Alto Adige	1,049	17.21	17,121	1.80	15.41
Veneto	55	0.90	112,886	11.86	−10.96
Friuli Venezia Giulia ..	205	3.36	27,075	2.84	0.51
Emilia Romagna	417	6.84	110,611	11.62	− 4.78
Marche	313	5.14	32,056	3.37	1.77
Toscana	158	2.59	91,123	9.57	− 6.99
Umbria	222	3.65	16,822	1.77	1.88
Lazio	1,393	22.84	69,276	7.28	15.56
Centre-North	6,098	100.00	951,744	100.00	
South	6,529	51.71	208,687	17.98	33.72
Italy.................	12,627	100.00	1,160,430	100.00	

Source: Based on data by ISTAT and LA NOCE M. [27].

"oriented" towards some sectors (Law 675 of 1977, part of the Law 46, the interventions of the Fund for the Development of the South of Italy, etc.). Hence a possible regional diversion in favour of those areas where the boosted sectors are more present; *b)* the industrial policies aare sometimes deliberately addressed to SMEs (Law 696 of 1983, 399 of 1987, DPR 902 of 1976, Law 1329 of 1965), while in other cases they privilege in fact large firms beyond the targets stated by the policy-makers (10). Regional distribution could then be affected not only by the relative amount of production, but also by the dimensional structure of the firms in the various areas of the Centre-North; *c)* the industrial policy laws which are now under examination are only a part of the interventions carried out in Italy.

The evolution of production may therefore appear not to be synchronic with the analysed incentives, but may actually prove to be faithful to the evolution of the productive structure when considering all the public transfer payments to firms: CIG, GEPI, cut in social securities for the firms increasing first-job employment, etc.

Moreover, the wish to emphasize, especially in the more recent legislation, the interventions in the field of technological innovations might have caused — owing to the different innovation level of the various sectors — further elements for a diversion between the dynamics of the regional industrial value added and the evolution of the industrial incentives.

In order to verify the possible influence of the firms size on the course of the incentive flow, we reorganized data according to the traditional division into areas with similar characteristics for what concerns the firm size structure (11): the Centre-North-East regions, where the medium and small sized units are prevailing, and units with less than 20 employees are widespread; the North-West regions of the original industrial triangle, where, despite the weight reduction of large firms, the medium and large sized firm is still prevailing; the residual regions, showing a lesser stability of the size division and strong inner dynamics (12).

---

(10) Some analyses showed without a shadow of doubt that some measures of selective industrial policy, as for instance Law 46, favoured in the period 1983-1988 large firms for obvious reasons of superiority in the cognitive routines, lower search-cost and, in general, better ability to fulfill procedures. See ANTONELLI C. - GINESTRI S. [1].

(11) Such a classification is obviously simplified and is based on census data which do not record the latest trends. However, for our purposes it is necessary to verify the ratio between incentives and industrial production in areas which are as homogeneous as possible. In any case, this classification is the same used in the most recent literature. See GIANNOLA A. [20]; TASSINARI F. [38].

(12) The territorial division we used does not correspond to the geographic one, as it was defined on the basis of the homogeneity of the size structure of the firms. In particular: *A)* territory of the Centre-North-East: Emilia-Romagna, Marche, Toscana, Veneto; *B)* territory of the North-West: Liguria, Lombardia, Piemonte, Val d'Aosta; *C)* territory of the residual regions (RE): Friuli Venezia Giulia, Lazio, Umbria, Trentino Alto Adige.

Even using this classification, the comparison between incentives and production does not give clear results as regards the courses of the incentive flows (Table 3 and 4).

On the one hand the Centre-North-East territory seems to be at a disadvantage, with SMEs prevailing; such disadvantage is also true for the regions of the industrial triangle, where the large and medium sized firms are prevailing. The fact that the concentration of incentives as compared to production takes place in the residual regions, where the size structure of firms is less devined, accounts for a very little influence of the firm size on the determination of the territorial distrubition of incentive flows. In other words, even if the financial resources had in fact privileged SMEs (except for the opposite case of the Law 46), such privilege does not seem to be evenly distributed in the Centre-North territory of Italy.

At this point it is crucial to examine closer the analyses at a sectorial level to verify whether or not the sector-orientation characterized the Italian industrial policy in the 1980s, determining the territorial distribution of the industrial incentives.

TABLE 3

INVESTMENTS FINANCED THROUGH THE MAIN INDUSTRIAL
INCENTIVE LAWS IN THE PERIOD 1980-1987
INCLUDING THE SABATINI LAW (*)
(billion lira at 1980 prices)

Region (**)	Financed investments (a)	% (b)	Industrial value added 1980-1987 total (c)	% (d)	Concentration index (b)-(d)
Centre-North-East regions	4,595	19.93	346,676	36.43	− 16.50
North-West regions	8,173	35.44	474,773	49.88	− 14.44
Residual regions	10,292	44.63	130,294	13.69	30.94
Centre-North	23,059	100.00	951,744	100.00	

(*) The Sabatini Law data refer to the 1980-1987 period.
(**) Regions of the CNE: Veneto, Emilia Romagna, Marche, Toscana; regions of the NW: Piemonte, Valle d'Aosta, Liguria, Lombardia; residual regions: Trentino-Alto Adige, Friuli Venezia Giulia, Umbria, Lazio.
Source: Based on data by Istat, Mediocredito and La Noce M. [27].

Maurizio Tenenbaum

Table 4
APPROPRIATIONS ACCORDING
TO THE MAIN INDUSTRIAL INCENTIVE LAWS
IN THE PERIOD 1980-1987
EXCLUDING THE SABATINI LAW
(billions lira at 1980 prices)

Region (*)	Appropria-tions (a)	% (b)	Industrial value added 1980-1987 total (c)	% (d)	Concentration index (b)-(d)
Centre-North-East regions	943	15.47	346,676	36.43	− 20.96
North-West regions	2,285	37.48	474,773	49.88	− 12.41
Residual regions	2,869	47.06	130,294	13.69	33.37
Centre-North	6,098	100.00	951,744	100.00	

(*) See table 3.
Source: Based on data by Istat, Mediocredito and La Noce M. [27].

3. - Industrial Policies, Sectorial Dynamics and Regional Development

In order to verify the influence of the sector-orientation on the determination of the territorial distribution of the industrial incentives in areas and regions of the Centre-North, one should be able to effect a cross-section, by sector and region, of the data of the individual laws with the corresponding data of the industrial value added. While for the latter aggregate it was possible to reconstruct the sector-region matrix (see Appendix I), analogous matrices with reference to the main industrial incentive laws are not available; only in the case of the Sabatini Law (Law 1329 of 1965) Mediocredito Centrale supplied the basic data, which so far do not seem to have been used in literature. In the case of other laws, the availability of data, though not connected, by sector and by region allowed to draw some conclusions into the merits concerning whether or not a diversion of the incentive flow with regard to the evolution of the industrial production was present, even if in the case of the Sabatini Act the analysis was obviously more complete and analytical.

The trend of the regional value added in the period 1982-1987 points out the main trends of the sectorial redistribution in our industrial system (Table 5): higher than average growth in the food, woodworking, mechanical, chemical and paper sectors; nocticeable fall of the iron and steel and of the manufacturing sectors in general. It is evident that such a low disaggregation level cannot account for the different technological content at sectorial level, mainly in the light of the spreading of product and process innovations also in the more mature sectors.

Nevertheless, it seemed useful to reclassify the productive sectors in three groups on account of higher or lower capital intensive productive processes: group *A)* (metal products and iron metallurgy, chemistry and synthetic fibers, non-metalliferous mineral working) with capital intensive technology; group *B)* (means of transportation and mechanical sector) with no precise characterization as to capital intensity; group *C)* (food, clothing, textile, hide and leather footwear, wood furniture and others) with the prevalence of low capital intensive technology.

The results are given in table 6*A*, showing for the period 1982-1987 a steady growth of group *B* (which we may define, for simplicity's sake, medium capital intensive) over the two other groups. This trend (Table 6*B*) is even more noticeable if we reduce the time series (eliminating the 1982-1983 crisis); setting 1984 as the basis of the new index, the results in terms of average annual growth rate are the following: group *A)*: 2.29%; group *B)*: 5.16%; group *C)*: 3.07%. The productive development of the Italian industry seems to centre on the mechanical and the means of transportation sectors, within a general frame of remarkable growth for all the manufacturing sector: 2.12% as annual average for the period 1982-1987, 3.33% in the period 1984-1987.

The sectorial dynamics for groups of sectors cannot but be reflected at geographical area level, favouring the regions where the most dynamic sectors are present.

Tables 7, 8 and 9 show the recorded growth by region and geographic area. The first remark concerns the performance of the Centre-North-East (were the SMEs are prevailing), which seems to be better considering both the 1982-1987 and the 1984-1987 periods

Maurizio Tenenbaum

TABLE 5

INDEX NUMBERS OF THE INDUSTRIAL VALUE ADDED AT FACTOR COST BY SECTOR
(1980 constant prices, 1982 = 100)

Sectors	1982	1983	1984	1985	1986	1987	Average annual growth rate (%)
Food	100.00	103.72	103.91	109.51	112.68	121.79	4.02
Textile and clothing	100.00	96.98	101.01	102.70	103.30	103.25	0.64
Hide and leather	100.00	99.91	104.38	106.41	107.52	107.65	1.49
Wood working	100.00	98.51	103.39	100.73	111.08	128.14	5.08
Metallurgy	100.00	94.17	91.08	92.76	90.72	95.62	−0.89
Metal working	100.00	101.49	104.95	110.96	116.31	122.05	4.07
Chemical	100.00	105.01	111.22	117.13	117.51	122.00	4.06
Paper	100.00	101.41	108.59	110.56	112.45	122.76	4.19
Quarrying	100.00	95.49	101.83	104.40	102.17	105.83	1.14
Energy	100.00	101.29	100.23	105.83	105.83	110.13	1.95
Non-metalliferous mineral work.	100.00	101.01	104.93	104.32	103.03	106.21	1.21
Building	100.00	103.17	102.46	106.33	108.48	110.12	1.95
Other manufacturing	100.00	94.11	94.25	97.02	96.40	96.89	−0.63
Total	100.00	100.14	102.38	105.79	108.11	112.96	2.47

Source: Based on ISTAT, BANK OF ITALY and MINISTRY OF THE BUDGET data.

TABLE 6*a*

INDEX NUMBERS OF THE INDUSTRIAL VALUE ADDED AT FACTOR COST
(1980 constant prices, 1982 = 100)

Groups (*)	1982	1983	1984	1985	1986	1987	Average annual growth rate (%)
Group A)	100.00	98.45	99.82	102.49	102.27	106.83	1.33
Group B)	100.00	101.49	104.95	110.96	116.31	122.05	4.07
Group C)	100.00	100.50	102.71	105.39	107.84	112.46	2.38
Total	100.00	100.14	102.38	105.79	108.11	112.96	2.12

(*) Group A) metallurgy, chemical, quarrying, energy, non metalliferous mineral working; Group B) mechanical; Group C) food, textile and clothing, hides and leather, paper, building, other manufacturing.
Source: Based on ISTAT, BANK OF ITALY and MINISTRY OF THE BUDGET data.

TABLE 6*b*

INDEX NUMBERS OF THE INDUSTRIAL VALUE ADDED AT FACTOR COST
(1980 constant prices, 1984 = 100)

Groups (*)	1984	1985	1986	1987	Average annual growth rate (%)
Group A)	100.00	102.67	102.45	107.02	2.29
Group B)	100.00	105.74	110.83	116.30	5.16
Group C)	100.00	102.61	105.00	109.49	3.07
Total	100.00	103.32	105.60	110.33	3.33

(*) See note under table 6a.
Source: Based on ISTAT, BANK OF ITALY and MINISTRY OF THE BUDGET data.

TABLE 7a

INDEX NUMBERS OF THE INDUSTRIAL VALUE ADDED AT FACTOR COST BY REGION
(1980 constant prices, 1982 = 100)

Region (*)	1982	1983	1984	1985	1986	1987	Average annual growth rate (%)
North-West regions	100.00	97.2	98.5	101.6	103.3	108.2	1.58
Centre-North-West regions	100.00	107.2	109.7	114.2	116.7	122.4	4.12
Residual regions	100.00	93.8	98.7	100.8	104.7	107.7	1.50
Centre-North	100.00	100.1	102.4	105.8	108.1	113.0	2.47

(*) see note Table 3.
Source: Based on ISTAT, BANK OF ITALY and MINISTRY OF THE BUDGET data.

TABLE 7b

INDEX NUMBERS OF THE INDUSTRIAL VALUE ADDED AT FACTOR COST BY REGION
(1980 constant prices, 1984 = 100)

Region (*)	1984	1985	1986	1987	Average annual growth rate (%)
North-West regions	100.00	103.1	104.9	109.8	3.16
Centre-North-West regions	100.00	104.1	106.4	111.5	3.70
Residual regions	100.00	102.1	106.1	109.1	2.96
Centre-North	100.00	103.3	105.6	110.3	3.33

(*) See note table 3.
Source: Based on ISTAT, BANK OF ITALY and MINISTRY OF THE BUDGET data.

TABLE 8

INDEX NUMBERS OF THE INDUSTRIAL VALUE ADDED
AT FACTOR COST BY REGION
(1980 constant prices, 1982 = 100)

Region	1982	1983	1984	1985	1986	1987	Average annual growth rate (%)
Piemonte-Valle d'Aosta	100.00	95.69	97.37	101.66	105.69	110.68	2.05
Liguria	100.00	90.61	93.75	95.11	96.65	99.97	− 0.01
Lombardia	100.00	98.71	99.58	102.25	103.02	107.98	1.55
Trentino Alto Adige	100.00	93.07	101.56	101.63	103.71	105.90	1.15
Veneto	100.00	109.25	116.03	122.38	128.69	136.31	6.39
Friuli Venezia Giulia	100.00	97.28	96.44	103.23	106.73	108.91	4.13
Emilia-Romagna	100.00	101.46	105.08	105.65	106.93	115.30	2.89
Marche	100.00	115.87	111.49	116.89	119.48	124.65	4.50
Toscana	100.00	109.19	107.78	114.88	114.49	114.54	2.75
Umbria	100.00	106.30	105.89	104.41	103.81	105.15	1.01
Lazio	100.00	89.90	97.34	98.90	104.43	108.31	1.61
Centre-North	100.00	100.14	102.38	105.79	108.11	112.96	2.47

Source: Based on ISTAT, BANK OF ITALY and MINISTRY OF THE BUDGET data.

Maurizio Tenenbaum

TABLE 9

INDEX NUMBERS OF THE INDUSTRIAL VALUE ADDED
AT FACTOR COST BY REGION
(1980 constant prices, 1984 = 100)

Region	1984	1985	1986	1987	Average annual growth rate (%)
Piemonte-Valle d'Aosta	100.00	104.41	108.55	113.68	4.37
Liguria	100.00	101.45	103.10	106.64	2.17
Lombardia	100.00	102.69	103.46	108.44	2.74
Trentino Alto Adige	100.00	100.07	102.13	104.28	1.41
Veneto	100.00	105.47	110.91	117.48	5.52
Friuli Venezia Giulia	100.00	107.03	110.67	112.92	4.13
Emilia-Romagna	100.00	100.55	101.76	109.73	3.14
Marche	100.00	104.85	107.17	111.80	3.79
Toscana	100.00	106.59	106.23	106.28	2.05
Umbria	100.00	98.60	98.04	99.30	−0.23
Lazio...........................	100.00	101.61	107.29	111.28	3.63
Centre-North	100.00	103.32	105.60	110.33	3.33
South	100.00	97.70	97.36	102.42	0.80
Italy...........................	100.00	102.13	104.24	107.98	2.59

Source: Based on Istat, Bank of Italy and Ministry of the Budget data.

(these results remain the same when setting 1981 as the basis). In this case, the role played by the growth of the mechanical sector in the development of the Centre-North-East is evident.

Consistent with the adopted classification are also the good results obtained in 1982-1987 by the North-West and by the other residual regions; among the latter, Lazio's good results stand out, which are probably owed to the presence in the regional territory (as in the case of Veneto in the Centre-North-East) of areas subject to the intervention of the Fund for the Development of the South of Italy.

On the other hand, the sectors-regions cross section confirms the presumed ratio existing between firm size and capital intensive technology (Table 10):*a)* the industrial value added of the sectors under group *A)* (capital intensive) is concentrated for over 52% in the North-West regions, where large firms are prevailing, and only marginally in the group of the residual regions; *b)* the industrial value added of the sectors of group *C)* (low capital intensive) is concentrated in the Centre-North-East, where SMEs predominate, and in the North-West, while it is less present in the residual regions (it is to be noticed that group *C)* represents 47% of total production); *c)* over 60% of the industrial value added of group *B)* (medium capital intensive) seems to be located in the North-West regions, thus confirming the switch from large-sized firms to medium-sized ones recorded in the 1980s in the most industrialized areas.

Analysing the territorial distribution of the contribution given by the three groups of sectors on the total industrial value added it is evident that: group *C)* covers about 67% of the production of the Centre-North-East and 53% of the residual regions, while group *A)* and *B)* (large and medium firms) reach 61% of the industrial value added of the North-West regions.

Now it must be verified whether the incentive flows of the various industrial policy laws in favour of the SMEs followed a course favouring the Centre-North-East areas or not, and, in the hypothesis of a convergence between SMEs and low capital intensive sectors, in favour of the sectors of group *C)*. In the case of laws aimed at promoting technological innovation, since an orientation in favour of the capital intensive and large firm sectors is not explicit, it must be verified whether the courses of incentive flows spread or not in all

TABLE 10*a*

INDUSTRIAL VALUE ADDED AT FACTOR COST, 1982-1987
(in % of total)

Sector (*)	NW	CNE	Residual regions	Total
Group A)........	11.63	7.30	3.39	22.31
Group B)........	18.56	8.51	3.10	30.16
Group C)........	19.64	20.62	7.26	47.52
Total........	49.83	36.42	13.75	100.00

(*) For the composition of the groups and the territorial division see notes, tables 6*a* and 3.
Source: Based on ISTAT, BANK OF ITALY and MINISTRY OF THE BUDGET data.

TABLE 10*b*

INDUSTRIAL VALUE ADDED AT FACTOR COST, 1982-1987
(in % by region)

Sector (*)	NW	CNE	Residual regions	Total
Group A)........	52.10	32.70	15.20	100.00
Group B)........	61.53	28.20	10.27	100.00
Group C)........	41.34	43.39	15.28	100.00
Total........	49.83	36.42	13.75	100.00

(*) For the composition of the groups and the territorial division see notes, tables 6*a* and 3.
Source: Based on ISTAT, BANK OF ITALY and MINISTRY OF THE BUDGET data.

TABLE 10*c*

INDUSTRIAL VALUE ADDED AT FACTOR COST, 1982-1987
(in % by sector)

Sector (*)	NW	CNE	Residual regions	Total
Group A)........	23.33	20.04	24.67	22.31
Group B)........	37.25	23.36	22.53	30.16
Group C)........	39.42	56.61	52.80	47.52
Total........	100.00	100.00	100.00	100.00

(*) For the composition of the groups and the territorial division see notes. tables 6*a* and 3.
Source: Based on ISTAT, BANK OF ITALY and MINISTRY OF THE BUDGET data.

three groups of sectors, and consequently in all three territories considered.

3.1 *Incentive Laws in Favour of SMEs*

The main laws which are specifically addressed to small and medium-sized firms are the Law 696 of 1983 and its follow up through the Law 399 of 1987. They deal with incentives equal to 25% of the cost of the tool machinery purchased up to a maximum amount between 500 million lira (according to Law 696) and 350 million lira (according to Law 399). The fields of application of these laws have been made wider, and nowadays they include not only mechanical and electronic equipment, but also systemic integration and software.

Being targeted to the development of SMEs or to the sectors more in need of electronic plant renovations, the incentive flows should have been mainly directed to the productive areas of the Centre-North-East, of the residual territory, and to the sectors of group *C)*.

Tables 11 and 13*A* show the regional and sectorial distribution of the payments effected in the period 1984-1987 compared to the value of the industrial production. Though a substantial uniformity in the territorial distribution of the two variables (with a 98% correlation) may be observed, the regions which are able to use the incentive to a greater extent than their percent weight in terms of production are Lombardia, Veneto, Piemonte and Emilia Romagna, while all the other regions, except for the South of Italy, which is totally absent, receive incentives to a lesser extent than their contribution to the industrial production.

Grouping the regions by homogeneous groups as to their size structure (Table 13*A*) it is clear that the North-West territory receives the greatest portion of incentives: having 49% of the industrial value added, it receives 55% of the grants paid; the Centre-North-East territory follows with + 3%, while the group of residual regions is consequently disadvantaged; among these, the Lazio region stands out for the size of the negative deviation, as it alone absorbs 65% of the diversion.

TABLE 11

LAWS 696 OF 1983 AND 399 OF 1987: APPROPRIATIONS BY REGION,
1984-1987 (billion lira at 1980 prices)

Region	Appropria-tions (a)	% (b)	Total industrial value added 1980-1987 (c)	% (d)	Concentration index (b)-(d)
Piemonte-Val d'Aosta ..	47.6	17.29	67,849	14.12	3.17
Liguria	3.1	1.12	16,295	3.39	− 2.27
Lombardia	100.1	36.39	151,312	31.49	4.90
Trentino Alto Adige	0.6	0.22	8,904	1.85	− 1.64
Veneto	43.6	15.85	59,073	12.29	3.56
Friuli Venezia Giulia ..	5.9	2.14	13,789	2.87	− 0.73
Emilia Romagna	38.3	13.93	56,171	11.69	2.24
Marche	5.8	2.09	16,012	3.33	− 1.24
Toscana	22.6	8.21	46,316	9.64	− 1.43
Umbria	2.5	0.92	8,157	1.70	− 0.78
Lazio	5.1	1.86	36,699	7.64	− 5.78
Centre-North	275.2	100.00	480,577	100.00	
South	8.0	2.82	107,989	18.35	− 15.53
Italy................	283.2	100.00	588,565	100.00	

Source: Based on Istat and Ministry of Industry data.

The analysis by sector should therefore verify the "orientation" expressly stated by the law, and therefore favour the sectors which are more in need of the introduction of electronics and informatics.

In Table 12 the sectors are shown which record the highest relative incentive flow; these are the mechanical, followed at a great distance by the textile and clothing and by groups of sectors (Table 13*B*), GROUP *B)* (means of transportation and all the mechanical sector) shows the best performance: 23% of the industrial value added "catches" 47% of the incentives.

It is clear that the course of the incentive flows to the SMEs does not reflect the characteristics previously discovered by crossing the data of the industrial production value by groups of sectors with those relative to the identified districts. In other words, if the target was to boost SMEs, the prevalence of Centre-North-East areas, and therefore of the sectors of group *C)* would have been rightly expected (Table

TABLE 12

LAWS 696 OF 1983 AND 399 OF 1987:
APPROPRIATIONS BY SECTOR, 1984-1987
(billion lira at 1980 prices)

Sectors	Appropria-tions (a)	% (b)	Total industrial value added 1984-1987 (c)	% (d)	Concentration index (b)-(d)
Food	11,7	4,12	40.675	8,46	− 4,35
Textile clothing	35,9	12,68	32.029	6,66	6,02
Hides and leather	7,5	2,65	33.462	6,96	− 4,31
Wood working	15,2	5,37	23.661	4,92	0,45
Metallurgy	7,6	2,69	45.463	9,46	− 6,77
Mechanical...........	133,0	46,96	110.308	22,95	24,01
Chemical	3,5	1,24	30.473	6,34	− 5,10
Paper	26,8	9,46	25.343	5,27	4,19
Quarrying	2,1	0,75	7.427	1,55	− 0,80
Energy	0,2	0,05	25.853	5,38	− 5,33
Non-metalliferous min-eral working	14,5	5,12	20.051	4,17	0,95
Building	0,2	0,06	66.078	13,75	− 13,69
Other manufacturing ..	25,1	8,85	19.753	4,11	4,74
Total	283,2	100.00	480.577	100,00	

Source: Based on ISTAT and MINISTRY OF INDUSTRY data.

10); actually the sector-orientation as stated in the law favoured the sectors of group *B)* (medium capital intensive technology) and consequently the regions of the North-West, which alone account for over 60% of the total value added produced by such sectors in the period 1982-1987.

It is convenient to point out that only through the comparison of the relative weight of the incentives with that of the industrial productions it is possible to assess the actual amount of the transfer payments effected at territorial level. On the contrary, all the main analyses available in literature only give the absolute flows of the transfer payments, which alone do not account for the actual level of the sectorial and regional incentives (13).

---

(13) See among others GROSS-PIETRO G.M. - OCCHIFREDDI D. - ROLFO S., and VITALI G. [22].

TABLE 13*a*

LAWS 696 OF 1983 AND 399 OF 1987:
APPROPRIATIONS BY TERRITORIES, 1984-1987
(billion lira at 1980 prices)

Region (*)	Appropria-tions (a)	% (b)	Industrial value added 1984-1987 total (c)	% (d)	Concentration index (b)-(d)
Centre-North regions ..	110.3	40.07	177,571	36.95	3.12
North-West regions	150.8	54.80	235,456	48.99	5.80
Residual regions	14.1	5.13	67,549	14.06	− 8.93
Centre-North	275.2	100.00	480,577	100.00	

(*) See note table 3.
Source: Based on ISTAT and MINISTRY OF THE INDUSTRY data.

TABLE 13*b*

Groups (*)	Appropria-tions (a)	% (b)	Total industrial value added 1984-1987 (c)	% (d)	Concentration index (b)-(d)
Group A)	27.9	9.85	129,268	26.90	− 17.05
Group B)	133.0	46.96	110,308	22.95	24.01
Group C)	122.3	43.19	241,001	50.15	− 6.96
Total	283.2	100.00	480,577	100.00	

(*) See note table 6*a*.
Source: Based on ISTAT and MINISTRY OF THE INDUSTRY data.

3.2 *Incentive laws in favour of SMEs in the Centre-North of Italy*

DPR 902 of 1976 together with the Law 675 form the main interventions in favour of the industrial reorganization within the sector-oriented approach prevailing in the first half of the 1970s. In particular, DPR 902 regulates the grants in favour of industrial SMEs for small investments in the form of soft loans for new plants, renovations and enlargement of existing ones.

The allowance for new plants, however, may be paid only in the specific areas which are defined as depressed areas. Owing to this fact, the effectiveness of the law was delayed by some years, as its enforcement started in 1989 (and in any case with a minimum amount of allowances paid) and was fully applied in 1982-1983.

As compared to Laws 696 and 399, DPR 902 seems oriented explicitly at a territorial level (Centre-North), and implicitly at a sectorial level: by tying the investments for new plants to the depressed areas, this law is in fact addressing the facilities towards economic areas where low capital-intensive sectors are prevailing (group *C* in our classification). Hence a further territorial specification follows, to the advantage of the Centre-North-East areas, where the SMEs prevail in low capital-intensive sectors.

Data analysis (Tables 14, 15 and 16) confirms only in part the orientations directly and indirectly expressed by the legislator: 1) at territorial level the concentration ratios show a higher facilities flow than the weight of the industrial production in Emilia Romagna, Marche and Toscana, while Veneto records a rather remarkable negative diversion (the incentive flows are ove 3% lower than the weight of the industrial value added). On the whole, however (Table 16*A*), the Centre-North-East seems to be the territory getting the highest incentive share as compared to the weight of its production. To the opposite, the North West seems to have been disadvantaged by the prevalence of large enterprises; 2) at sectorial level, instead, the expected symmetry is not proved: the good results of the food, textile, clothing and wood working sectors are more than made up for by the the non-metalliferous mineral working and by the metallurgic sector. It follows that at a general level the group of sectors that receives more incentives compared to the weight of production in group *A)* (capital intensive).

In the case of DPR 902 it must be observed that the facilities flows seem to be distributed over the territory more evenly as compared to other laws. The pointed out diversions are actually due mainly to the exceptional performance of the region of Umbria for what concerns the territorial distribution, that must be crossed with the similar sectorial results of the non-metalliferous workings and of metallurgy.

TABLE 14

DPR 902 OF 1976: TRANSFER PAYMENTS BY REGION, 1981-1987
(billion lira at 1980 prices)

Region	Amounts paid (a)	% (b)	Total industrial value added 1981-1987 (c)	% (d)	Concentration index (b)-(d)
Piemonte-Val d'Aosta ..	23,8	10,14	118.973	14,28	− 4,13
Liguria	7,2	3,09	27.263	3,27	− 0,18
Lombardia	75,4	32,16	269.048	32,29	− 0,13
Trentino Alto Adige	1,9	0,80	14.850	1,78	− 0,98
Veneto	20,4	8,70	99.640	11,96	− 3,26
Friuli Venezia Giulia ..	0,2	0,09	23.326	2,80	− 2,71
Emilia Romagna	27,3	11,64	96.220	11,55	0,09
Marche	15,1	6,43	27.960	3,36	3,07
Toscana	29,0	12,37	80.042	9,61	2,77
Umbria	29,6	12,63	14.553	1,75	10,88
Lazio	4,6	1,95	61.391	7,37	− 5,42
Centre-North	234,5	100,00	833.268	100,00	

Source: Based on ISTAT and MINISTRY OF INDUSTRY data.

TABLE 15

DPR 901 OF 1976: TRANSFER PAYMENTS BY SECTOR, 1981-1987
(billion lira at 1980 prices)

Sectors	Amounts paid (a)	% (b)	Total industrial value added, 1981-1987 (c)	% (d)	Concentration index (b)-(d)
Food	31,7	13,52	68.411	8,11	5,31
Textile, clothing	27,5	11,72	62.081	7,45	4,27
Hides and leather......	12,8	5,47	50.177	6,02	− 0,55
Wood working	14,0	5,96	40.068	4,81	1,16
Metallurgy	14,2	6,07	17.345	2,08	3,99
Mechanical...........	61,1	26,06	250.600	30,07	− 4,01
Chemical	13,6	5,80	82.566	9,91	− 4,10
Paper	9,9	4,22	42.314	5,08	− 0,86
Quarrying	1,4	0,59	12.311	1,48	− 0,89
Energy	0,1	0,02	38.108	4,57	− 4,55
Non metalliferous mineral working	34,4	14,67	34.794	4,18	10,49
Building	0,0	0,01	125.266	15,03	− 15,02
Other manufacturing ..	13,8	5,87	9.228	1,11	4,77
Total	234,4	100,00	833.268	100,00	

Source: Based on ISTAT and MINISTRY OF INDUSTRY data.

TABLE 16*a*

DPR 902 OF 1976: TRANSFER PAYMENTS BY TERRITORY, 1981-1987
(billion lira at 1980 prices)

Regions (*)	Amounts paid (a)	% (b)	Total value added 1981-1987 (c)	% (d)	Concentration index (b)-(d)
CNE regions	91.8	39.14	303,863	36.47	2.67
NW regions	106.5	45.39	415,284	49.84	−4.44
Residual regions	36.3	15.47	114,121	13.70	1.77
Centre-North	234.5	100.00	833,268	100.00	

(*) See note table 3.
Source: Based on ISTAT and MINISTRY OF INDUSTRY data.

TABLE 16*b*

DPR 902 OF 1976: TRANSFER PAYMENTS BY GROUP OF SECTORS,
1981-1987 (billion lira at 1980 prices)

Groups (*)	Amounts paid (a)	% (b)	Total value added 1981-1987 (c)	% (d)	Concentration index (b)-(d)
Group *A)*	63.6	27.15	185,123	22.22	4.93
Group *B)*	61.1	26.06	250,600	30.07	−4.01
Group *C)*	109.7	46.79	397,545	47.71	−0.92
Total	234.4	100.00	833,268	100.00	

(*) See note table 6*a*.
Source: Based on ISTAT and MINISTRY OF INDUSTRY data.

3.3 *Incentive Laws for Technological Innovation*

The attempt to orient the incentives to the factors of production was made through Law 46 of 1982; in particular, applied research and technological innovation were boosted by means of two different funds: the Special Fund for Applied Research (FSRA) and the Special Fund for Technological Innovation (FSIT); the first is managed by IMI, the second by MICA.

While FSRA seems clearly oriented to the development and the transfer of new technologies to the SMEs also through the involbement of the regional governments, FSIT is not firm-oriented; instead, it indicates some sectorial priorities: motorcars and components, electronics, iron and steel, aeronautics, chemistry. It is evident that Fsit is much influenced by the "philosophy" on which the sector plans mentioned in the Law 675 are based, hence the contradiction between an industrial policy devised to be horizontal and a legislation which is still oriented to the keeping of vertical organization requirements in the production incentives.

The sectors listed under Fsit in Law 46 show an evident homogeneity as to the industrial localization (North-West), enterprise size (large and medium) and capital intensity of the boosted sectors (group *A)*).

The results of the first years of law implementation prove the high sectorial concentration indices for firm sizes and capitalistic level of productions.

TABLE 17

LAWS 46 OF 1982 FSIT: TRANSFER PAYMENTS BY REGION, 1984-1987
(billion lira at 1980 prices)

Region	Amounts paid (a)	% (b)	Total industrial value added 1984-1987 (c)	% (d)	Concentration index (b)-(d)
Piemonte-Val d'Aosta ..	54.9	23.28	67,849	14.12	9.17
Liguria	0.9	0.37	16,295	3.39	− 3.02
Lombardia	100.2	42.48	151,312	31.49	11.00
Trentino Alto Adige	0.7	0.29	8,904	1.85	− 1.57
Veneto	11.7	4.94	59,073	12.29	− 7.35
Friuli Venezia Giulia ..	5.9	2.49	13,789	2.87	− 0.38
Emilia Romagna	44.4	18.83	56,171	11.69	7.15
Marche	0.9	0.40	16,012	3.33	− 2.93
Toscana	5.9	2.49	46,316	9.64	− 7.15
Umbria	0.4	0.16	8,157	1.70	− 1.54
Lazio	10.0	4.26	36,699	7.64	− 3.38
Centre-North	235.9	100.00	480,577	100.00	
South	8.5	3.49	107,989	18.35	− 14.86
Italy.................	244.4	100.00	588,565	100.00	

Source: Based on ISTAT and MINISTRY OF INDUSTRY data.

Piemonte, Lombardia, and Emilia Romagna show a much higher incentive flow than the relative weight of their industrial production, while the disadvantage of the South of Italy is evident: having 18% of the domestic industrial value added it only gets about 3.5% facilities. Other areas in the Centre-North-East which are at a strong disadvantage are: Veneto − 7%; Marche − 3%; Toscana − 7%.

In the sectorial division some "peculiarities" may be observed which make the symmetry between groups of sectors and regional districts less consistent (Table 19*B*). Though the mechanical and chemical sectors record an exceptional sectorial concentration index (+ 43% and + 14%, respectively), the aggregation by sectorial groups shows that group *B)* (medium capital intensive technology) gets the greatest amount of facilities: with 23% of the industrial value added it receives 66% of the facilities.

In this case the unbalance clearly results form the regional distribution of the chemical sector, that somehow reduced the relative

TABLE 18

LAW 46 OF 1982 FSIT: TRANSFER PAYMENTS BY SECTOR, 1984-1987
(billion lira at 1980 prices)

Sectors	Amounts paid (a)	% (b)	Total industrial value added 1984-1987 (c)	% (d)	Concentration index (b)-(d)
Food	2.4	0.98	40,675	8.46	− 7.48
Textile and clothing	4.4	1.80	32,029	6.66	− 4.87
Hides and leather......	1.8	0.74	33,462	6.96	− 6.22
Wood working	4.3	1.78	23,661	4.92	− 3.15
Metallurgy	2.3	0.95	45,463	9.46	− 8.52
Mechanical...........	161.9	66.25	110,308	22.95	43.30
Chemical	49.9	20.43	30,473	6.34	14.09
Paper	1.4	0.59	25,343	5.27	− 4.68
Quarrying	0.2	0.09	7,427	1.55	− 1.46
Energy	0.4	0.14	25,853	5.38	− 5.24
Non metalliferous mineral working	1.9	0.77	20,051	4.17	− 3.40
Bouilding	1.1	0.45	66,078	13.75	− 13.30
Other manufacturing ..	12.3	5.03	19,753	4.11	0.92
Total	244.4	100.00	480,577	100.00	

Source: Based on Istat and Ministry of Industry data.

TABLE 19*a*

LAW 46 OF 1982 FSIT: TRANSFER PAYMENTS BY TERRITORY, 1984-1987
(billion lira at 1980 prices)

Region (*)	Amounts paid (a)	% (b)	Total industrial value added 1984-1987 (c)	% (d)	Concentration index (b)-(d)
CNE regions	62.9	26.66	177,571	36.95	− 10.29
NW regions	156.0	66.14	235,456	48.99	17.15
Residual regions	17.0	7.20	67,549	14.06	− 6.86
Centre-North	235.9	100.00	480,577	100.00	
South	8.5	3.49	107,989	18.35	−14.86
Italy.................	244.4	100.00	588,565	100.00	

(*) See note table 3.
Source: Based on ISTAT and MINISTRY OF INDUSTRY data.

TABLE 19*b*

LAW 46 OF 1982 FSIT: TRANSFER PAYMENTS BY GROUP OF SECTOR, 1984-1987 (billion lira at 1980 prices)

Groups (*)	Amounts paid (a)	% (b)	Total industrial value added 1984-1987 (c)	% (d)	Concentration index (b)-(d)
Group *A)*	54.7	22.38	129,268	26.90	− 4.52
Group *B)*	161.9	66.25	110,308	22.95	43.30
Group *C)*	27.8	11.37	241,001	50.15	−38.78
Total	244.4	100.00	480,577	100.00	

(*) See note table 6*a*.
Source: Based on ISTAT and MINISTRY OF INDUSTRY data.

advantage of the North-West regions, which receive over 4.5% less than their contribution in terms of industrial value added.

Also in this case it is evident that by comparing the incentive flow data with the groups of detected sectors — with the limits due to such a simple classification — it was possible to detect some particular territorial repercussion of the specific industrial policies that a simple examination of the payment flows had no been able to detect.

3.4 *Facilities Favouring the Acquisition*
   of Individual Plants Regardless of the Firm Size (Sabatini Law)

The Law 1329 of 1965 is undoubtedly the intervention which recorded the best succes in terms of utilization of the available resources.

The good working of this law should not be so much brought back to the simplicity of the operation mechanisms, as it is often maintained, and to the diffusion over the territory of medium term credit institutions allowed to operate with Mediocredito Centrale. The reason of its success in our opinion ought to be found in the very instrument used for financing: the discounting of bills (and invoices) issued against the purchase of new machinery.

The possibility to monetize the sale of machinery within a very short time has caused the commercial structure of the salespeople to become the prime movers of trading, through their door-to-door action with prospective buyers: the latter, in turn, have seen in this way the burden of their preliminary inquiries at Mediocredito Centrale reduced to a minimum and have solved through the discount of bills their problems of obtaining financings assisted by government incentives.

Being not oriented to the firm size, nor to specific territorial areas, in addition to not requiring special commercial networks or access capacities to complex preliminary stages, the Sabatini Act seems to evenly distribute over the Centre-North territory, exactly following the value of industrial production.

Tables 20 and 21 show the distribution by region and sector of the granted amounts compared to the corresponding industrial value added.

It is immediately clear that the granted amounts are distributed at regional level in a balanced way, so that the diversion between incentives and production value is very limited: only Emilia Romagna, Veneto, and Umbria record a higher incentive flow than the relative weight of the regional value added, to the detriment, though limited, of Lazio and Lombardia. The other regions show lower deviations that − 2%.

Also at sectorial level the diversion incentive vs.value added is

TABLE 20

LAW 1329 OF 1965: TRANSFER PAYMENTS BY REGION, 1982-1987
(billion lira at 1980 prices)

Region	Amounts paid	%	Total industrial value added 1982-1987	%	Concentration index
	(a)	(b)	(c)	(d)	(b)-(d)
Piemonte-Val d'Aosta ..	453	12.89	99,812	14.16	− 1.27
Liguria	53	1.52	24,353	3.46	− 1.94
Lombardia	1.048	29.81	224,142	31.81	− 2.00
Trentino Alto Adige	32	0.92	13,069	1.85	− 0.93
Veneto	527	14.99	83,628	11.87	3.12
Friuli Venezia Giulia ..	70	2.00	20,339	2.89	− 0.88
Emilia Romagna	589	16.77	82,308	11.68	5.09
Marche	163	4.62	23,327	3.31	1.31
Toscana	300	8.53	67,765	9.62	− 1.08
Umbria	137	3.90	12,170	1.73	2.17
Lazio	142	4.05	53,739	7.63	− 3.58
Centre-North	3.515	100.00	704,652	100.00	

Source: Based on ISTAT and MEDIOCREDITO data.

TABLE 21

LAW 1329 OF 1965: TRANSFER PAYMENTS BY SECTOR, 1982-1987
(billion lira at 1980 prices)

Sector	Amounts paid	%	Total industrial value added, 1982-1987	%	Concentration index
	(a)	(b)	(c)	(d)	(b)-(d)
Food	576.4	16.40	59,175	8.40	8.00
Textile, clothing	471.8	13.42	90,654	12.87	0.56
Hides and leather	48.0	1.37	5,919	0.84	0.53
Wood working	107.7	3.06	34,256	4.86	− 1.80
Metallurgy	99.2	2.82	14,431	2.05	0.77
Mechanical	853.4	24.28	214,112	30.39	− 6.11
Chemical	253.1	7.20	71,451	10.14	− 2.94
Paper	215.7	6.14	36,577	5.19	0.94
Quarrying	68.7	1.95	10,476	1.49	0.47
Energy	4.7	0.13	32,811	4.66	− 4.52
Non metalliferous mineral working	302.2	8.60	29,682	4.21	4.39
Building	455.2	12.95	97,491	13.84	− 0.88
Other manufacturing ..	58.8	1.67	7,616	1.08	0.59
Total	3,515.0	100.00	704,652	100.00	

Source: Based on ISTAT and MEDIO CREDITO data.

limited: only the food sector experiences a remarkable relative flow of incentives (+ 8%), while the mechanical sector is disadvantaged (− 6%) and all the other sectors are showing a sectorial diversion lower than 5%.

In order to express synthetically the concentration level of the territorial flows by sector compared to the distributions of the industrial value added we proceeded to calculate two concentration indices of the incentives, defined as follows:

$$(1) \quad IC_s = \left(\frac{1}{2} \sum_i \left| \frac{INC_{ij}}{INC \cdot j} - \frac{Prod_{ij}}{Prod \cdot j} \right| \right) * 100 \quad \text{index of sectorial concentration}$$

$$(2) \quad IC_r = \left(\frac{1}{2} \sum_j \left| \frac{INC_{ij}}{INC \cdot i} - \frac{Prod_{ij}}{Prod \cdot i} \right| \right) * 100 \quad \text{index of sectorial concentration}$$

where:
INC = approved amounts of incentives;
$Prod$ = industrial value added;
i = 1...n sectors of production;
j = 1...m regions.

The two proposed ratios compare the relative distribution of the incentives granted in a given sector (or region) with the relative distribution of the industrial value added in a given sector (or region). The two ratios vary between 0 and 100: the lower limit indicates the equality between the two distributions for each sector (or region), thus implying that the incentives were evenly distributed without sectorial (or regional) concentration, and therefore that the incentives reflect perfectly the sectorial (or regional) distribution of production. Values near 100 instead indicate the rise of the degree of sectorial or regional concentration of incentives vs. production.

The obtained results are the following:

$$IC_s = 21.36$$
$$IC_r = 11.69$$

Wishing to supply elements for a further analysis, it is possible to calculate the global index of sectorial and regional concentration by putting as denominator the line and column totals, obtaining the global concentration level, which was equal to 30.21. Hence it is evident that the low level of the concentration ratios shows that the incentives granted under the Sabatini Law are distributed to both the sectorial production and its geographical distribution in a similar way.

Moving to the analysis by geographical areas and groups of sectors, the results are further confirmed: 1) at geographic area level the deviations between distribution of the approved amounts and distribution of the industrial value added (Table 16) seem limited, and

TABLE 22*a*

LAW 1329 OF 1965: TRANSFER PAYMENTS BY TERRITORY. 1982-1987
(billion lira at 1980 prices)

Region (*)	Amounts paid (a)	% (b)	Total industrial value added 1982-1987 (c)	% (d)	Concentration index (b)-(d)
CNE regions	1,578	44.91	257,028	36.48	8.43
NW regions	1,554	44.22	348,307	49.43	− 5.21
Residual regions	382	10.87	99,317	14.09	− 3.22
Centre North..........	3,515	100.00	704,652	100.00	

(*) see note, Table 3.
Source: Based on ISTAT and MEDIOCREDITO data.

TABLE 22*b*

LAW 1369 OF 1965: INDEX NUMBERS OF TRANSFER PAYMENTS BY TERRITORY
(1980 constant prices, 1982 = 100)

Region (*)	1982	1983	1984	1985	1986	1987	(%)
CNE regions	100.00	79.8	88.7	86.4	147.9	312.9	25.63
NW regions	100.00	86.6	83.6	100.6	133.8	376.1	30.33
Residual regions	100.00	70.9	64.8	90.5	157.4	386.8	31.07
Centre-North............	100.00	81.8	84.0	92.9	142.9	347.7	28.30

(*) see note Table 3.
Source: Based on MEDIOCREDITO data.

TABLE 23a

LAW 1329 OF 1965: TRANSFER PAYMENTS
BY GROUP OF SECTORS. 1982-1987
(billion lira at 1980 prices)

Groups (*)	Amounts paid (a)	% (b)	Total industrial value added 1982-1987 (c)	% (d)	Concentration index (b)-(d)
Group A)	727.9	20.71	158,851	22.54	−1.83
Group B)	853.4	24.28	214,112	30.39	−6.11
Group C)	1,933.7	55.01	331,689	47.07	7.94
Total	3,515.0	100.00	704,652	100.00	

(*) see note Table 6a.
Source: Based on ISTAT and MEDIOCREDITO data.

TABLE 23b

LAW 1329 OF 1965: INDEX NUMBERS OF TRANSFER PAYMENTS
BY GROUP OF SECTORS
(1980 constant prices, 1982 = 100)

Groups (*)	1982	1983	1984	1985	1986	1987	Aver. annual growth rate
Group A)	100	85.02	90.06	77.42	91.78	195.09	14.30
Group B)	100	79.61	71.91	89.67	179.86	358.56	29.10
Group C)	100	80.96	86.38	103.07	153.85	428.05	33.75
Total	100	81.76	84.00	92.87	142.87	347.69	28.30

(*) see note Table 6a).
Source: Based on MEDIOCREDITO data.

TABLE 24*a*

LAW 1329 OF 1965: TOTAL TRANSFER PAYMENTS, 1982-1987 PER CENT DISTRIBUTION AMONG REGIONS

Sectors (*)	NW	CNE	Residual regions	Total
Group *A)*	41.13	51.37	7.50	100.00
Group *B)*	48.18	44.97	6.85	100.00
Group *C)*	43.64	42.44	13.92	100.00
Total	44.22	44.91	10.87	100.00

(*) For the group composition and the territorial division, see notes, Tables 6*a* and 3.
Source: Based on MEDIOCREDITO data.

TABLE 24*b*

LAW 1329 OF 1965: TOTAL TRANSFER PAYMENTS, 1982-1987 PER CENT DISTRIBUTION AMONG SECTORS

Sectors (*)	NW	CNE	Residual regions	Total
Group *A)*	19.26	23.69	14.28	20.71
Group *B)*	26.45	24.31	15.29	24.28
Group *C)*	54.29	51.99	70.43	55.01
Total	100.00	100.00	100.00	100.00

(*) For the group composition and the territorial division, see notes, Tables 6*a* and 3.
Source: Based on MEDIOCREDITO data.

the better results obtained by the Centre-North-East is evident. In dynamic terms, the average annual growth rate of incentives is in that area lower than recorded in the two other territorial districts. The high erraticism with which from time to time funds are paid makes the level of annual growth rate not much meaningful; 2) the analysis by groups of sectors (Table 17) is in line with the regional analysis, as group *C)* is the most boosted one also at dynamic level, as rightly expected, given the good performances of the Centre-North-East territory.

Referring to Appendix I for detailed data on the sectors/regions matrices of the incentives granted under the Sabatini Law, we summarize in Table 18 the cross-sections by geographic areas and groups of sectors. Data show that: *a)* the North-West and Centre-North-East territories receive about 89% incentives (versus 86% industrial value added produced in the period under examination); *b)* the *C)* group of sectors (low capital intensive) collects 55% incentives, contributing with 48% to the industrial value added; *c)* data concerning the group of residual regions and other sectorial groups confirm the ability shown by SMEs fo have access to funds under the Sabatini Law, in confirmation of what was previously asserted on the charatteristics of the access procedure to funds, which takes on the shape of an outright factoring.

4. - Industrial Policy Lines at Regional Level

The delegation to the regions to legislate in the field of industrial areas with infrastructures and of industrial syndicates triggered the expansion of the interventions by the individual regions, which were also stimulated by the recent regional reequilibrium policies carried out by the EEC (Regulations 2052 of 1988, Resider Programme for iron metallurgy, Regulations 2616 of 1980 for degraded sites, etc.).

After an initial period when the legislative initiative was focused on the endowment of financial instruments which could carry out a first intervention in the areas where the productive crisis was more marked, the field of intervention of the regional administrations expanded and even touched almost all the typical field of the national industrial policy: from the support of productive activities (Law of the Lombardia region 33 of 1981) to the area integrated projects, to the research and technological innovation projects in favour of SMEs (Law of the Lombardia region 34 of 1985).

In addition to the legislative interventions by the regions, which suffer from the scarcity of financial means compared to the national resources, there is a whole series of financing channels which were activated by the regions in order to strengthen, though indirectly, the productive structure in their own territory. The main source which was activated in the period 1982-1988 concerned the financings under the Investment and Employment Fund (FIO); such financings could not be destined to directly productive activites, nevertheless in many cases they were used to reinforce the basic infrastructures: road conditions and trasportation, industrial waterworks, energy supplies, etc.

A detailed analysis of the regional interventions by area, or of the contents and operational evolution of the regional legislation is not possible owing to the enormous dispersion of initiatives and to the lack of a systematic analysis by 14 region and productive section (14).

However, there are several studies on areas in a state of crisis clearly showing the difficulties and the inandequacies of the national industrial policy, not so much for what concerns available resources as to the difficulties of having access to financings and coordinating the promoted initiatives. On the other hand, it is evident that whatever be the approach prevailing in the future (target-oriented incentives, and therefore very selective, or automatic, less selective incentives) the lack not only of a coordination, but also of a real interaction between regional and national policies cannot but prevent, or in the best of cases delay, the adoption of efficient and effective measures.

In order to determine some operational proposals deriving from the studies and the debate of these last years at local level — a debate that only rarely is reflected in literature — we close some studies of areas in crisis in central Italy from which the need appears for a new subject of industrial policy at regional or industrial are level to be introduced, which may be able to link the market to the local authorities, and the latter to the central government.

We defined such subject «local agency for the industrial development of SMEs», and as we shall see, this agency should have both a coordinating function and production planning and development functions (15).

---

(14) The only updated and thorough bibliographic sources on the regional industrial policy are those by the Lombardia Region, previously mentioned. It is evident that in this case we are in front of a privileged habitat which is not representative of the average situation in the Centre-North.

(15) The definition and the operational structure of the local agency for the development of SMEs explained below on was effected in the course of a research directed on behalf of CLES by appointment of the Toscana Region-Italimpianti, that was carried out during 1988-1989.

While referring to the appendix for a short summary of the results of the field analyses, which obviously are not able to identify all problems and cannot be representative of the whole national productive structure, it is convenient to point out that under no circumstances the enterprises referred to the national industrial policy laws as a reference point able to provide resources for the support of the productive development of the enterprises.

4.1 - An Operational Proposal; the Local Agency for the Development of SMEs: Structure, Targets, Intervention Tools

Passing from the analysis of the industrial policies at national level to that of an area or industrial district causes a radical change both in the contents under discussion and in the operational proposals following the intervention difficulties of the institutions operating in the territory. While at a national level the proposals for an industrial policy are placed in a context of reference in which the strategic targets are essentially aimed at improving the productive efficiency and the domestic or international competitiveness of the industrial system, at a local level the problems concern more society as a whole than firms. It follows that problems like employment, need for the intersectorial mobility of the labour force and territorial reequilibrium of the productive activities, environmental impact of old and new productions, represent the elements of the same problem, concerning which the Central Government is from time to time made reference to.

Although the industrial firms is a more informed and dynamic subject than other operators, the gap between the national industrial policies and the difficulties of the individual industrial areas is so great and specific as to originate a widespread enstrangement attitude, mainly in SMEs, from public intervention, which is considered only as a possible supplier of financial resources, which may be certainly taken, but should not be cosnsidered as a strategic contribution to the firm plans.

On the other hand, the requirements of the firms at local level pay for the need to come in touch with local authorities and social forces which are acting locally and often do not align with the economic policy trends on which the national legislation in favour of the industry is based.

In the literature, however, the separation between national, regional and territorial policies reflects the task separation that delegations and attributions have from time to time codified. Therefore we have a situation of total confusion in which the enterprise may choose among several financing channels to which to address their requests, the regions have seen the subjects (Italian and EC ones) to which to refer for their economic policy multiply, and the industrial areas have in fact lost their role, their functions and financial resources.

In such situation of operational and informational difficulty SMEs have either privileged the recourse to the banking market or have used the Sabatini Act for small investments. In all the analysed field surveys the firms expressed the need for a "new subject" of industrial policy able to act as a link between national and regional policies and local authorities; such subject has been identified in a "local agency for industrial development" with functions and characteristics which are original in comparison with those of other subjects operating in the industrial system (Asi, industrial syndicate, etc.), and can be summarized in the coordination of the initiatives which can be activated for the industrial development and the supply of real services to SMEs.

From the information drawn from the field surveys, which are schematized in the Appendix, the operational targets that the local agency for industrial development should pursue are evident: *A)* promote and coordinate the initiatives of the various subjects that contribute to the creation and the support of industrial activity. In this action, the ability of the agency to become a point of reference for old and new entrepreneurs is of fundamental importance as regards the possibility to use the structural intervention instruments. Moreover, the action of the agency should consist in the coordination of public financial resources coming from different sources and subjects (regional, national and community funds), each of which ties the availability of its resources to its own rules, so as to make such resources available to the logical development. It is greatly advisable that the agency be a privileged interlocutor for the subjects managing the financial instruments that potentially can be activated locally. The target is to direct the funds to integrated interventions programmes defined within the firm planning, and thus help the fulfillment of the requirements for the financing of such programmes; *B)* guarantee the supply of real basic services to the firms having special management difficulties or wishing to expand their production. Such services, which will be better examined below, are roughly identifiable in the consulting services for the technical-economic procedures for the financing of projects through the capital and/or operating accounts, in the consulting services for the planning of such projects, in the assistance to the start up.

Therefore, two complementary functions are envisaged for the agency: the coordination of the interventions for the industrial development in agreement with the local authorities and the supply of real basic services to firms.

These tasks are added to the competences and the specific role of the industrial syndicates (if they exist) which have the direct management of all the problems regarding the industrial areas and their effective infrastructuring.

A delicate and important task for the agency regards the creation of new firms. The new entrepreneurial initiatives may be created both by springing from a mother firm which, developing, externalizes some cycle stages giving them an autonomous operational horizon, and by workers which, being provided with the necessary professional competence, leap towards an entrepreneurial size.

One of the main problems in the starting of new firms concerns the acquisition of the areas and the initial expenses for the re-organization and the carrying aut of the industrial infrastructures. It is then evident that the financial and real functions should fall within the competence of the agency for the industrial development of SMEs.

Finally, the adressee of the direct support interventions must be discussed, i.e. the actual and potential entrepreneurs able to respond to the incentives offered to entrepreneurial expectations and ideas present in the area (especially within defined and targeted contexts: trained young people, small entrepreneurs in sectors considered of greater interest, former employees of other firms with expendable skills) must be one of the first tasks of the agency's promoting activity.

The above described general target of enterprise support consist of the folloving specific targets: *a)* favour the expansion of the firms present in the industrial area; *b)* favour the entrance of new firms from outside the area; *c)* foster the birth of new entrepreneurial activities; *d)* favour the relocation in the industrial area of neighbouring firms currently located in towns, or in any case in non suitable areas, intended for a different use.

4.1.1 - Services Supplied by the Agency

The indicated targets will be achieved through a service network that the agency will offer to its associates and to external entrepreneurs interested in new locations, that will form the agency's income. In particular, the agency's functions can be summarized as follows: *a)* coordination and evaluation of new initiatives in the light of the market forecasts, of the area availability and of the utilization constraints on the available space; *b)* finding of all available financing sources, whether facilitated or not; processing of the files up to the achievement of the financing; *c)* coordination, organization and management of formative initiatives; *d)* supply of real services to firms; *e)* studies and researches aimed at the finding of new market spaces; *f)* organization of congresses and meetings to advertise the area productions and favour trade agreements; *g)* real and financial operations.

In general, as said above, the agency's specific task should be to coordinate the various subjects which, as it already now happens in part, contribute to the creation of new entrepreneurial initiatives and to support generally and specifically the already operational productive activities. In particular, the subjects are: 1) technical staff of large groups, vocational training centres, professional officies and consulting firms for what concerns the intangible real services; 2) programming companies, service firms for real services of a traditional kind; 3) local authorities, credit institutions, financial enterprises, regional, national and community funds for financing; 4) schools, trade-unions, entrepreneurs' associations, training centres, for the finding and the starting of new entrepreneurial capabilities.

4.1.2 - The Agency Intervention Instruments and Organizing Procedures

The general target concerning which the agency acts as a supervisor and coordinator is therefore the industrial development of SMEs and the productive reequilibrium of the industrial area of reference. To this end the agency must have a strategy able to safeguard the area total level of industrialization and employment.

Within this context, it is convenient to find first of all the subjects that may be involved and, in some respect, have some advantage in the general strategy of industrial development.

The agency's attention should focus on the firms connected with the typical sectors of the area and on the medium and small firms that during the last years have shown more dynamic productive or employment-related development.

The agency's contribution consists in the starting of interventions relating to several services put at the disposal of the users (firms, new firms, entrepreneurs): technical, productive and managerial capabilities covering a series of factors which are lacking in small firms thus inhibiting, or creating problems to, their growth, their strengthening and/or their development on the market.

The agency's activity is strongly different from the service organizing structure and the functions because, even though it tries to fill a gap in real services, it operates in the territory as a filter between the various entrepreneurial and formative initiatives on one side and the range of usable real and financial services on the other. Therefore, the agency offers its consulting services to the firms (old and new ones) with the purpose of finding a solution to the typical problems it deals with.

This kind of intervention should not be regarded as merely passive, in which the agency adapts to the requests coming from the population of enterprises: the agency itself might carry out a job of selection of the firms (or of some of them) which could be involved in the programme, directing the choice on the basis of the above discussed sectorial reequilibrium. Concerning the ways in which the coordinating intervention (typical of the agency) could be carried out, the suggestion is to work with an agile, motivated and autonomous

Maurizio Tenenbaum

GRAPH 1

HYPOTHESIS OF WORKING SCHEME FOR THE LOCAL AGENCY
FOR INDUSTRIAL DEVELOPMENT

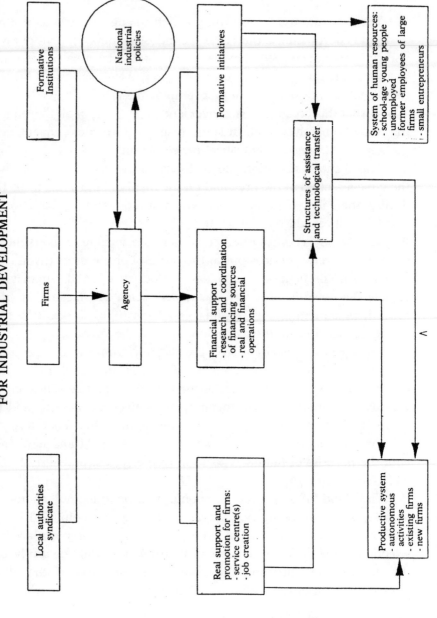

structure. Then, as regards the promotion of development, the agency may offer a range of different services, on account of the specific area problems, starting from a series of competences which are necessary to the entrepreneurs in their areas of interest.

In short, the filter formed by the agency may consist in the following kinds of services: 1) technical consulting; 2) financial and real advice; 3) consulting for the finding procedures of investment financings; 4) assistance to the innovation of production processes; 5) marketing; 6) management consulting; 7) export consulting; 8) planning of infrastructures.

The coordination carried out by the agency refers both to public and private initiatives within the above mentioned fields, possibly operating in the territory, and to a range of quite different actions (services to firms, job creation, training intiatives) each of which forms a specific field of interventions. The schematic figure in graph 1 shows all these facets.

A necessary and priority-condition for the good working of the described strategy is obviously the full involvement of the local, institutional, associative and social forces.

We shall see in the final remarks that the bill on the development of SMEs recently introduced by Minister Battaglia contains in embryo some signs in this direction, even if these are not organized in an agency as is instead proposed here (16).

5. - Some Final Remarks

The patient reader that has followed the analysis so far could ask at this point which connections there are between a national industrial policy destined to strategic and/or sectorial targets and an operational proposal at local level like the one presented here.

The national policy is adressed to the industrial system as a whole, where the firm is autonomous and independent of the social-institutional context and the transfer payments of the public sector are

---

(16) MINISTRY OF THE INDUSTRY, COMMERCE AND CRAFTSMANSHIP [29]. The Bill introduced by Minister Battaglia was passed by the Council of Ministers on 5th Dec. 1989.

aimed at improving the ability of the firm to stay on the domestic and international market.

In the local agency for the industrial development instead the firms comes into contact with a mixed structure where the interaction — and the consequent conditioning — with the institutions and the social forces might seem to herald troubles and autonomy restrictions.

The reduced effectiveness of the national industrial policies, at least for what concerns the orientation targets in favour of SMEs or the spreading of innovations within the whole productive system is so well-known that in our opinion it cannot but require a greater integration with the social-economic realities at a territorial level. On the other hand, the only effective law seems to be the Sabatini Act, which does nothing else but spread its incentives like rain without any explicit "orientation". The fact that SMEs are the main recipients of incentives is, as above shown, the simple results of a very low level of sectorial and territorial concentration of the Sabatini Law.

Such comments have in part been absorbed — though in a totally different context — in the bill introduced by the Minister of Industry, where, under Art. 23 (composition of syndicates and of public and private non-profit companies) and mainly under Art. 38, the public and private non-profit companies are defined as the subject to which the typical tasks of the agency are to be assigned: advice and assistance in the creation of new entrepreneurial activities and their strengthening, professional training for new technologies, financial assistance and consulting, purchase and management of industrial areas with infrastructures, etc.

Though being convinced that the industrial policy measures must be coordinated better and managed in a unitary way, the emphasis placed in the new bill for the industrial policy on the public and private non-profit companies goes in the right direction of interventions aimed at strenghtening the industrial environment as a whole, instead of simple transfer payments tending to improve the operating accounts of the individual firms.

Methodology of Estimates
and Data on the "Sabatini Law"

1. - Methodological Note
on the Estimate of Industrial Production

The reconstruction of the series of industrial production divided into the main activity sectors involved no little difficulties of a statistical character. All the studies we have examined in the literature using information at this level of territorial and sectorial disaggregation refer almost exclusively to data gathered by ISTAT through its surveys on *sales and gross product of industrial enterprises*. These surveys, however, show considerable gaps in information mainly due to the variability of the population of enterprises referred to. Furthermore, the data refer only to firms with more than 20 employees; in fact, surveys covering smaller enterprises (6 to 19 employees) do exist, but only cover few years (1983, 1985, 1986) and therefore require further approximation.

In our case, we tried to complete the ISTAT series by using the 1981 industry census data described below. In spite of this, a comparison of the series so obtained with the aggregate values for he whole industrial sector provided by the new ISTAT regional accounting shows remarkable divergences between the two historical series both in absolute terms and, particulrly, in the percent composition of the contribution given by the individual regions to the total industrial production. A similar comparison carried out on the index numbers of industrial producton by sectùor of activity as rearranged by the Bank of Italy, shows further divergences in terms of comparative evolution between the different sectors.

Within this frame, and having carried out an empirical check of a number of alternative estimate methods, we verified (by means of a suitable index of statistical dependence) that the error margin could be minimized by applying the following procedure: *A)* reconstruction of the historical series of industrial production by sector and region through the ISTAT surveys on sales and gross product of industrial enterprises, with the chief aim of obtaining information on the evolution of the percent contribution to the total production given over the years by the individual components x_{ij} (production of the ith sector of the jth region); *B)* reconstruction of the same historical series by an alternative method: in the first place the total value of the 1981 industrial production at factor cost (consistent with the new national accounting) was divided by sector and region through the composition learned in the ISTAT census on industry employees (turned into production on the basis of the average production/employee ratio as found in the statistics referred to at point *A)* above); in the second place, these values were projected to 1987 through the indexes of industrial production as processed by the Bank of Italy for the various sectors except for the "building" one. For the latter we used the production values at consistant prices, as per the 1989 report by the Budget Ministry, disaggregated on a regional basis by means of the above mentioned data on sales and gross product of enterprises (see point *A)*); *C)* finally, on the series so calculated we imposed the observance of a constraint being represented by the corresponding values gathered year by year from the new national accounting — keeping the internal composition of the individual $x_{ij}s$ as unchanged as possible (to the detriment, of course, of a greater consistency of the column sum vectors with the index numbers of the Bank of Italy).

TABLE 1.1

LAW 1329 OF 1965: TOTAL TRANSFER PAYMENTS IN THE PERIOD 1982-1987
(million lira at constant prices)

Sectors	Piemonte Val d'Aosta	Liguria	Lombardia	Trentino Alto Adige	Veneto	Friuli Venezia Giulia	Emilia Romagna
Food	139,530	19,598	216,321	8,612	178,651	26,328	215,508
Textile.............	160,337	1,052	462,556	2,552	89,618	11,736	15,655
Hides and leather	1,623	86	5,445	0	56,254	2,047	2,448
Wood working	12,685	106	49,478	2,230	39,916	5,964	31,755
Metallurgy	34,046	215	71,337	466	34,294	3,505	15,476
Mechanical	205,839	27,757	517,756	4,661	259,875	55,814	335,056
Chemical	83,343	3,732	204,997	2,183	73,684	5,354	46,846
Paper	80,558	2,280	127,407	5,467	47,501	1,028	33,488
Quarrying	12,294	4,641	21,375	1,465	15,945	2,463	12,121
Energy	376	0	1,662	0	859	65	694
Non met. min. wor.	28,797	13,823	57,805	9,265	78,629	2,586	193,512
Building	55,727	22,980	150,993	18,974	91,001	16,878	143,846
Other manufact.	8,500	807	50,636	628	10,042	1,494	8,616
Total	823,655	97,077	1,937,728	56,503	976,269	135,262	1,055,021

Maurizio Tenenbaum

Table 1.1 *continued*

LAW 1329 OF 1965: TOTAL TRANSFER PAYMENTS IN THE PERIOD 1982-1987
(million lira at constant prices)

Sectors	Marche	Toscana	Umbria	Lazio	Centre-North total	South total	Total
Food	62,796	73,258	87,064	65,982	1,093,648	193,039	1,286,687
Textile..............	11,746	100,543	6,054	1,816	863,665	10,065	873,730
Hides and leather	9,715	10,418	1,247	0	89,283	779	90,062
Wood working	25,829	14,085	5,750	1,816	189,614	1,894	191,508
Metallurgy	4,074	7,336	1,979	1,076	173,804	3,783	177,587
Mechanical	66,695	43,139	33,797	16,534	1,566,923	23,319	1,590,242
Chemical	24,195	14,961	6,285	4,195	469,775	5,939	475,714
Paper	11,026	69,429	5,561	9,004	392,749	2,464	395,213
Quarrying	8,908	29,527	4,833	10,370	123,942	46,523	170,465
Energy	25	5,112	172	106	9,363	289	9,652
Non met. min. wor.	19,123	78,659	26,001	15,595	523,795	81,513	605,308
Building	51,894	88,588	62,901	138,683	842,465	337,384	1,179,849
Other manufact.	5,716	7,493	5,087	840	99,859	2,598	102,457
Total	301,742	542,880	246,731	266,017	6,438,885	709,589	7,148,474

(*) Only the amounts relative to the industrial sector were considered.

TABLE 1.2

LAW 1329 OF 1965: TOTAL TRANSFER PAYMENTS IN THE PERIOD 1982-1987
(million lira at 1980 constant prices) (*)

Sectors	Piemonte Val d'Aosta	Liguria	Lombardia	Trentino Alto Adige	Veneto	Friuli Venezia Giulia	Emilia Romagna
Food	73,434	10,208	113,419	4,390	93,032	13,462	115,923
Textile	90,193	534	250,861	1,297	48,725	6,024	8,414
Hides and leather	898	61	3,123	0	29,894	1,081	1,329
Wood working	7,314	56	27,540	1,389	22,456	3,209	18,106
Metallurgy	19,226	116	41,029	251	19,058	1,915	9,391
Mechanical	113,187	15,607	282,372	2,604	139,986	28,891	184,290
Chemical	46,060	2,015	117,745	1,206	39,533	2,712	25,611
Paper	44,047	1,260	69,378	2,825	25,968	564	18,708
Quarrying	6,889	2,614	11,433	782	8,901	1,387	6,926
Energy	189	0	831	0	437	35	352
Non met. min. wor.	16,675	7,753	32,825	5,025	43,888	1,519	114,194
Building	29,863	12,707	74,077	12,290	49,160	8,894	80,299
Other manufact.	5,244	483	29,118	359	5,708	752	5,777
Total	453,221	53,415	1,047,752	32,419	526,746	70,444	589,320

(*) Only the amounts relative to the industrial sector were considered.

TABLE 1.2 *continua*

LAW 1329 OF 1965: TOTAL TRANSFER PAYMENTS IN THE PERIOD 1982-1987 (million lira at 1980 constant prices) (*)

Sectors	Marche	Toscana	Umbria	Lazio	Centre-North total	South total	Total
Food	32,493	38,129	47,963	33,977	576,431	91,745	668,176
Textile............	6,195	55,241	3,254	1,089	471,826	5,424	477,250
Hides and leather	5,374	5,556	729	0	48,045	401	48,446
Wood working	14,695	8,370	3,254	1,040	107,698	1,010	108,708
Metallurgy	2,454	3,956	1,233	576	99,205	1,917	101,122
Mechanical	36,066	23,461	18,344	8,584	853,392	12,674	866,066
Chemical	10,314	8,241	3,445	2,220	253,103	3,404	256,507
Paper	5,917	38,679	3,383	4,936	215,665	1,369	217,034
Quarrying	5,277	16,248	2,750	5,471	68,679	25,300	93,979
Energy	13	2,746	87	53	4,743	151	4,894
Non met. min. wor.	10,986	45,421	14,799	9,111	302,197	46,487	348,684
Building	29,024	49,467	34,625	74,808	455,216	181,117	636,333
Other manufact.	3,426	4,393	3,076	446	58,782	1,467	60,249
Total	162,503	299,908	136,942	142,312	3,514,982	372,467	3,887,448

(*) Only the amounts relative to the industrial sector were considered.

TABLE 1.3

LAW 1329 OF 1965: TOTAL TRANSFER PAYMENTS IN THE PERIOD 1982-1987
PER CENT DISTRIBUTION BY SECTOR BASED ON VALUES AT CONSTANT PRICES (*)

Sectors	Piemonte Val d'Aosta	Liguria	Lombardia	Trentino Alto Adige	Veneto	Friuli Venezia Giulia	Emilia Romagna
Food	16.2	19.1	10.8	13.5	17.7	19.1	19.7
Textile..............	19.9	1.0	23.9	4.0	9.3	8.6	1.4
Hides and leather	0.2	0.1	0.3	0.0	5.7	1.5	0.2
Wood working	1.6	0.1	2.6	4.3	4.3	4.6	3.1
Metallurgy	4.2	0.2	3.9	0.8	3.6	2.7	1.6
Mechanical	25.0	29.2	27.0	8.0	26.6	41.0	31.3
Chemical	10.2	3.8	10.7	3.7	7.5	3.8	4.3
Paper	9.7	2.4	6.6	8.7	4.9	0.8	3.2
Quarrying	1.5	4.9	1.1	2.4	1.7	2.0	1.2
Energy	0.0	0.0	0.1	0.0	0.1	0.0	0.1
Non met. mineral work.	3.7	14.5	3.1	15.5	8.3	2.2	19.4
Building.........	6.6	23.8	7.1	37.9	9.3	12.6	13.6
Other manifact.	1.2	0.9	2.8	1.1	1.1	1.1	1.0
Total	100	100	100	100	100	100	100

(*) Only the amounts relating to the industrial sector were considered.

Maurizio Tenenbaum

TABLE 1.3 *continued*

LAW 1329 OF 1965: TOTAL TRANSFER PAYMENTS IN THE PERIOD 1982-1987
PER CENT DISTRIBUTION BY SECTOR BASED ON VALUES AT CONSTANT PRICES (*)

Sectors	Marche	Toscana	Umbria	Lazio	Centre-North total	South total	Total
Food	20.0	12.7	35.0	23.9	16.4	24.6	17.2
Textile.............	3.8	18.4	2.4	0.8	13.4	1.5	12.3
Hides and leather ...	3.3	1.9	0.5	0.0	1.4	0.1	1.2
Wood working	9.2	2.8	2.4	0.7	3.1	0.3	2.8
Metallurgy	1.5	1.3	0.9	0.4	2.8	0.5	2.6
Mechanical	22.2	7.8	13.4	6.0	24.3	3.4	22.3
Chemical	6.3	2.7	2.5	1.6	7.2	0.9	6.6
Paper	3.6	12.9	2.5	3.5	6.1	0.4	5.6
Quarrying	3.2	5.4	2.0	3.8	2.0	6.8	2.4
Energy	0.0	0.9	0.1	0.0	0.1	0.0	0.1
Non met. mineral work.	6.8	15.1	10.8	6.4	8.6	12.5	9.0
Building.............	17.9	16.5	25.3	52.6	13.0	48.6	16.4
Other manufact.	2.1	1.5	2.2	0.3	1.7	0.4	1.5
Total	100	100	100	100	100	100	100

(*) Only the amounts relating to the industrial sector were considered.

TABLE 1.4

LAW 1329 OF 1965: TOTAL TRANSFER PAYMENTS IN THE PERIOD 1982-1987
PER CENT DISTRIBUTION BY SECTOR BASED ON VALUES AT CONSTANT PRICES (*)

Sectors	Piemonte Val d'Aosta	Liguria	Lombardia	Trentino Alto Adige	Veneto	Friuli Venezia Giulia	Emilia Romagna
Food	11.0	1.5	17.0	0.7	13.9	2.0	17.3
Textile, clothing	18.9	0.1	52.6	0.3	10.2	1.3	1.8
Hides and leather	1.9	0.1	6.4	0.0	61.7	2.2	2.7
Wood working	6.7	0.1	25.3	1.3	20.7	3.0	16.7
Metallurgy	19.0	0.1	40.6	0.2	18.8	1.9	9.3
Mechanical	13.1	1.8	32.6	0.3	16.2	3.3	21.3
Chemical	18.0	0.8	43.6	0.5	15.4	1.1	10.0
Paper	20.3	0.6	32.0	1.3	12.0	0.3	8.6
Quarrying	7.3	2.8	12.2	0.8	9.5	1.5	7.4
Energy	3.9	0.0	17.0	0.0	8.9	0.7	7.2
Non met. mineral work.	4.8	2.2	9.4	1.4	12.6	0.4	32.7
Building	4.7	2.0	11.6	1.9	7.7	1.4	12.6
Other manufact.	8.7	0.8	48.3	0.6	9.5	1.2	9.6

(*) Only amounts relative to the industrial sector were considered.

Maurizio Tenenbaum

TABLE 1.4 *continued*

LAW 1329 OF 1965: TOTAL TRANSFER PAYMENTS IN THE PERIOD 1982-1987
PER CENT DISTRIBUTION BY SECTOR BASED ON VALUES AT CONSTANT PRICES (*)

Sectors	Marche	Toscana	Umbria	Lazio	Centre-North total	South total	Total
Food	4.9	5.7	7.2	5.1	86.3	13.7	100.0
Textile, clothing	1.3	11.6	0.7	0.2	98.9	1.1	100.0
Hides and leather	11.1	11.5	1.5	0.0	99.2	0.8	100.0
Wood working	13.8	7.7	3.0	1.0	99.1	0.9	100.0
Metallurgy	2.4	3.9	1.2	0.6	98.1	1.9	100.0
Mechanical	4.2	2.7	2.1	1.0	98.5	1.5	100.0
Chemical	4.0	3.2	1.3	0.9	98.7	1.3	100.0
Paper	2.7	17.8	1.6	2.3	99.4	0.6	100.0
Quarrying	5.6	17.3	2.9	5.8	73.1	26.9	100.0
Energy	0.3	56.1	1.8	1.1	96.9	3.1	100.0
Non met. mineral work.	3.2	13.0	4.2	2.6	86.7	13.3	100.0
Building........	4.6	7.8	5.4	11.8	71.5	28.5	100.0
Other manufacturing	5.7	7.3	5.1	0.7	97.6	2.4	100.0

(*) Only amounts relative to the industrial sector were considered.

Characteristics of the Areas and Summary
of the Field Surveys Carried Out

1. - Characteristics of the Areas Investigated

1.1 - *Industrial Area of Terni*

The development model is based upon the organization of large estabilishments in the chemical and especially in the iron and steel sectors. Terni can be described as a company town: its productive apparatus has grown in connection with the presence on the spot of a few big industries.

On this background, the present situation can be outlined by the following points: 1) employment crisis owing to a reduction of the labour employed directly by the large firms, without an equivalent increase in indirect or tertiary employment; 2) inadequate management; 3) lack of entrepreneurship (the tendency is for minor enterprises to develop oñ protected markets, guaranteed by subcontracts with large industries); 4) little productive tertiarization.

1.2 - *Industrial Area of Valdarno Superiore*

The local productive system is marked by a diffusion of activities over the territory, particularly in the following sectors: leather, shoes, hides, working of non-metalliferous minerals, some metalworking activities.

The structure is close to that of an industrial district.

The 1980s were characterized by: 1) increasing integration between firms; 2) steady employment by small and medium firms despite a small decline in the profitability; 3) a positive evolution of medium-large firms; 4) a remarkable concentration of infrastructural investments; 5) a local policy favouring industrial localization which are also determined by the availability of areas, their low price, and the promixity of important mainroads.

1.3 - *Industrial Area of Val di Cornia-Piombino*

The productive system is based on the presence of the public and private iron and steel pool (a similar situation was seen in Terni). The presence of an ENEL power plant is to be noted.

At the beginning of the 1980s the iron and steel crisis determined: 1) a high increase of unemployment; 2) a productive reality unable to create a market of its own, independent of the iron and steel firms. Moreover, the following is to be noted: 3) the little independence of the management of the large local firms, as the latter refer to national groups whose decisional centres are located outside the area; 4) as a result, it appears that the true constraint on the development of initiatives of reindustrialization in Val di Cornia is the scarcity of entrepreneurial resources.

1.4 - *Apuan Industrial Area of Massa Carrara*

The area is characterized by a productive dichotomy: on the one hand, the presence of large firms in the basic sectors (chemistry, iron metallurgy) that are in a state of crisis since the beginning of the 1980s due to economic reasons (crisis of the iron metallurgy sector) and to environmental ones (chemistry); on the other, the spreading over the territory of marble quarrying and working activities, as also the production of machinery for the transforming industry of non metalliferous minerals.

In the 1980s the "traditional" sectors responded to the crisis of the basic sectors (with consequences similar to those earlier described) by creating an alternative employment. In order to fully recover a development path it is important to face a series of questions: 1) problems of environmental compatibility due to the spread of polluting productive activities over the territory; 2) lack of entrepreneurship in sectors other than the marble one; 3) lack of industrial areas with infrastructures far away from towns; 4) reconversion of the labour force expelled by the large firms.

2. - Field Surveys at the Firms

2.1 *Industrial Area of Terni*

Characteristics: 1) interviews to 3 large groups present in the area (Società Terni, Montedison, Ternichimica); 2) sample surveys at the firms of the area of Narni, Amelia and Terni. Sixty-two manufacturing firms were interviewed, equal to 21.4% of the firm population: all the manufacturing firms employing more than 20 persons, and a representative sample of the firms employing from 6 to 50 persons.

The aim of the survey was to examine the evolution of the productive structure in the light of technological innovation phenomena.

Firm and area weakness facators (constraints on development) for large firms: *a)* difficulty in creating employment given the trend in the demand for iron and steel productions; *b)* the local industry suffers the consequences of the freeze of the energy domestic plan ;*c)* in Terni there are mainly manufacturing plants belonging to the groups of reference; *d)* organizational and physical distance of the main markets of reference.

For what concerns the remaining productive structure: *a)* lack of independence of small and medium firms which supply services to the large ones, but do not have their own market; *b)* insufficient size of the productive tertiary; *c)* presence of a demand (which is not met) for services connected to the position on the market: strategic marketing, market surveys, assistance to and mediation in the import-export, finding and training of personnel.

Proposal: interventions of reindustrialization by the State Shareholdings. Job creation initiatives and realization of a Bic (GEPI-

SPI); creation of a local agency for industrial development coordinating the interventions and the subjects concerning the technical
procedures, the financing and the assistance in planning the carrying
out of new entrepreneurial initiatives.

2.2 - *Industrial Area of Valdarno Superiore*

Characteristics: 73 firms were interviewed, equal to 2.5% of the
industrial enterprises and 25% of total employment (3,700 workers).
The purpose of the survey was to identify the existing project routes,
and to analyse the constraints on, and the needs of, the firms.

Firm and area weakness factors (constraints on development):
scarce creation of internal resources to be employed in the firm;
finding of technical personnel and of skilled blue-collar workers;
unmet demand for services to be supplied to the firms in the fields of
marketing, training of managers, research and development; the
larger firms also show shortcomings in the infrastructures and the
problem of the disposal of manufacturing waste.

Proposals: creation of a Council of productive and financial
subjects of Valdarno Superiore Sud aiming at improving the environment in which the SME is operating.

The work of this Council should focus on: *a)* coordination of the
town-planning instruments; *b)* realization of an economic observa-
tory; *c)* opening of an information counter for small firms for the
purpose of mediating between firms and local service market.

2.3 *Industrial Area of Val di Cornia-Piombino*

Characteristics: surveys at 13 large-medium firms, in order to
identify the existing relation between large firms and related and
upstream industries, and to find new productive initiatives.

Firm and area weakness factors (constraints on development):
lack of a network of firms downstream from the iron and steel sector;
related and upstream industries characterized by the mere supply of
services to the large firms (maintenance, equipment); occupation

centred on the employment by firms: difficulty for the development of entrepreneurial initiatives.

Proposals: creation of a centre for firms and innovations acting as an agency for job creation and diversification of production. The centre should also supply services of a formative, financial, and technological kind; creation of a "quality guarantee syndicate"; finding of new productive initiatives for local reindustrialization purposes; creation of an agency with tasks of promotion service arrangement and organization, and research activities to foster the economic activities in Val di Cornia; the agency should supply real services and help the local entrepreneurs in general, and in particular it should take action in the following fields: *a)* synergy of environment, agriculture and tourism; *b)* agriculture-industry; *c)* exploitation of artistic and handicraft activities; *d)* preparation of vocational training and refresher programmes.

2.4 *Apual Industrial Zone (ZIA) of Massa Carrara*

Characteristics: about 250 firms (industrial and non-industrial ones) located in ZIA (equal to 75% of the population) answered the interviews; the aim of the survey was to identify the general problems of ZIA and find development initiatives.

Firm and area weakness factors (constraints on development): the environmental problem is indicated by 43% of the firms as the main obstacle to development; lacking offer of industrial areas, with or without infrastructures; lack of availability of financial means necessary for moving the processings; difficulty in the treatment of manufacturing waste; lack of support activities and structures for firms: real basic and strategic services, difficulty in the development of productive activities in sectors other than the marble one.

Proposals: creation of an agency with tasks of: 1) coordination of subjects and services working for the reindustrialization of ZIA; 2) supply (or coordination) of financial and real services to firms; 3) coordination and creation of plans for vocational training and reconversion; 4) fostering, assistance, and support of new entrepreneurial activities.

296   *Maurizio Tenenbaum*

BIBLIOGRAPHY

[1] ANTONELLI C. - GINESTRI S.: «Politica industriale, razionalità limitata e asimmetrie. Il caso del fondo rotativo innovazione tecnologica», *Cespe Papers*, no. 6, 1989.

[2] ANTONELLI C. - MOMIGLIANO F.: «Aree economiche, modelli di sviluppo alternativi e politiche di intervento in Italia», *L'industria*, no. 3, 1980.

[3] ARTONI R. - PONTAROLLO E.: *Trasferimenti, domanda pubblica e sistema industriale*, Bologna, il Mulino, 1988.

[4] AVITABILE R. - GALLO R. - SCARANGELA D.: «Il finanziamento pubblico dell'innovazione tecnologica», *L'industria*, no. 1, 1985.

[5] BANCA D'ITALIA: *Appendice alla relazione annuale della Banca d'Italia*, 1989.

[6] BARCA F. - MAGNANI M.: *L'industria fra capitale e lavoro: piccole e grandi imprese dall'autunno caldo al risanamento*, Bologna, il Mulino, 1989.

[7] BARCA F. - BRASCA F.M.: «Risanamento e prospettive di sviluppo dell'industria italiana», in BATTAGLIA A. - VALCAMONICI R. [8], pp. 224-80.

[8] BATTAGLIA A. - VALCAMONICI R. (ed.): *Nella competizione globale. Una politica industriale verso il 2000*, Roma, Bari, Laterza, 1989.

[9] BECATTINI G. (ed.): *Mercati e forze locali: il distretto industriale*, Bologna, il Mulino, 1987.

[10] BRUSCO S.: «The Emilian Model: Productive Decentralization and Social Integration», *Cambridge Journal of Economics*, no. 6, 1982.

[11] CER «Mercato e politica industriale. Terzo rapporto sull'industria e la politica industriale» Bologna, il Mulino, 1989, pp. 293-7.

[12] CLES: *Studi e ricerche per la «conferenza economica e cittadina»*, Mimeo, Terni, 1987.

[13] — —: *Analisi e prospettive economiche della Val di Cornia*, mimeo, Piombino, Associazione intercomunale Val di Cornia, 1988.

[14] — —: *Materiali per la «conferenza economica»*, Mimeo, Firenze, Associazione intercomunale Valdarno Superiore sud, 1988.

[15] — —: *La reindustrializzazione della zona industriale apuana*, mimeo, Firenze, Regione Toscana-Italimpianti, 1988.

[16] CONFINDUSTRIA: «Per una politica industriale: le proposte degli imprenditori», Atti del Convegno, Genova, 9-10 ottobre 1981, *Rivista di politica economica*, August-September 1982, pp. 1086-93.

[17] FAINI R.-SCHIANTARELLI F.: «Incentives and Investment Decisions: the Effectiveness of Regional Policy», in *Oxford Economic Papers*, no. 39, 1987.

[18] FILIPPI E. - MOMIGLIANO F.: «La politica per l'innovazione in Italia, l'esperienza del primo periodo di applicazione della legge no. 46 del 1982», *L'industria*, no. 4, 1985.

[19] FLORIO M.: «Grande impresa e sviluppo endogeno nei sistemi locali» *L'industria*, no. 4, 1986.

[20] GIANNOLA A.: «Il ruolo delle piccole e medie imprese nel recente sviluppo industriale italiano», Isve, *Institute Papers*, no. 27, 1988.

[21] GRILLO M. - SILVA F.: *Impresa concorrenza e organizzazione*, Roma, Nis, 1989.

[22] GROSS PIETRO G.M. - OCCHIFREDDI D. - ROLFO S. - VITALI G. (eds.); *Dalla politica industriale ad una politica per l'industria*, Associazione per Tecnocity, 1989.

[23] GROS-PIETRO G.M.: «L'innovazione nell'industria italiana: situazione e problemi», *L'industria*, no. 2, Apr.-June 1985.

[24] ISTAT: *Fatturato, prodotto lordo, investimenti delle imprese industriali, del commercio, dei trasporti e comunicazioni*, Roma, ISTAT, 1981-1982.

[25] —— : *Fatturato, prodotto lordo, investimenti delle imprese industriali, del commercio, dei trasporti e comunicazioni e di alcuni tipi di servizi*, Roma, ISTAT, 1983, 1984, 1985.

[26] —— : *I conti economici delle regioni 1980-1987*.

[27] LA NOCE M.: *Linee di intervento delle politiche di incentivazione industriale*, in BATTAGLIA A. - VALCAMONICI B. [8], pp. 251-80.

[28] MINISTERO DEL BILANCIO E DELLA PROGRAMMAZIONE ECONOMICA: *Relazione generale sulla situazione economica del paese*, vol. 1, 1989.

[29] MINISTERO DELL'INDUSTRIA, DEL COMMERCIO E DELL'ARTIGIANATO: *Relazione illustrativa dello schema di disegno di legge recante: interventi per l'innovazione e lo sviluppo delle Pmi industriali*, Roma, January 1990.

[30] —— : *Rapporto della commissione per lo studio delle problematiche delle Pmi*, Roma, May 1988.

[31] MOMIGLIANO F. (ed.): *Le leggi della politica industriale in Italia*, Bologna, il Mulino, 1986.

[32] NOMISMA: *Politica industriale, servizi reali e opportunità di sviluppo a livello locale*, Bologna, Nomisma, November 1985.

[33] PASINETTI L. (ed.): *Mutamenti strutturali del sistema produttivo*, Bologna, il Mulino, 1986.

[34] REBECCHINI F.: «Documento conclusivo della indagine conoscitiva sulla politica industriale della Commissione industriale del senato», *L'industria*, no. 4, 1985.

[35] REGIONE LOMBARDIA: *Interventi regionali nel settore industriale*, Milano, Regione Lombardia, 1990.

[36] —— : *Le politiche regionali per la rilocalizzazione industriale*, Milano, F. Angeli, 1984.

[37] SCANAGATTA G.: «L'attuazione degli interventi di politica industriale per le piccole e medie imprese» in BATTAGLIA A. - VALCAMONICI R. [8], pp. 281-301.

[38] TASSINARI F. (ed.): *Industria manifatturiera e terziario avanzato per le imprese*, Milano, F. Angeli, 1989.

III - INNOVATION
AND COMPETITIVENESS:
PERSPECTIVES OF INDUSTRIAL
POLICY FOR THE 90s

Industrial Policy
and Technological Innovation (*)

Bruno Lamborghini - **Cesare Sacchi**
Olivetti, Ivrea   Fiat, Torino

1. - Introduction

The purpose of this paper is to re-evaluate the role of industrial policy in favour of technological and organizational innovation in Italy. This will not be undertaken purely for the sake of analysis; rather, an attempt will be made to provide some answers with regard to the possible role of industrial policy measures if innovation is to be promoted and diffused effectively among Italian enterprises.

To interpret the relationship between industrial policy and the technological and organizational innovation of firms, an effort was made to identify the internal and external "driving forces" underlying the innovation of firms during the 1970s and 1980s, periods of growth in Italian industry.

In a recent interview with Richard Nelson, Sidney Winter, the founder of the theory of evolution of the firm (which implies that enterprises are selected by the market in Darwinian fashion), said: "For each firm, the primary source of innovation may be external or internal. Within the system as a whole, innovation is entirely a question of economics, but at the some time it is closely connected with the progress of science and national policies. One cannot begin to understand the path followed by modern economies without exploring the relationships which exist between the innovation that takes place internally, and the broader context within which it occurs".

(*) We wish to thank Roberto Maglione for his contributions to this paper.

The parameters used to measure the overall effect of internal and external action of industrial policy (or of economic policy in general) took the form of evaluations by comparison of the development of Italian industry and of its competitiveness at the international level.

This study has intentionally been limited to several macrovariables; the scarcity of available data and the need for *ad hoc* research would have precluded a more detailed analysis. Given the nature of this paper, it was considered preferable to draw conclusions, based on past experience, particularly on the first-hand experience of firms, which could play a useful role in shaping Italian innovation policy in the 1990s.

In the latter part of the paper, we endeavoured to verify the validity of a new approach which could serve to implement a coherent policy while creating the necessary conditions for the emergence of a truly competitive market. The changes awaiting Europe in the near future are destined to topple even the last barriers shielding certain areas of Italian industry, such as the services sector, from international competition.

Market integration will extend even farther than expected to include Central and Eastern Europe, and will increase the presence of leading American and Asian producers. Nonetheless, quality and innovation prevail as the resources which can be tapped by Italian industry in order to maintain and increase involvement in high technology, to remain competitive in "traditional" sectors, and to improve its position on international markets. It is necessary, therefore, to delay no further in developing an industrial policy for innovation that takes into account the high stakes involved and the behaviour of competitors.

2. - The "Driving Forces" of Innovation in Italy from a Historical Perspective

Analysis of the experience of past decades has revealed two "driving forces" of innovation: *a)* external forces (linked to the economy as a whole, and *b)* internal forces (affecting the decisions of firms). External forces result from the interaction of a series of variables, namely the level of public R&D expenditure, the degree of internationalization, developments in the national scientific and technological framework, the infrastructure, and, last but not least, industrial policy (coupled with institutional support fostering the development and diffusion of technological innovation).

Internal forces involve the optimality and the improvement of the production cycle, the search for increasingly flexible management and production methods, the ability to benefit from existing technological opportunities (both inside and outside the firm). Understanding the characteristics of these forces and how they work may provide some insight into the relationship between the innovative processes of firms and industrial policy measures fostering innovation.

2.1 *The 1960s*

Italy's industrial base grew at a rapid pace. Innovation was directed toward filling the technological gap between Italy and other most industrialized countries (such as the US).

Enterprises viewed technological innovation as a way to boost the Taylorist efficiency of the production process (by cutting down production time) on the one hand, thereby lowering production costs, and, on the other hand, as a means of differentiating their products.

2.2 *The 1970s*

Development entered a state of crisis, due in part to the oil shocks which occurred during the decade. Production and hierarchical reference models were beginning to fall out of favour (from a social standpoint as well). Industrial policy attempted not so much to stimulate innovation as to stop up the gaps in Italian industry, most notably in the staple sectors. Moreover, it was thought that market forces alone were unable to redress certain disequilibria and structural shortcomings: the search for sector-by-sector intervention policies (Law 675 of 1977) began as a result. Enterprises speeded up production process innovation so as to fragment production cycles, rendering them more responsive to the peaks and troughs of the business cycle (the decentralization of production).

Technological innovation therefore became a means of overcoming crisis situations even as it offered new organizational solutions. Small- and medium-sized firms also began to benefit from the transfer of technological innovation achieved by large-sized enterprises during the 1960s; a direct consequence of this was the exceptionally high birthrate of small business during the early 1980s.

2.3 *The 1980s*

The exponential rise in new technology (particularly in electronics and computers), the shortening of product life-cycles, new consumer needs and profound changes in international competition (with the ever-increasing presence of Japanese competitors) were the variables that shaped innovative processes during this decade.

Technology became the truly determinant factor in the globalization of markets.

During the first half of the decade, this rapid change of perspective caused enterprises to redouble their R&D efforts by increasing the amount of skilled labour and financial resources during a period of unsteady economic and financial development; this despite mounting uncertainty concerning the prospect of an economic recovery and about viable technological solutions. With the risk to investors in R&D activity on the increase, enterprises were compelled by financial constraints to make harsh decisions which affected not only these activities, but also, in a broader sense, structural costs, so as to lower the break-even point.

These conditions, once limited to a few sectors were now imposed on industry as a whole. Understandably, the extent to which they apply varies with each sector's sensitivity to changes in technology and in the competitive context. There is a growing need for an industrial policy which provides some sort of insurance against technological risk and relieves the heavy financial burden (caused in part by real interest rates, which are much higher in Italy than in other industrialized countries).

This turn of events brought a shift away from the "by-sector" approach and toward a "by-factor" approach; broadly speaking, the latter expression refers to the workable competition with other industrial countries.

From a legal viewpoint, the approval in 1982 of Law 46, which set up the Fund for Technological Innovation, partially satisfied this need. However, insufficient knowledge of the workings and of the goals of innovation caused this source of financial aid to be over-estimated, and no serious attempt was made to bring the overall structure and the specific services required in line with the production process. Nonetheless, despite the fact that the solutions put in place were not entirely satisfactory, at the time Law 46 adequately accelerated the innovation programmes of many firms.

During the second half of the decade, enterprises continued to invest in the renewal and the rationalization of production processes while focusing on product innovation, seeking to gain value added not only at the manufacturing stage, but also at the post-manufacturing stage (product-related services and systems, follow-up assistance, quality, and so on).

Large-sized industrial groups grew both as a result of the enlargement of their structures (growth in size) and because of a large number of international alliances, cooperation agreements and acquisitions (growth caused by networks external to firms). This increases the degree of internationalization of industry and the technology acquired can be directly applied to internal innovative processes.

Technological innovation became increasingly linked to financial and organizational innovation. Small- and mid-sized enterprises systematically turned to technological innovation in order to acquire competitive advantage (especially in international markets), in high-technology sectors and in more mature ones. Geographically defined concentration of information and experience with respect to innovation continued to rise. A few territories developed into actual integrated systems emphasizing the expertise of local production (these were known as "industrial districts"). Enterprises attempted to reach the necessary critical mass (the minimum economic, financial, and organizational requirements of size) to survive the challenge of the

European single market. At the end of the 1980s, this became the primary objective of the decisionmaking of firms.

The independent commitment of enterprises to innovation and internationalization existed side by side with the progressive failure of industrial policy instruments aimed at strengthening innovative processes, particularly those of large enterprises, which received the lion's share of innovation in the 1980s. Financial aid in support of industrial research and technological innovation, which during the 1980s had reached unprecedented levels of allocation, was readjusted and reformed toward the end of the decade. This was caused by the fact that firms seemed to be increasingly capable of financing their own initiatives, and by the worsening of public finances. EEC guidelines concerning what was considered to be an excessively high number of transfer payments to Italian enterprises also served to influence the decisions of institutional authorities.

In the case of the IMI Fund, Law 346 of 1988 (which introduced interest account contributions) aimed at clearing the backlog of applications for financing that could not be accommodated by the more limited refinancing scheme under Law 46 of 1982. In a sense, the former law was proposed as a measure to deal with the unsatisfied requests rather than an innovative measure to support industrial research.

During the late 1980s, the opportunity to replace direct financial intervention with automatic tax concessions similar to those offered in other countries such as France was suggested once again (in the form of a draft bill), but received scant attention in Parliament. Entrepreneurs became increasingly aware that incisive action and appropriate intervention were unlikely to come from the public sector, because of the uncertainty concerning which objectives to pursue and which measures to adopt. That substantial improvement in conditions within the system could not possibly be provided within the time limits set by changing technology and competition was equally evident.

At the beginning of the 1990s, the somewhat positive experiment of direct support conducted during much of the 1970s and the 1980s seems to be drawing to a close. The direction, intensity and methods associated with innovative processes seem to be determined exclusively by the internal "driving forces" of both large and small firms.

The experiences of other countries, which we will summarize in the next chapter, clearly reveal that the overall advancement of innovation in industry cannot be guaranteed merely by the decisions of firms, though these decisions may be completely rational, or by their resources even when used in the most efficient manner. Competition increasingly measures not only individual firms, but also entire national economic systems.

Direct intervention mechanisms in support of industrial innovation (even in countries which blatantly exhibit laissez-faire behaviour, suc as England, under Thatcher) are being replaced by forms of indirect intervention geared toward creating a climate conducive to the internal shift of firms toward innovation.

3. - Comparison of Innovation Policies

Despite their shared objective, to increase the competitiveness of industry through the use of large-scale modernization, the industrial policies promoting research and development adopted by the leading European countries from the 1960s on differ with respect to the emphasis placed on specific sectors considered at some stage in the country's economic development to be of strategic importance, and as far as the instruments used to achieve stated objectives are concerned. A few noticeable stages of development can be defined.

Since the 1960s, the emergence of new strategic sectors has been matched by that of national policies geared predominantly toward individual sectors. The aims of these policies were essentially: 1) to broaden technological horizons, particularly by means of direct subsidies to national corporations, and 2) the diffusion of technology throughout national industry through support to research associations, agreements between universities and industry, the creation of high-level technology transfer centres and so on.

In France, the internationalization of the economy and the specialization of industrial production are pursued in tandem by means of extensive subsidization of large-sized enterprises and through the use of large-scale international projects focusing on individual products or sectors (such as Concorde or the nuclear plan).

In Germany, state intervention is directed particularly at maintaining conditions of workable competition; although extensive intervention is avoided, its broad objectives are the rationalization of markets, minimizing the social cost of structural changes in the economy, restoring geographic equilibrium and the support of innovation. As regards the latter item, the most significant form of public intervention is the creation of a network of public and private research centres (the Fraunhofer Society).

In Italy, since the mid-1960s enterprises have benefited from the transfer of public funds. Soft loans and cash grants had become the major instrument of industrial policy, actually taking the place of ordinary credit. In this context, salvage operations and subsidies based on need prevailed at the expense of initiatives geared toward the modernization of industry. It was during this decade that two important laws for technological innovation were approved: Law 139 of 1965, better known in Italy as the Sabatini law, which provides for the discounting at subsidized rates of the bills of exchange used to purchase tool machinery and is aimed specifically at small- and medium-sized enterprises; and Law 1089 of 1968, which created the IMI Fund for Applied Research to stimulate industrial research and the transfer of technological expertise to small- and medium-sized enterprises, at least formally through the use of a wide range of intervention measures.

Even an agency such as the National Research Council, created in 1923 and reorganized in 1937 and again in 1945 for the purposes of promoting, coordinating and regulating scientific research and fostering scientific and technical progress, encounters enormous difficulties in transferring information acquired from industry and in building an efficient network of private, public and university research centres.

During the 1970s there was a growing need for the planning and coordination of various initiatives concerning scientific research and the introduction, diffusion and transfer of the technology of firms.

In France, industrial policy strategy focuses on specific infrastructural projects (the *VII Plan* sets a limit to the number of *Programmes d'actions prioritaires*) and on selective intervention in sectors considered to be of strategic importance. The mandate of the

Comité d'orientation et de dèveloppement des industries stratégi-ques, formed by Raymond Barre in 1979, centres on six major objectives: office automation, robotics, bioindustry, energy conservation, large plants and undersea projects.

The major directions of strategy in Germany are twofold: foremost is the promotion of a strong national electronics industry led by a large-sized private-sector enterprise such as Siemens; the second involves the bailout of troubled industrial sectors (a case in point is the intervention received by AEG-Telefunken).

In Italy, a wave of economic change from 1975 on brought a shift toward structural policies aimed at industrial and financial reconversion in the short-to-medium term. Law No. 675 of 1977 approved the industrial planning of productive sectors for the purposes of coordinating industrial restructuring, reconversion of production, and development initiatives by rationalizing the previous measures. During this effort to organize the numerous instruments of industrial policy (which will involve streamlining, coordinating and narrowing the margins of discretion built into existing laws) an attempt which only partially succeeded, in 1976 Law 183 was approved to redirect southern Italy incentives toward small- and medium-sized exporting firms operating specifically in highly innovative sectors.

The principal policy measure to stimulate the technological modernization of medium-sized firms nationwide was Presidential Decree (DPR) 902 (set out in Law 183) which provided for the granting of subsidized investment in new plant and equipment, enlargement or modernizaiton to firms belonging to extractive or manufacturing industries. This initiative (in place since 1980) was initially proposed as a means of restoring regional equilibrium; however, the bulk of its assistance flows toward technological modernization projects of small-sized enterprises located in the Centre-North.

In the United Kingdom, between the end of the 1960s and the end of the 1970s, both Labour and Conservative governments elected, on the one hand, to provide firms and large groups in a crisis state with support (thereby shifting the focus from regional intervention to intervention by sector with the introduction of the *Industry Acts*) and on the other hand to ensure a significant amount of public-sector involvement in industries considered to be of strategic importance, such as computers, telecommunications equipment, and biotechnology.

Despite noticeable differences from country to country, the general tendency in Europe favours the integration of policies fostering new technologies (microelectronics, biology, optoelectronics, new materials, and so forth) and more sector-by-sector or geographically defined policies.

As regards those sectors considered to be of strategic significance (and in which high-level technology is applied), the following industrial policy decisions prevail: *a)* the creation of interministerial committees of coordination and of technology transfer agencies; *b)* the approval of programmes for the diffusion of new technology among small- and medium-sized enterprises, both regionally and by sector; *c)* special agreements between governments and exceptionally dynamic enterprises (at times by means of real venture capital operations); *d)* increased public-sector demand geared toward stimulating innovative activity, horizontally (new technologies would cross over into all sectors of production and services) as well as vertically (when sectors are rigidly delineated); *e)* the creation of new instruments, especially fiscal measures, promoting technological and organizational innovation; *f)* increased focus on real services to firms, in certain regions only.

During the 1980s, the frame of reference of national innovation policies was transformed. The rapid pace of internationalization and growing worldwide competition among the three major industrialized areas (the United States, Japan and Europe) led to the re-evaluation of European policies for innovation.

If, on the one hand, promoting the introduction, transfer and diffusion of technological and organizational innovation became an imperative for every government (as well as a return to the extensive promotion of basic research in specific strategic sectors such as microelectronics, biotechnology and new materials), on the other hand both the push of enterprises for the internationalization of national economic systems and the need to create synergies at the Community-wide and international levels made their presence felt with growing intensity.

In France, the rise to power in 1981 of the Socialist Mitterand government led to the nationalization of important industrial groups (Rhône-Poulenc, Saint-Gobain, CGE, Thomson) and of most of the private banking system. Efforts to promote strategic sectors were also intensified by means of selective intervention and through a rise in international cooperation.

The strategic lines of industrial policy adopted at the end of the 1980s again changed course, favouring at once the reprivatization of the large industrial groups and their expansion into international markets, and abandoning to some extent the concept of the technological *filière* underlying the measures supporting technological innovation in the early 1980s.

In Germany, direct intervention for innovation is non-existent. Nonetheless, public-sector demand serves as the principal means of giving incentives to sectors considered to be of strategic importance to the national economy. Two objectives are pursued simultaneously: the first involves the modernization of the industrial structure as a whole, with a view to enhancing the competitiveness of manufacturing industries deemed more mature (by increasing the productivity of factors of production through process innovation); the second involves the computerization of society, that is, creating consumer demand for the new tools made available by screen-based technology.

In Italy during the late 1970s and the early 1980s, the failed implementation of Law 675 and the ongoing difficulties encountered by large industrial groups caused the objectives pursued in relation to sector-by-sector planning to be abandoned. Public policies with structural objectives were generally considered impraticable. Whereas intervention was aimed at restoring equilibrium (through the use of regulatory measures) or at financial restructuring (Law 787 of 1978) in the case of large-sized firms fallen victim to industry crisis or poor management, small- and medium-sized firms were nonetheless considered fully capable of adjusting without benefit of aid to financial strife.

Since 1982, albeit with some delay compared with most of the other industrialized countries, Law 46 has aided in strengthening support of industrial research and development by dealing, at least on paper, not only with the problems associated with R&D activities (through the usual financing or subsidy channels), but also with the transfer and diffusion of technological innovation to industry as a whole (for more information, please see Law 696 of 1983, which promotes the purchase of high-level production equipment by small- and medium-sized enterprises, and Law 64 of 1986, instrumental in the reform of the Ministry for Special Intervention in Southern Italy).

In the United Kingdom, since 1979 when the Conservative government of Margaret Thatcher rose to power, the concept of public intervention in support of industry has shown a decisive shift. The prevailing viewpoint is that private market participants are better able to allocate financial resources for investment than the public sector. Yet traditional industrial policy measures have not been abandoned, nor has there been a lessening of the commitment to support innovation, especially in small- and medium-sized firms and in specific regions. This commitment is chiefly fulfilled by the switching of resources from general and regional grants to financial assistance for science and technology (for example, *Support par Innovation* and the Alvey programme) and through high-level technological coope-ration with Japan and the United States.

As for the speeding up of the internationalization process, not until the late 1970s and the early 1980s did the objectives of dividing the risk and the cost of innovation initiatives among EEC Member States while creating pan-European alliances become a priority. In 1983, the Community-wide ESPRIT programme fostering R&D in information technology was created. Linked to other Community-wide research initiatives, this pioneer programme led to the approval of the EUREKA programme. Thus the beginnings of a pan-European policy framework for technological research and development were being gradually constructed; until the late 1980s, however, this base would remain inferior to individual Member State policies.

In sum, the behaviour of policy in Italy and in other European nations with regard to the modernization of industry via organi-zational and technological innovation gives rise to a few observations. The shared objectives of these policies are as follows: *a)* a rise in the productivity and competitiveness of industry; *b)* the promotion of sectors and/or manufacturing industries considered to be of strategic importance to the national economy (particularly as regards defence); *c)* the transfer and diffusion of innovation by sector (and by size of firm) as well as by region; *d)* the coordination and rationalization of intervention; *e)* the expansion of industry to international markets.

Agencies such as ANVAR, DATAR and INODEV are used in France to form inter-industry alliances that are directly accountable to government, led by large-sized enterprises in high-technology sectors. This approach has caused public demand to show strong support for the development of highly innovative sectors/firms/products, and has opened national industry to international cooperation.

Germany and the United Kingdom have adopted a similar approach, though industry in both countries has moved at a more moderate pace and has shown less adaptability. Emphasis has been placed on incentives which, rather than maintaining supply levels (the national champions policy), serve to stimulate user demand for the innovative products and services and to create an extensive, coordinated network of public, private and university research centres capable of transferring the results of technological advancement to industry as a whole (especially to small- and medium-sized enterprises).

Although Italy is headed in the same direction, its innovation initiatives are consistently late in coming compared with those of other countries. It should be stressed that Italian intervention to support innovation, in existence for the past ten years, has had a very brief history. Given the complexity of the institutions responsible for setting, controlling, coordinating and implementing intervention policies, the Italian system is crearly trailing behind those of the other governments examined. Taking into account the lime lag between policymaking, lawmaking and actual implementation, this situation is destined to worsen considerably.

The following constraints on the achievement of stated goals cast Italian industrial policy for innovation in a negative light with respect to those of the other countries examined:

1) the need for one authoritative body structured so as to ensure continued intervention and to truly coordinate various programmes;

2) the lack of accountability and the complexity of procedures, both of which deter firms seeking incentives (particularly in the case of small- and medium-sized enterprises);

3) the vagueness of geographically defined and sector-by-sector technology transfer objectives, and the resultant lack (or the virtual absence) of efficient structures to provide small- and medium-sized firms with aid in connection with scientific and technical projects.

The policy measure adopted by European countries to further tbe above-mentioned objectives may be grouped as follows: *a) direct incentives*, including: 1) non-selective incentives in the form of sub-sidized credit or capital account contributions, 2) selective incentives in special sectors or technologies and for particular areas or sizes of firm, again as soft loans or capital account contributions, and 3) public procurement (including large-scale projects); *b) indirect incentives*, such as: 1) fiscal incentives, 2) a patenting system and 3) technological and organizational consulting and assistance (real services to firms); *c) aid to research facilities.*

Germany makes extensive use of fiscal incentives to reward R&D activity (special amortization of capital expenditure and credit, and tax concessions for overall expenditure. Small- and mid-sized firms are also entitled to cash grants toward the costs of R&D staff and outside research contracts in the case of firms without the necessary in-house facilities). Financial incentives are directed toward the R&D and innovative activity of enterprises in sectors/programmes of national interest.

France is the country with the most intricate industrial policy for innovation with regard to intervention schemes, measures in place, variety of approaches (horizontal, inter-industry, by sector/program-me and leading firm) and development issues under review.

The United Kingdom frequently provides aid by tax allowances on innovative activity, and tends to focus financial incentives (cash grants for the research and development projects of firms and for the development costs and industrial investment of specific programmes) on two clearly defined areas: the reconversion and development of troubled areas and the strengthening of higher technology.

The Italian case presents the following characteristics: 1) with regard to *direct measures*, financial incentives (soft loans and cash grants) are the most widely received. Though provided for, national research contracts (under Law 46 of 1982), public demand and large-scale national projects are seldom used to stimulate R&D

activity; 2) as for *indirect incentives*, it is important to note the following: the almost total absence of suitable measures to promote innovative processes or sustained R&D activity (as regards the cost of labour and capital account expenditure); an antiquated patenting law (wheras in France, for instance, the ANVAR palys a useful role in patenting, a key function if research is to be displayed to its fullest advantage); and the lack of coordination, of any kind, of technological and organizational consulting (real services to firms, to promote the innovation of products and processes); 3) similarly, aid to *research facilities* (incentives to research consortia, the setting up of experimental stations, and so on) falls disappointingly short when compared with the efforts of the other countries examined (Germany in particular).

4. - Effects of Innovation Policy on the Competitiveness of Italian Industry

To evaluate the effectiveness of decisionmaking to provide incentives for innovation throughout Europe, it is useful to compare several important indicators. However, given the dissimilarity of conditions in each country and the heterogeneity of both statistical sources and the criteria used to interpret data, some measure of caution is needed to make such a comparison.

The validity of industrial policy decisions concerning innovation may be evaluated by analyzing the competitiveness of Italian industry as a whole (the macroeconomic view) and within individual firms (the microeconomic view). In macroeconomic terms, the commitment of the countries examined to promote R&D and innovative activity may be quantified, albeit partially, by the following input indicators: *a)* total expenditure, number employed, public-sector financing of R&D activity expressed in relation to the total R&D expenditure of enterprises (Table 1); *b)* public-sector financing of R&D for socioeconomic reasons.

Not only do these data underscore the inadequacy of Italian human and financial resources in comparison with other European countries, but they also confirm the grouping of strategic (and

Bruno Lamborghini - Cesare Sacchi

TABLE 1

MAIN R&D INDICATORS, 1987

	US	Japan	Germany	France	UK	Italy
Total R&D expenditure ($ bn)	125.6	64.7	30.3	20.5	16	9.4
Per capita expenditure ($)....	515	530	495	368	293	165
R&D expenditure/GDP	2.8	2.7	2.7	2.3	2.5	1.3
Researchers (000) in 1985	762	473	144	102	94	64
Researchers per 10,000 inhabitants, 1985	32	39	24	19	17	11
R&D expenditure per researcher, ($000), 1985	147	78	139	147	149	109
public financing/R&D expenditure (%)	51.5	19.4	35.8	53.1	39.8	51.4
Public financing of R&D of firms (%), 1985	33.6	6.2	16.1	23.5	23.2	16.9

Source: Based on OECD data.

practical application) decisions of countries provided earlier. From 1974 to 1987, France and the United Kingdom (and Japan, whose share rose from 14.3% to approximately 24.0%) increased their shares of the total R&D expenditure of the major OECD countries. Germany's share fell (from 12.8% to 11.3%) while the United States' share experienced a more dramatic decline (from 56.6% to 47.0%); nonetheless, these two countries continue to finance the largest portions of R&D expenditure, the former within Europe, and the latter worldwide.

   As regards research facilities, in France and in Italy the share of R&D expenditure incurred by firms is relatively small, whereas in Germany and in the United States this portion is substantially larger. The analysis of public-sector funding of R&D for socioeconomic reasons confirms what was mentioned earlier concerning the priority given by each country to sectors/programmes of national importance. Defence, university research, industrial productivity incentives and energy respectively receive most of the public-sector R&D financing provided in France, Germany and the United Kingdom.

Italy allocates a high percentage of its R&D resources to the energy sector, to promote indutrial productivity, and to space research. Lower-than-average levels of financing are used to further objectives such as defence, infrastructure at the nationwide level, and environment.

Let us now turn to the output indicators to be examined, even though these are recognized as being partial — and controversial — measures of technology transfer: 1) the number of patent applications made in each country; 2) trends in the technological balance of payments (Graph 1).

GRAPH 1

TECHNOLOGICAL BALANCE OF PAYMENTS
BALANCES
(values in billion lira)

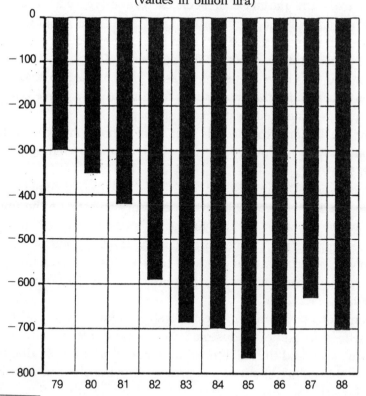

Source: Based on ENI (National Hydrocarbon Agency) RESEARCH CENTRE data.

These data give rise to the following considerations: 1) Germany and the United Kingdom are on the leading edge of patenting activity in Europe; Italy, weighed down by the backlog accumulated in its patents office, is relegated to last place. If the number of patents applied for by residents is taken into account, then Italy makes an even poorer showing, with only 21% of total applications, against percentages ranging from 25% in France to 99% in Japan; 2) the Italian technological balance of payments closed in 1988 with a deficit of L703 bn, with a worsening in trade other OECD countries. Of these, the United States and France respectively absorbed 70% and 25% of the deficit.

The United Kingdom is the largest European centre for the international diffusion of technology.

Italy is a country which processes and exports technologies derived from the purchase of licences with more scientifically and technologically advanced countries. Less favourable conditions exist in these countries for the execution of licensed projects. Whereas 52% of total expenditure is used for the purchase of licences and further 24% for the purchase of technical assistance related to know-how, total revenues under the latter item are equal to 40%, while only 28% of revenue is generated by the sale of licences.

Trends in Italian export levels over total exports at the worldwide level put Italy in last place with respect to its major trading partners (Graph 2).

International comparison has revealed that much remains to be done to reach the acceptable levels necessary to activate the upward spiral which consists of the following steps: increased research, increased innovation, higher productivity levels in industry, better positioning of products on markets and/or lower production costs, higher overall competitiveness, increased financial resources to be devoted to research.

Some of the obvious causes of Italy's unfavourable position are the ineffectiveness of industrial policy measures at the macro-economic level and the still limited diffusion of innovation, due to the impenetrable nature of industry at present. The transfer and diffusion of technological and organizational innovation (closely linked to the broader concept of overall quality) is in fact the weakest link in the chain.

GRAPH 2

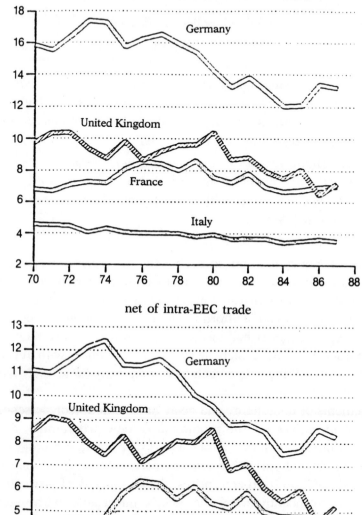

SHARES OF EXPORTS OF HT PRODUCTS
(ratio of national exports to worldwide exports)

net of intra-EEC trade

Source: CER: *Report.*

The final point for review is the first-hand experience of enterprises (the microeconomic view) concerning recourse to industrial policy measures and the effects of this intervention on company management.

The roles of innovation policy as it applies to entrepreneurial decisions have essentially been threefold:

1) as a start-up measure at the development stage of innovation programmes. The availability of aid caused enterprises to examine a wider range of possible innovative activity and to select higher-level projects (in the belief that these would be looked upon more favourably by agencies during the review process);

2) as reinforcement at the management stage of innovation programmes, since financial subsidies led to a rise in overall investment in beneficiary firms, with a multiplier effect on the modernization of industry structure;

3) as partial insurance against increased risk caused by the outcome of innovation and, in particular, of research projects.

It may be concluded that incentives have clearly fostered the creation of innovative investment programmes at the microeconomic level. Enterprises could ill afford to include these programmes in their budgets during the first half of the 1980s. However, this intervention was characterized by a high degree of uncertainty (with regard to financing in the Budget Law each year) and delay (in actually making the payments).

Elements of uncertainty and delay have undoubtedly lessened the effects of incentives for the promotion of new programme, limiting the role of intervention to that of supporting expenditure programmes initiated or carried out with resources internal to firms. In the case of small- and medium-sized enterprises, the complexity of procedures to gain access to incentives and the relative uncertainty with regard to actual payment certainly placed a sizeable obstacle in the way of small- and medium-sized enterprises wishing to benefit from this type of financing. The commitment of Italian firms to large-scale innovation projects and to the rationalization and restructuring of industry as a means of optimizing the factors of production (capital and labour) has clearly had positive results. International comparison also reveals:

1) the steady progress of labour productivity. In fact, the OECD sets the 1988 index based on 1980 at:

> *139 for Italy*
> 126 for Germany
> 126 for France
> 153 for the United Kingdom
> 129 for Japan
> 141 for the United States

2) consistent growth in the ratio of gross operating margin to invested capital, which in recent years, according to the OECD, reached levels comparable to those of other most industrialized countries:

(1986-1988 average)	
Italy	*16.2%*
Germany	17.2%
France	14.2%
United Kingdom	10.3%
Japan	19.8
United States	16.6%

3) the satisfactory performace of overall productivity, considered to be a good indicator of technological progress, which rose from 1979 to 1986 (the last year for which the OECD provides data) at an average annual rate of:

> *2.0% for Italy*
> 1.6% for Germany
> 0.8 for France
> 2.4% for the United Kingdom
> 4.4% for Japan
> 2.6 for the United States

During the late 1980s, Italian manufacaturing sectors also succeeded in maintaing virtually the same share of the total exports of

OECD countries (similar to the experience of other industrialized countries). Whereas Italy's position on domestic markets seems to have improved, with a decline of 2-3 percentage points in the ratio of imports to domestic demand from 1980 to 1986 (OECD data), France and Germany both registered an increase in imports during the same period.

As for financial results of firms, our interpretation of BACH data on company balance sheets is that Italian enterprises experienced an upturn in profitability in the 1980s, despite the fact that Italy was still in last place compared with other most industrialized countries.

TABLE 2

PROFITABILITY OF FIRMS
(result of fiscal year plus taxes expressed as a percentage of product)

	1983	1988
Italy	2.3	4.2
Germany	5.8	6.6
France	1.8	5.3
United Kingdom	4.0	5.1
Japan	4.0	4.8
United States	5.9	8.1

Source: CONFINDUSTRIA RESEARCH CENTRE elaboration of BACH data.

This brief international comparison reveals an industrial system which has achieved important objectives over the past decade and has succeeded in matching its competitors in many areas. Innovation has played a key role in this development, and industrial policy is central to innovation. Nonetheless, the May 1990 Bank of Italy *Annual Report* reminds us that during the late 1980s, this positive trend began to show signs of a slowdown: the productivity of labour for the processing industry, up 6.2% in 1988, rose by an unusually low 2.6% in 1989; as a consequence, the unit cost of labour was driven upward by 7.7%, seriously undermining the competitiveness of Italian industry compared with other industrialized countries, Furthermore, given that competitors consider real interest rates to be unfavourable, the lowering of the ratio of self-financing to investments (once more at levels below unity) dealt yet another blow to firms.

5. - Conclusions

The analysis of Italian innovation policy in the 1980s gives rise to a few observations:

1) during the 1980s, a sharp upturn in Italian industry brought large- and small-sized firms out of the slump of the 1970s even as it increased their involvement in production and organizational restructuring and introduced process innovation (and, to some extent, product innovation);

2) this transformation was largely due to the "driving forces" of firms, namely a strong commitment to increasing productivity, to innovative production methods and to cost control;

3) though insufficient, the innovative effects on industry on small-sized firms (chiefly growth in terms of subcontractor networks) as a result of the transformation of large- and medium-sized enterprises have been positive;

4) during the 1980s industrial policy, especially innovation policy, clearly attempted to introduce innovative instruments geared toward promoting the technological and production-related renewal of enterprises. Examples are incentives for applied research, assistance to promote the technological innovation of products and processes, and investment incentives for new plant and equipment in the case of small- and medium-sized enterprises. Others are the introduction, in recent legislation for the Mezzogiorno (Law 64 of 1986), of measures to promote research and innovative services, and the signing of the first *Contratto di programma* between the state and enterprises (planned contracts had been proposed as an innovative planning measure in previous industrial policy recommendations, but had never before been put in place);

5) most of these measures aimed at providing direct assistance, and were fraught with difficulties, delays and uncertainty as far as the access to funds and actual payment were concerned.

This ran counter to the turn of events in other European countries where direct, centralized subsidies were being replaced by decentralized forms of indirect intervention. Despite their role in stimulating many of the independent restructuring and innovation projects undertaken by enterprises (chiefly large- and medium-sized enterprises), these incentives were the instruments of a secondary policy rather than a policy directly aimed at adding to innovation to Italian industry (this situation is therefore diametrically opposed to the situation in Germany and France);

6) during the 1980s the trnasformation and redress of Italian industry also enjoyed a favourable external economic climate, characterized by the gradual lessening of inflationary factors resulting from the cost of raw materials and by exceptional growth in industrial economies. Conversely, a persistently wide gap between domestic Italian costs and external costs represented a stumbling block to Italian competitiveness, periodically readjusted by means of the exchange rate;

7) the latter half of the 1980s saw a worsening of these conditions, with a gradual slowdown in economic growth, and with the creation in Europe of a framework for the regulation of exchange rates that provided for increasingly limited fluctuation. In addition, international competition within Europe and elsewhere enjoyed unusually high rates of growth (in anticipation of market integration), and the diffusion of new technologies of products and processes took on an increasingly important role;

8) at the beginning of the 1990s, the yardstick for the comparison of industrial systems internationally has changed. The innovative and competitive capacity of individual enterprises, once the standard parameter, has been replaced, and entire economic systems are compared in this increasingly internationalized context of competitive markets. The importance of innovation policy in determining the success of national industry, rather than diminishing, has increased. Italian industry will be called upon to meet this deadline at a time when industrial policy has no clear direction, and even as the positive effects of the rationalization and innovation process undertaken in recent years begin to dwindle away;

9) it is therefore suggested that the objectives and policy instruments fostering innovation be re-evaluated; nowadays, policymaking in support of innovation implies: *a)* policymaking to promote the development and modernization of infrastructures, networks and services in industry; *b)* creating the necessary conditions for a truly

competitive market, fitted into the Community-wide framework and open to international comparison.

Markets, industry, networks and services must be closely interconnected to meet the competitive challenge of the 1990s. Innovation policy has assumed a more significant role than in the past, not as a policy which is specifically aimed at sectors (strategic or non-strategic, as they used to be described during the 1970s and 1980s) or at factors (as proposed in the 1980s), but as a policy in support of the integration of industry (industrial structure, infrastructure and services).

Within this policy, a dominant role must be given to the implementation of large-scale programmes (developed by public-sector authorities or by the private sector) aimed at renewing the infrastructure and services which constitute the industrial system (telecommunications and computer networks, transport, education, health services at all levels, environmental protection, safeguarding and management of artistic and cultural heritage and services offered by public-sector authorities centrally as well as locally). The effect of these programmes is twofold: the creation of large-scale investment projects and new demand, boosting the level of technological and organizational innovation in industry nationwide, and the renewed efficiency, quality and productivity of Italy's infrastructure and services, which have direct bearing on the productivity and competitiveness of industry. These programmes must also lead to the integration of the Italian system in today's European context. It should be stressed that skilled human capital is fast becoming the "raw material" central to the success or failure of industry in the international market. Thus the accumulation of this resource by improving the quality of education, science and technology is the best investment possible in order to safeguard innovation in industry and to guarantee its survival. Indicators of the involvement of national industries in these two areas provide the clearest signal of their success, both present and future;

10) developing new strategies and instruments to promote innovation involves the re-evaluation and the reform of existing industrial policy measures, taking into account the complex interrelationship among the following facators: *a)* the context (nationwide as opposed to central, European as opposed to national); *b)* those

directly involved (large enterprises, SMEs, financial operators, public research agencies, universities); *c)* the type of policy measure (direct, indirect, automatic, and so on). It also becomes necessary to work toward the intelligent use of fiscal policy measures, which play a fundamental role in other countries. Fiscal policy is increasingly considered a stimulus to the "driving forces" of firms as far as research investment is concerned (French fiscal policy is an interesting case in point; in Italy, however, the use of fiscal policy as a means of promoting innovation and investment in firms is still strictly forbidden ground). For the re-evaluation of policy measures to be truly effective, government must have a clear understanding of its role in setting well-defined rules as a guide for participants in an innovative market, the new scene for the competition of industry in the 1990s. The instruments put in place must be capable of ensuring that both private- and public-sector participants obey the new rules;

11) in brief, an industrial system can only be rendered innovative and competitive if a real market exists. By no means does this imply the absence or weakness of the state. A real market can only exist if the state plays an important role in setting and enforcing clearly defined rules, in reducing the sheltered portion of the market, and in combatting situations which lack transparency or which privilege some participants at the expense of others. Recently a trend has developed which in the past had cast a negative light on government behaviour with respect to industrial policy: the role of state-owned firms as the focal point of industrial policy in certain sectors considered to be of strategic importance and as the principal instrument of innovation policy in high-technology areas. This direction not only appears to be diametrically opposed to past models of industrial policy — not to mention policy to promote innovation — adopted by other countries (even taking into account the failed "national champions" experiment which adversely affected the electronics and computer industries in France and in other countries). It is also ill-suited to the current direction of decisionmaking in major European countries, where the necessary conditions are being created to increase the competitiveness of industry as a whole. In these countries, the success of policies in favour of high-technology innovation is closely connected to the capacity to create new, dynamic enterprises ready to

accept the increased risk to investors in new technolgy. Investing state-owned firms with the responsibility for the achievement of specific industrial policy objectives could create non-market conditions, or inhibit market development, undermining the competitiveness of private-sector firms, especially in the high-technology areas which are in constant contact with international competitors. These sectors can only be strenghtened if high-risk investment is stimulated by means of direct and indirect subsidization of research, and if modern financial instruments are used to create enterprises capable of developing synergies "within the external environment";

12) the competitive challenge will be played out differently in the 1990s than in the past. The central role of integrated national systems is evident even at the initial stages of globalization and market integration. Competitive advantage will be determined by comparing national economic systems as well as individual firms. Technological innovation has become a complex instrument requiring national commitment; the individual activity of firms, regardless of size, is no longer sufficient to achieve this objective. To be competitive, innovation must involve true synergy between enterprises and the national economic system, as the triumphs of Japan and Germany illustrate beyond the shadow of a doubt. To this end, Italy's policy for innovation must be re-evaluated, with the objective to bridge the gap between Italy and the other economic systems. This gap prevented the creation of true synergy between the driving forces of innovation internal and external to firms. A context of real competitive market conditions must be created in which state intervention is quantitatively lower, and yet qualitatively higher.

BIBLIOGRAPHY

[1] BANCA D'ITALIA, 1990: *Annual Report 1989*, Roma, Banca d'Italia, 1990.

[2] BATTAGLIA A. - VALCAMONICI R. (eds.): *Nella competizione globale. Una politica industriale verso il 2000*, Bari, Laterza, 1989.

[3] BIANCHI P.: «Riorganizzazione produttiva e condotte strategiche nella ristrutturazione dell'apparato produttivo italiano», *Rivista di politica economica*, September 1989.

[4] CER: «L'Italia nel commercio mondiale dei prodotti ad alta tecnologia», *Terzo rapporto*, Roma, CER, 1989.

[5] CER - IRS: «Un'industria in Europa» *Secondo rapporto sull'industria e sulla politica industriale italiana*, Bologna, il Mulino, 1988.

[6] — —: «Il mercato e la politica industriale», *Terzo rapporto sull'industria e sulla politica industriale italiana*, Bologna, il Mulino, 1989.

[7] CONFINDUSTRIA - CENTRO STUDI: «Progresso tecnico, investimenti e politiche industriali» *XI rapporto Csc*, Collana l'Industria italiana, Roma, Sipi, May 1989.

[8] GROS G. - ODIFREDDI P. - ROLFO M. - VITALI S.: *Dalla politica industriale ad una politica per l'industria. Analisi delle principali esperienze europee e la proposta di Tecnocity*, Torino, Associazione per Tecnocity, 1989.

[9] LAMBORGHINI B.: «La politica industriale in Italia di fronte all'Europa del 1992» intervento alla Tavola rotonda: *Indirizzi di politica industriale ed evoluzione dell'assetto produttivo italiano*, Torino, Comitato Giorgio Rota, 14 November 1987.

[10] MAGLIONE R.: «L'integrazione delle politiche nazionali per l'innovazione a livello comunitario», *Secondo rapporto sull'industria e sulla politica industriale italiana*, mimeo, Cer-Irs, August 1987.

[11] — —: «Politiche per la ricerca e l'innovazione: una sfida per l'Italia», Torino, Banca Crt, 1988, *Osservatorio economico*, no. 3, 1989.

[12] MALAMAN R. - RANCI P. (eds.): *Le politiche industriali della Cee*, Bologna, il Mulino, 1988.

[13] MOMIGLIANO F. (eds.): *Le leggi della politica industriale in Italia*, Bologna, il Mulino, 1986.

[14] MOMIGLIANO F.: «Convenienze e prospettive di una politica industriale europea», intervento al Convegno: *Europa conviene?*, Milano, Istituto Rosselli, 1987.

[15] NOMISMA - LABORATORIO DI POLITICA INDUSTRIALE: 1989, *Ristrutturazione industriale e piccole imprese*, Bologna, Nomisma, 1989.

[16] OECD: 1990 «Industrial policy in OECD countries», *Annual Review*, 1989, Parigi, OECD, 1990.

[17] SENATO DELLA REPUBBLICA: *La politica degli aiuti alle imprese*, Indagine conoscitiva svolta dalla Commissione industria e dalla Giunta per gli affari delle Comunità europee, Roma, 1990.

[18] SORCE A. - OTTIER E.: 1990 «Bilancia tecnologica dei pagamenti italiana anni 1979-1988», Roma, Eni, Studi economici ed energetici, *Note di ricerca*, no. 3, March 1990.

[19] ZANETTI G. (eds.): *Analisi dello sviluppo d'impresa*, Bologna, il Mulino, 1990.

Index